BLOOD & IVY

MASS MEDICAL COLLEGE.

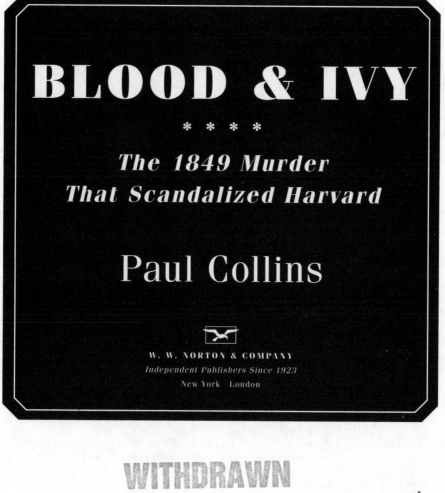

BLOOD & IVY

✳ ✳ ✳ ✳

The 1849 Murder
That Scandalized Harvard

Paul Collins

W. W. NORTON & COMPANY
Independent Publishers Since 1923
New York London

WITHDRAWN

For information about permission to reproduce selections from this book, write to
Permissions, W. W. Norton & Company, Inc., 500 Fifth Avenue, New York, NY 10110

For information about special discounts for bulk purchases, please contact
W. W. Norton Special Sales at specialsales@wwnorton.com or 800-233-4830

Manufacturing by Quad Graphics Fairfield
Book design by Lovedog Studio
Production manager: Julia Druskin

Library of Congress Cataloging-in-Publication Data

Names: Collins, Paul, 1969– author.
Title: Blood & ivy : the 1849 murder that scandalized Harvard /
Paul Collins. Other titles: Blood and ivy
Description: First edition. | New York, N.Y. : W. W. Norton & Company, Inc., [2018] |
Includes bibliographical references and index.
Identifiers: LCCN 2017057354 | ISBN 9780393245165 (hardcover)
Subjects: LCSH: Parkman, George, 1790–1849. | Webster, John White, 1793–1850. | Harvard
University—History—19th century. | Murder—Massachusetts—Boston—Case studies.
Classification: LCC HV6534.B6 C65 2018 | DDC 364.152/3092—dc23
LC record available at https://lccn.loc.gov/2017057354

W. W. Norton & Company, Inc., 500 Fifth Avenue, New York, N.Y. 10110
www.wwnorton.com

W. W. Norton & Company Ltd., 15 Carlisle Street, London W1D 3BS

1 2 3 4 5 6 7 8 9 0

For Richard & Shirley Thick,
with gratitude for all your help

Contents

IV. THE ACCUSED

V. THE TRIAL

VI. THE VERDICT

And this is good old Boston,
The home of the bean and the cod,
Where the Lowells talk to the Cabots,
And the Cabots talk only to God.

—JOHN COLLINS BOSSIDY (1910)

BLOOD & IVY

A Note on the Text

THE COVERAGE OF THIS CASE—INCLUDING A MULTITUDE OF newspaper accounts, letters, journals, court transcripts, and memoirs— allowed me to draw on many eyewitness sources. All dialogue in quotation marks comes directly from their accounts; lines rendered without quotation marks are paraphrased. While I have freely edited out verbiage from quotations, not a word has been added.

—P.C.

Prologue

January 5, 1868

It was a miserable New Year.

The holidays should have been a delight for Charles Dickens; he was on a triumphant stage tour of the United States, his first in twenty-five years. To welcome him back to America, Boston threw off all its customary reserve. The city, the poet Henry Longfellow marveled, was "Dickenized," its streets swept for his arrival and store shelves stuffed with copies of *Great Expectations* and *David Copperfield*. The eight thousand tickets for his first four shows sold out in hours. Protected from fans by his entourage—"our men sit outside the room door and wrestle with mankind," Dickens reported—he paced about a suite at the Parker Hotel, musing at the strangeness of it all. Boston was hardly the place he'd left behind in 1842.

"The city has increased enormously in five-and-twenty years," he wrote to his daughter. "It has grown more mercantile—it is like Leeds . . . but for smoke and fog you substitute an exquisitely bright light air." And it had only one catch: "The cost of living is enormous."

This was not for lack of Americans offering to host him. Even after carefully limiting his social engagements to his old literary friends, he spent his days in a whirl of lunches and dinners with the likes of Longfellow, Emerson, and Oliver Wendell Holmes. True, their numbers were diminished by the losses of Thoreau and Hawthorne, and Longfellow's leonine mane had given way to a long white beard worthy of Father Christmas. Yet the poet found Dickens much the same as when he'd last seen him: "So many years—twenty-five! He looks somewhat older, but is as elastic and quick in his movements as ever."

Dickens's manner of coping with his fame also remained unchanged: he walked away from it. As was his habit, during his tour he hiked at least seven miles through the city every morning, often alone, but sometimes with fellow authors struggling to keep up with the fifty-five-year-old. If he paused to look in a shop window—now busily hawking Little Nell Cigars and Pickwick Snuff—crowds stopped to see what had drawn their visiting celebrity's gaze. Crossing the bridge over the Charles River, Dickens found that, unlike Boston, "Cambridge is exactly as I left it." Time had stood still around Harvard Square. Just as merchants were the presiding spirit of Boston, so authors were in Cambridge. Here he was just one among many in a town where, Bret Harte joked, "you couldn't fire a revolver from your front porch without bringing down a two-volumer."

These authors attended Dickens's first show en masse; the group lacked only Melville, who came to a later show. Longfellow, though admitting that "Boston audiences are proverbially cold," felt unusually jaunty on a moonlight ride to the theater. So did other Bostonians, as it happened. Dickens's half-recited and half-acted readings—played out around a stage set of his writing desk—were met with sheer delight. Even the usually reserved Emerson, one spectator observed, "laughed as if he might crumble to pieces." A correspondent for the *New-York Tribune*, watching the roaring Boston crowd in amazement, wrote simply, "I thought the roof would go off."

The tour was generating so much money that Dickens and his road crew almost didn't know where to put it all. "The manager," he reported, "is always going about with an immense bundle that looks like a sofa-cushion."

Yet success couldn't save Dickens from a glum Christmas. He woke up that morning to a fever and a cold—an exotic and punishing American variety he couldn't shake. "I have tried allopathy, homeopathy, cold things, warm things, sweet things, stimulants, narcotics, all with the same result," he groaned. "Nothing will touch it." It even stood up to his hotel manager's cure: a cocktail dubbed a Rocky Mountain

Sneezer, which shook together snow with "all the spirits ever heard of in the world."

It was as well, then, that Dickens took Oliver Wendell Holmes Sr. as his visitor on the morning of January 5. Though he was famed as a poet and an essayist—and had a promising son who'd just passed the bar exam—Holmes's daily work was still as a professor at Harvard's medical school. There was only so much he could do for a cold, yet his company was salutary and bracing amid Boston's polite gentility. For the job of a physician, Dr. Holmes would muse, made one something of a seer: you could stare into an apparently healthy man's future and see that he was about to die.

His old friend Dickens had nothing to worry about—yet.

With the ailing author as restless as ever, they made their way through the snow to the banks of the Charles River, and to the Massachusetts Medical College. Inexorably, their steps went along Grove Street, tracing those of two men whose history weighed upon them. For a tragedy had passed in Dickens's long absence, one shared between the authors and society worthies he had met in Boston: a shocking morality play enacted in their burgeoning city, back when their youth and their country were both beginning to darken.

The murder, Dickens asked. *Show me where it happened.*

Part I

* * * *

SCENES OF
THE CRIME

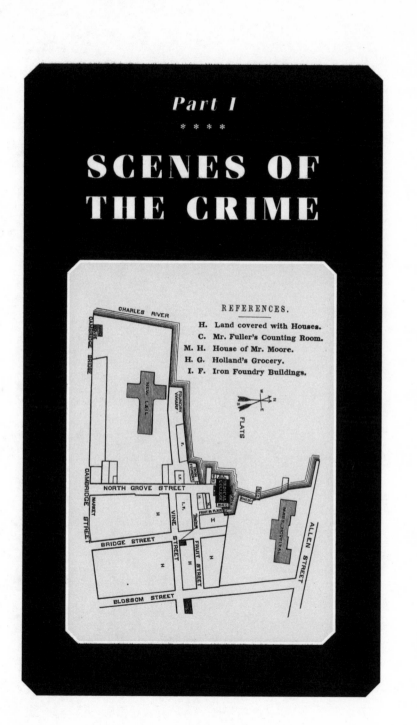

REFERENCES.

H.   Land covered with Houses.
C.   Mr. Fuller's Counting Room.
M. H.   House of Mr. Moore.
H. G.   Holland's Grocery.
I. F.   Iron Foundry Buildings.

1

THE WAY INTO HARVARD

JULY 1849 SAW THE BOYS ARRIVING IN CAMBRIDGE AS THEY had for years: coming over the bridge from Boston, down dusty streets shaded by old elms, and disembarking at a sweltering omnibus station. "ICE! ICE! ICE!" promised an ad from a store next to the depot, but even that was no relief. For the boys arriving into town during one of the hottest weeks of the year, there was little else to do but find the local inns or the homes of family friends or relatives, and there, in spare rooms and guest beds, to lie in the oppressive summer night and wait. If they couldn't sleep, there was staring at the ceiling and out the window to occupy them, wondering if they were ready, and if they were even willing, until exhaustion shut their eyes.

When they awoke, it was still dark out.

As the sun rose, they came in from all sides of Cambridge, scores of them, down Harvard Street and Holmes Place, some sauntering across the Cambridge Common, others earnestly keeping to the paths. Harvard's campus was empty on this early Monday morning, a deceptive calm before the commencement to be held later that week. Soon the bunting would be hung, lecterns positioned for the governor and other worthies to declaim from, the grass flattened by crowds of proud parents, and pitchers lined up for the much-needed tumblers of lemonade.

All this remained out of reach for now, as the boys seeking admission to Harvard were ushered into University Hall, Room 16. Parents and other family were left outside; the applicants were on their own. In this creaking old room were the others who would become their classmates— and some that wouldn't. The tableau was the same every year.

"Young men, some standing, others sitting, in different postures—some full of dread and apprehension, half afraid to meet the eye of others," one applicant wrote of Room 16. "Some were full of confidence and bold—full of self respect,—observing others,—laughing at the awkward or diffident."

Divided into smaller groups by proctors, they were called out, one at a time, into the two adjoining exam rooms. A tutor began with a simple request: State your name, age, month born, and the name of your father.

John Quincy Adams, said one. *I am fifteen years old. Born September. My father is Charles Francis Adams.* An unnecessary introduction, perhaps; his namesake grandfather had been president, and his father was on the university's Board of Overseers.

Moses Henry Day. Heir to a twine and a cordage manufactory—one of two twine heirs that day, in fact. *I am seventeen. Born in May. My father is Moses Henry Day Sr.*

William Dorsheimer, boomed an improbably sonorous voice. The boy had the beard and bearing of a man of forty. *I am seventeen years old. Born in February. My father is Philip Dorsheimer.* A German immigrant's son from New York; new money.

Nathan Henry Chamberlain. I am twenty years old, born in December. My father is Artemas White Chamberlain. A Cambridge policeman's son. No money.

The rolls continued with each group as they came through the exam rooms. There was Samuel Shaw, whose father was the state's chief justice and another university overseer; there was Albert Browne, a thirteen-year-old abolitionist firebrand in the making—and, as if to balance him out, John Daves, an equally fiery young North Carolinian. Scores more passed through the room, and once the tutor had finished conducting each roll, a printed sheet of sentences in English was placed before every boy.

Translate those into Latin, they were told.

In the next room, more exercises—this time translating Latin into

English. Then the same exercises, but with Greek. One could also expect to face a professor of Greek for one or two sudden point-blank questions: What cases do verbs of admiring or despising govern? *The genitive and the dative, sir.* Or, perhaps, a wildly long-haired professor, by turns bemused, distracted, and then remarkably intense, suddenly pouncing: What is (a + b) times (a - b)? *It's a squared minus b squared, sir.* As evening fell, the exhausted boys went back to their lodgings. Then, staggering awake in the predawn hours, they got up and did it all again. The most meaningful difference of the second day was that the number bothering to show would be noticeably diminished.

This went on until two in the afternoon, when suddenly, remarkably, the admissions exams were finished.

The boys lingered outside University Hall, shuffling and unsure. And then, one by one, the names were called out. Walking inside, each boy found a room full of faculty before them: there was the poet Longfellow, familiar from the engraved portraits in their books at home; the famed mathematician and astronomer Benjamin Peirce, recognizable as their wild-haired interrogator in algebra; and the kindly visage of Jared Sparks, newly appointed that summer as Harvard's president. Sparks had gone through the admissions exams nearly forty years before, a poor and largely self-taught carpenter's apprentice. It was said that he'd been so flustered that he very nearly failed to get in; of the boys gathered in Room 16 the day before, President Sparks would have been numbered among the anxious. So the words were all the more significant coming from him.

Welcome to Harvard.

As each young man emerged, the count of the Class of 1853 edged steadily upward. By the end of the day, there were eighty-seven of them, the largest incoming class the college had ever known.

* * * *

AND THEN, for six weeks every year, the town fell into dead silence.

"The average number of people that pass for twelve hours from 6 to 6, per hour, is 1/12," came the droll report of John Holmes, whose house lay on a street bordering the town common. "The only amusement we have is the burglaries."

Cambridge was hot, empty, and dusty. The students were away on their break, and the faculty afield to procure new specimens, dig into archives, deliver learned speeches, or just stroll the beach in Nahant. But by the end of August, the common began to fill again with new students. Some came across the quad, trunks stuffed and wagons piled, their fathers pointing out old dorms and former glories; others arrived alone, lugging trunks up unfamiliar stairs; and all of them poked their heads into their neighbors' rooms in the manner of new students from time immemorial. It was at about this time that the Cambridge Furniture & Carpet Ware Rooms could expect a run on the store; students had to provide their own enameled washbasins, their own rugs, and hang their own curtains in the dormitory rooms.

Only some lucky freshmen had procured dorm rooms, however. At Harvard, students longed to live *on* campus; the more senior the student, the more certain he was to be found in a dormitory, especially a desirable one like Hollis or Holworthy. The rooms there, one resident noted admiringly, were "large, with pleasant, high windows, and stout doors, which will defy many a hard kick."

Scattered through other dorms and boardinghouses were Harvard's graduate students, whose population was burgeoning. Along with its three hundred undergraduates, Harvard now boasted nearly as many students attending a divinity school, a law school, a medical school, and a newly formed scientific school. The Medical College started its term last—not until the November snows set in. This was just as well, as professors and interns alike were needed elsewhere to combat the deadly epidemics of an Indian summer. They were not much helped by what one doctor described as that year's favored cure for Bostonians: "to form groups at the corners of streets, and there boldly maintain that the doctors are all humbugs, and the city government is an anomalous mixture of old women and asses." More than six hundred cholera deaths later, Boston's street corners had turned rather quieter, and new students picking up their first issue of the *Cambridge Chronicle* received an ominous greeting.

"Death," it announced, "has been busy in our midst."

Still, such ills were largely a problem for Boston, a ten-cent horse-omnibus ride away across the bridge. In a charming town like Cambridge, the evils of the city could seem far away indeed.

* * *

THEY TRUDGED to morning prayers in the early light, across the newly fallen leaves in Harvard Yard, and with the tolling of the bell guiding their way. The bell could not be avoided, even after a mischievous student chemist poured sulfuric acid on it, even after another cut the bell rope and boarded up the tower; all this merely resulted in a janitor busting down the belfry door to ring the bell with a hammer. Morning chapel was not to be denied. The hour was so early that some students simply arrived in their nightgowns, a not entirely satisfactory solution, as the chapel was unheated. But attend they did; monitors kept lists of any backsliding students who slept in, and arriving after the bell stopped tolling lost a student eight points from the byzantine Scale of Merit they were allotted each term.

Getting written up was an inevitable, if nerve-jangling, rite of passage for freshmen. True, there was the guidance of the *Laws of Harvard University* booklet, but it ran forty pages, and in any case—up at *five-thirty*? In time, experience would reveal the merit system for what it was: a trade-off of cost and benefit. Absence, perversely, only cost two points, so as to prevent disruptions in the service. For a savvy upperclassman carefully tracking his venial sins through the twenty-week term, that meant chapel could safely be skipped once each week.

After chapel, the students shuffled out to a much-needed breakfast. This autumn, though, was different: they all headed back to their boardinghouses or to eating-houses, or they simply ate in their dorms. It was the first time the students hadn't gone across the Yard to the dining commons in University Hall. For two centuries, Harvard's students had dined together on campus, in a tradition as ancient and roundly resented as morning prayers. Commons breakfast—coffee "cooked in a dirty copper boiler and tinctured strongly with verdi-gris," a doughy lump of bread, and butter "not fit to grease cartwheels with"—had so often occasioned riots that the tables and chairs in the dining hall were bolted to the floor. Alas, the same preventive measure could not be taken for the college's crockery, and most of it was smashed in an 1818 student fracas.

The dining commons had also had the misfortune of being centrally located in University Hall, where it had been hungrily eyed for classroom space. Now it was gone, and it was hardly missed, at least initially: by the previous spring, sympathetic faculty members had been granting so many special permissions to avoid the commons that only one-sixth of the students had been showing up anyway. Yet the end of shared meals hinted that the old college was growing into a new university—into something larger and less intimate than the school their fathers and grandfathers attended.

Their morning classes, at least, remained recognizable. Despite some short-lived attempts at reform a generation earlier, Harvard's freshman curriculum remained stubbornly and almost shockingly retrograde. Of the sixteen hours of class time each week, fully eleven were spent in Greek and Latin. For the freshmen, this meant three hourly classes a day; on Monday, Wednesday, and Friday, it typically meant math and Latin in the early morning, and then an hour of Greek at noon. On Tuesday and Thursday: more Greek and Latin. The relief of an hour of history on those days proved illusory: it was Schmitz's *A History of Rome*. And then, on Saturday morning: more Greek and Latin.

You will please recite the next passage of Livy.

"Nuper divitiae avaritiam, et abundantes voluptates desiderium . . ."

The scratching of pencils would follow: *Of late years, indeed, opulence has introduced a greediness for gain . . .*

* * * *

THERE WERE also less elevated educational pursuits around campus. True, Harvard's annals were filled with earnest discussion groups like the Pythologian Society, which a young Emerson had belonged to—a debate club composed of "the fifteen smartest Fellows" of the sophomore and junior classes. But for the bottom of the class, there was the Navy Club, which with much pomp and travesty appointed as Lord High Admiral the student with the most suspensions; a Vice-Admiral, for the poorest grades; a Rear-Admiral, for the laziest student; and a Ship's Chaplain, for the most profane. Though the club's members were suitably attired in naval uniforms, their expeditions generally sank without a trace in the vicinity of the Porter Tavern.

Others, more serious in their maritime efforts, had noticed the regattas held on the Charles River by local mechanics and decided it was a splendid use for the College Wharf. In just a few years, rowing had become a passion for many at the college, with each class purchasing its own boat and forming its own club. That fall saw four boats streaking down the Charles and under the River Street Bridge, eight rowers and a coxswain apiece, and all decked in duck pants, white shirts with blue stars, and straw boaters. In time, some would find a less formal uniform to their liking.

"Upon these floats," one scandalized citizen who lived by the river wrote indignantly, "these would-be gentlemen deliberately expose themselves, *entirely naked,* and apparently glorying in their indecency and ill breeding."

Most of these campus clubs dissolved within a generation, sometimes under the glare of an unamused college president; others, like a Society to Discourage the Perpetration of Crimes, died instantly from a lack of interest. But one society had notably waxed, even as others waned: the Hasty Pudding Club. Having taken to staging ludicrous theatricals, it was coming off a fine production of battling gentleman nitwits, *Slasher and Crasher*. The latest production had starred Josiah Quincy—son of the mayor of Boston, grandson of a Harvard president—as the idiotic Mr. Slasher, and there was something salubrious in his being able to take to the stage as a raving, murderous toff.

"Let me get at him—let me annihilate him—reduce him to powder!" Quincy roared to his classmates' delight. *"I insist on reducing him to powder!"*

Where the Pudding wasn't able to provide comic relief, Professor John White Webster and his chemistry students could be relied upon to cook up laughing gas and then, as "an annual frolic," to sit on the common and inhale it. They dubbed themselves the Davy Society, after the pioneering chemist and noted nitrous oxide advocate. The more ardent student chemists of the lot took over a room in the basement of Massachusetts Hall, and Webster helped them cram the space with cast-off labware. The club's bylaws against making illicit fireworks were gleefully flouted; interrupting the Davy Club in this vital activity would bring jeers and yells of "Saw his leg off!" Yet Harvard's backroom chemists could also be public-spirited. After two college servants were overcome by carbon monoxide from burning coals, Webster's little group frantically cooked up bladders filled with pure oxygen to revive them, stoking the club's furnace so wildly that it briefly set Massachusetts Hall on fire. Webster later went to his duties across the river at the Medical College building with the cold comfort of having been able to save only one of the men.

The sole consolation for the other was, alas, perhaps the same as for any poor Bostonian who brained himself in a runaway carriage, laughed herself to apoplexy, or sank into a fever beyond the reach of Warburg's Tincture. Not for them, the terrors of Greek and Latin tests in Room 16. For in dying, they discovered the other way to get into Harvard: through its dissecting room.

2

ON PINS AND CROWBARS

WITH THE AUTUMN CAME THE KNOWLEDGE THAT SOON THE routes into Cambridge would be snowed out for days at a time, isolating the sleepy wooden cottages from the grimy brick of the thriving port city. But with the West Boston Bridge still easily passable, medical students and professors were streaming to and from the city, marking the first week of November the way they did every year: by converging on the opening lecture of the university's Massachusetts Medical College, now housed in a grand new building by the metropolitan end of the bridge. As if to remind the Harvard men that they were entering the dissolutions of the city, nearby was a fresh wreck: a drunk had galloped his carriage through the bridge toll to avoid paying the nine-cent fee and promptly collided with a horse omnibus, dislocating his shoulder. Sheer drunken luck saved the man's neck; a little less grace in being thrown onto the pavement, and it would have been just a short drag over to the college's cadaver storage.

Today, though, the haste was all in their newest professor, Henry Bigelow, who bounded up the building's front stairs two and three steps at a time. It had been only eight years since he'd been a Harvard medical student himself. But this spacious three-story brick building was hardly the old, cramped space where he'd taken his qualifying exams; the new building had been erected in 1846 on land donated by one of the medical school's wealthiest alumni, Dr. George Parkman. The steps led to the tall and expansive anatomy and chemistry lecture halls of the upper stories, as well as a library and professors' offices; one could easily miss the comparatively squat ground floor altogether, where more humble sets of side doors led into a chemistry lab, the janitor's quarters, a carriage shed, and a dissecting room that stretched out over the backwash of the Charles River.

In the building's grand anatomy lecture hall, the stage was crowded with skeletons dangling from frames; they gazed out upon rows of wooden seats raked sharply upward, like an amphitheater, sunshine streaming down upon them from skylights above. The rows were rapidly filling with Boston's physicians, surgeons, interns, lanky young students, and stout old alumni alike. One could trace the city's history in the names of the new class: Paul Revere had both a grandson and a great-grandson in the crowd, and the old Boston families of Choate, Eastman, Hitchcock, Osgood, and Shaw were all duly represented.

Prominent among the esteemed guests sitting at the front was Henry's father—Professor Jacob Bigelow, the most senior of the school's faculty. But then, the entire medical faculty always attended the introductory lecture, as did Harvard's president; the lecture was, next to graduation day, the medical school's most important occasion of the year.

"Gentlemen of the Medical Class," Henry's voice rang out.

A polite hush fell over the crowd.

"We are assembled in obedience to a healthy custom," their new professor continued. "It is well that those who are interested in this institution, should meet together once in the year, to testify to their good will to it. We recognize here the guardians of the University, some who look back as if it were yesterday when, like yourselves, they stood at the threshold of their profession."

For many on the faculty, it had not been so very long since they'd crossed that threshold. Three of the school's seven professors were recent hires—not least their dean, the poet and physician Oliver Wendell Holmes Sr. But of this new generation, Bigelow was both the youngest and a curious link to the past. His father, Jacob, was in his thirty-fourth year of teaching pharmaceuticals at the school, so Henry knew its traditions as only a faculty brat could. He'd been raised by one med school professor, trained by the three other elders still on the faculty, and even learned his undergrad chemistry from Professor Webster, who split his time between the medical and undergraduate lectures.

The memory of those days with Webster smarted a bit for Bigelow as he lectured. His lungs had suffered from youthful overindulging in nitrous oxide back in his Davy clubhouse days, though it was not exactly known how the damage occurred. And that, oddly, summed up medical science's dilemma in 1849: physicians knew that laughing gas worked as a sedative, and they knew that overindulging in it could harm the lungs; but they did not understand the mechanism for either of these phenomena.

"We still linger upon the lower steps of scientific progress," Bigelow mused to his new colleagues. "We stand without the edifice, and only gaze bewildered at the complicated manifestations of its exterior. We have only learned that certain occurrences are probable, but we do not know *why* they are probable."

In just the past three years, this reckless former student had been one of America's great experimenters and chroniclers for the discovery of surgical ether, authoring what some thought the most important paper the *New England Journal of Medicine* had ever published. It was Bigelow's friend Holmes, though, who had coined a new word for the substance—*anesthesia*—a choice that won out over "Letheon." For the students gathered in the lecture hall, a whole new field of medicine had opened up. Some had witnessed anesthesia's first successful use next door at Massachusetts General Hospital; indeed, this year's ranks of students also included a number of MDs, eager to pursue postgraduate studies at what was now the center of the most exciting experimentation in the country.

"Pain, but recently an object of insuperable terror, once prohibited many operations," Bigelow reminded them. "In these days, the surgeon has a lighter task."

There was one area, though, where their task had grown rather

heavier of late: courtroom testimony. With the rise of medical jurisprudence and the first successful prosecution using the Marsh test for
arsenic in 1840, doctors had come to have a credible and vital presence
in murder trials. Professor Webster, in particular, was in demand as
expert on poisoning; just the year before, he'd been called up to New
Hampshire to testify in the Roxanna Cook case, a sensational trial over
a mysterious death in 1834. The victim's husband was curiously indifferent to her sudden death, refused both a doctor and a coroner, and
afterward promptly married their young housekeeper. The Marsh test
having been invented since then, Roxanna's suspicious family had her
disinterred. The resulting trial epitomized the dilemma of courtroom
medicine: there was means and a motive, and Webster found arsenic in
the victim's body, but the husband walked free anyway. Understanding
the painstaking work and carefully weighed statements of a Harvard
medical professor, it seemed, was hard for jurors—harder, even, than
for the most recalcitrant freshmen.

"Suppose that a severe blow has been received upon the head, and
that a man thus assailed has fallen dead. Before whom is the question
brought to issue?" Bigelow scoffed. "Not before a jury who have spent
a lifetime acquiring an intimate knowledge of the human body—but
before *twelve average minds,* taken at random from the common walks
of life, profoundly ignorant of medicine."

Trust this unlettered public over a Holmes or a Webster, a Bigelow
or even a promising student? Why, the very teaching skeletons surrounding the stage seemed to smile at the notion.

* * * *

BIGELOW'S EXAMPLE of a severe head injury was not quite an acci-
dental one. Back at home, preparing for a Saturday night meeting of
the Boston Society for Medical Improvement, he had, in fact, been
thinking extensively upon the subject, not least because he was currently hosting a gentleman who'd had his brains blown out.

It was not in his usual run of cases, to be sure. Like most of the faculty, Dr. Bigelow still maintained a private practice in his home; and, always mindful of the poor, he even advertised the free excision of their "tumors, out-growths, or diseased enlargements" during his lunch hour. Such general practice work, above all, involved quickly judging probabilities: a sharp pain in the patient's side might indicate pericarditis, or perhaps a clot in the lung. But what if a sharp internal stabbing pain proved to be from—well, sharp internal stabbing? There had just been such a case here in town, with a doctor gently extracting a protuberance emerging from between a young man's ribs. It proved to be a needle that, prior to many internal wanderings, the unfortunate fellow had accidentally swallowed four years earlier.

But—that was just a pin. Bigelow's own newest case was altogether more unusual.

"A good sized crowbar," he explained incredulously to his colleagues, "was shot through a man's brain, *and he recovered.*"

So the young doctor was beginning his academic career with a most unlikely guest: Phineas Gage, the foreman on a construction gang for the Rutland & Burlington Railroad. The previous autumn, near Cavendish, Vermont, an errant detonation had sent a thirteen-pound crowbar through the bottom of Gage's head and clean out the top of his skull; the iron bar sailed high in the air and came clattering down eighty feet away. That Gage should survive or even remain conscious seemed impossible; carried to an inn, he proceeded to vomit blood and "about half a teacupful of the brain, which fell upon the floor." Yet Gage kept his wits about him, if not quite all his brains, and greeted the local physician drolly: "Doctor, here is business enough for you." After hurriedly dressing Gage's entry and exit wounds—through which the brain visibly pulsated with each beat of the foreman's heart—the doctor found himself with a patient not only stubbornly alive but insisting that he'd be back at work "in a day or two."

Phineas Gage was somewhat off in his guess. He faced two months of fevers and fungal infections, during which he'd wander deliriously out into the street, his head still clotted with gore. But, improbably, he rallied, and even tried reapplying for his old job. Gage clung to the crowbar—its surface oily to the touch from his brains—as his "inseparable companion." The sunken left side of his face and his protruding and blinded left eye hinted at their relation to his head wound—as did a strange, indefinable sense among his old friends that he was somehow "no longer Gage."

Dr. Bigelow had taken an immediate interest in the case after it appeared in newspapers under the headline "WONDERFUL ACCIDENT"—and, wary of a humbug, he wrote directly to the inhabitants of Cavendish for their accounts. Their responses were unequivocal, with reports from laborer to doctor to reverend, even down to the local justice of the peace, corroborating what one respondent called "the greasy feel and look of the iron, and the *fragments* of brain which I SAW upon the rock where it fell."

Phineas Gage, in short, was just the sort of man for Harvard.

It was this peculiar, indefinably altered man that Dr. Bigelow had brought to Boston at great expense that fall. The brilliant young Susan Bigelow, who after two years of marriage could already be considered long-suffering, had to bear him as the latest addition to her husband's strange menagerie. Henry kept a talking mynah bird in his consulting room and a kennel of hunting dogs out back; in his off-hours he liked to carve his own duck decoys, and his mechanical enthusiasms spilled out onto the house's shelves and filled its closets. Things with holes shot in them were, so to speak, a specialty of his already; as a student, Bigelow had nearly been kicked out of Harvard for keeping a small armory in his Hollis dorm room. It was said that the posts in his old room were still riddled with bullets from his impromptu bouts of target practice.

The hunter's love of the company of animals, curiously enough, was where Bigelow and Gage found a strange kinship. Since his shocking accident, Gage—once a sober, reliable sort—had turned rather childish and profane around his fellow man. He was only really happy in the unjudging company of animals.

Lie down over there, Gage was told. *And keep very still.*

The doctor had quills placed in the unfortunate foreman's nose—so that he might continue breathing—and then cold plaster was slathered over the patient's wondrously disfigured head. When it hardened, it would be a delicately detailed and calmly countenanced life mask—a fine addition for the anatomical museum.

Nor was this Bigelow's only re-creation of Gage's head. The doctor had taken, as he put it, "a common skull" from the medical school's generous supply and drilled through it to re-create the path of the crowbar. The iron bar, passed through the cranial cavity, would make for a dramatic bit of showmanship before his colleagues during Saturday night's meeting. After that, he could bring Phineas to his students in the anatomy lecture hall. These would be Bigelow's next great presentations that autumn—and surely the most sensational event of the season at the school.

* * * *

As the meeting of the Boston Society for Medical Improvement started that Saturday night, Bigelow first had one other vital discovery to present to his assembled brethren. With all due gravity, he commenced the meeting—*Gentlemen, Gentlemen!*—by holding up an immense . . . geological find.

"Remarkable Stalagmite," their secretary carefully recorded in the society's minutes for November 10, 1849. "*Remarkable for its singular resemblance to a petrified penis.*"

A roar of laughter was a fair start for any society meeting; they were all old friends. Henry's father had helped found the group two decades earlier, when they commenced meeting in a rented room over the Smith & Clark pharmacy. The three dozen current members were all local physicians, and almost every one a Harvard man. Before knowing each other in the society, many had spent their student days as part of a secret society, the "Med. Fac."—a travesty of the actual faculty, initiated through a hazing in a room draped with black, before "professors" dressed in ludicrous colonial-era wigs and knee buckles.

Many old Med Fac boys really *were* faculty now, right on up to the school's dean, Oliver Wendell Holmes Sr. Society gatherings fell somewhere between a Med Fac reunion and an actual department meeting; the entire Medical College faculty belonged to the society, save for Webster, the chemistry professor, and even he could be prevailed upon to contribute the occasional item to the society's journal. For tonight's meeting, though, the attention was all upon the newest professor and the extraordinary patient he'd brought with him.

I present to you a case of recovery from a passage of an iron bar through the head—Mr. Phineas P. Gage.

Gage peered out at them from his partly shattered face, perfectly conscious and voluble. "The iron entered there and passed through my head," he liked to say while pointing, and Bigelow hefted the brutal iron spike that had done the deed. It was three feet long, over an inch thick, and sharpened to a point on one end.

"The leading feature of this case is its improbability," Bigelow later explained. He handed the bar around for inspection. "This is the sort of accident that happens in the pantomime at the theatre, but not elsewhere."

The physicians of Boston ran their fingers along Gage's skull, gently examining the depression in the top of his head, where the pulsations of the brain could still be felt through the scar tissue. The top of his skull, Dr. Holmes marveled, had been pierced "as if it had been a pie-crust."

Bigelow had already secured a loan of the crowbar to the society from a hesitant Gage. The real prize was still in the patient's head, though, for the society had a sizable collection of fractured skulls in its anatomical display cabinets. Some had been split by sabers, others cracked by the kick of a horse, and one battered cranium was from a sailor killed by six years of epileptic attacks after he "fell through the decks of a man of war." But only one much resembled Gage's: the old skull of a coachman who'd lost a chunk of the parietal bone through a bad fracture, with the resulting opening sealed up by scarring on the brain's dura mater membrane, "very dense and as firm as parchment." *That* one had been donated by Dr. George Parkman, a founding member of the society. Dr. Parkman was still active, having just contributed an essay on the disordered mind of Jonathan Swift—and even though Parkman was busier these days as a wealthy landlord than as a physician, the society's "Monstrosities" cabinet still included an impressive mummified pair of conjoined twins from his doctoring days. But with all his years and his wealth, even Dr. Parkman couldn't top the curiosities Bigelow had brought to tonight's meeting.

For now, the bar alone would have to suffice. The society's collection remained an incomplete set; though the drilled-out demonstration skull was a fair enough facsimile, a proper display really required the actual matching skull—which, by some gentle negotiations later, Phineas might be induced to part with, after it was no longer in use. Harvard's medical men certainly couldn't be seen coveting the skulls of the still living, or outright stealing the bodies of the newly dead.

After all, they were in quite enough trouble about that already.

3

THE
SKELETON BOX

FOUR DAYS A WEEK THE FOOTSTEPS CREAKED, SHUFFLED, AND thudded across the ceiling of Professor Webster's laboratory—the sound of students trudging up the grand front stairs of the building and gathering in the lecture hall above. Underneath their dozens of feet, Webster had his sanctuary: a snug laboratory with one furnace to keep him warm, and another for high-temperature chemical assaying. A few steps away, across a wooden floor dotted with the inevitable alkali burns and acid splashes, a long table had been shoved up against a corner window. It looked out across a muddy lot to the neighboring Massachusetts General Hospital, a reminder of Webster's early days, some thirty years ago now, as a hospital dresser and a Harvard Med student. That was back before his attentions gravitated away from the corporeal body and over to the smooth glass beaker, when he ascended beyond bloodletting and alighted upon the chemical constituent parts of blood itself.

He finished his lecture notes under the sharp, cold light from the window. So much had changed since Webster's own student days; there was always more to keep up with. When he graduated with his MD in 1815, the medical school had just three professors and a six-week term; now it was seven professors and a seventeen-week term. Back then, the AMA hadn't been founded, and the stethoscope hadn't even been invented yet. And now? In just the last three years alone, ether had revolutionized surgery, doctors were beginning to wonder whether they should wash their hands before treating patients, and a woman—a *woman*—had graduated from a medical school in New York.

In the opposite corner from his desk, a tightly wound private staircase ascended to the back room of the lecture hall. Within easy reach for that moment was the dark coat he always wore for his lectures, and which he hadn't quite managed to destroy yet through chemical mishap. He would not need to don it today, nor ascend those back stairs to the lecture stage; it was a Monday, the one weekday when he did not have to lecture. As noon approached, the silence remained thankfully unbroken by students' footfalls; only the ministrations of the building's live-in janitor, Ephraim Littlefield, ever interrupted the Monday morning quiet, as he swept the floors and tumbled scoops of coal into the little stove. It was as well that Littlefield was working today; Professor Webster had cut his hand while trimming grapevines—raw material for yet another one of his experiments—so he'd need the janitor's help even more than usual. But before he could get under way on the day's work, Webster couldn't help but notice a puzzling absence in his lab: it didn't smell the way it used to.

That vault, he absently asked Littlefield. *Did it get fixed?*

It most certainly had been, the janitor proudly informed him. The medical building was only three years old, and Ephraim knew it as intimately as his own home, which indeed it was. He knew exactly where the retaining and load-bearing walls ran under which part of each room, and he knew what ailed the building, too. The coal pen off Webster's lab, heaped high with eight solid tons the previous winter, had cracked a wall in the medical school's subbasement, releasing foul air from a dissecting room disposal vault. And so during the summer, with the med school professors off collecting specimens and visiting family, Ephraim had overseen the descent of two hired men into the vault to repair it. This procedure struck Webster as impossible: Wasn't the only way into the vault through the small chute used for dumping body parts?

"We took up the brick floor in the dissecting room entry, and then cut a hole through the board floor," the janitor shrugged.

And that's the only way to get under the building? Webster asked.

"The only way."

It seemed a shame, because the vault itself could prove useful for research into the gases generated by decomposition. Couldn't, Webster suggested hopefully, a light still be lowered into the vault—say, a candle or a lantern?

"No," the janitor replied.

It was impossible: why, just a few days back he'd had trouble when Professor Ainsworth hung a severed head down there on a rope, letting it macerate so that he might eventually procure a clean demonstration skull. The problem was, the old rope they used rotted away, just like everything else in the vault, and the head tumbled into the charnel pile. Ephraim's unfortunate task from Ainsworth was to try to spot the head and fish it back up. Decomposition not only rendered the air unbreathable, it snuffed out the janitor's candles and made it impossible for him to see inside.

Still, there were good grounds for Webster to seek out that bad air: Boston and Cambridge were both struggling with overcrowded graveyards, which had become a festering public hazard and a hotly debated topic at city council meetings—a matter so pressing that, on that very day, Boston's mayor and city council were going on an outing to scout a new cemetery location. "It is not alone when the stench becomes intolerable, that burial grounds become injurious," the *Cambridge Chronicle* had warned that fall. "The subtle exhalations and gases impregnate the atmosphere, and, though it may not be perceived, bear their deadly influence in the community around." The wonders of Webster's chemistry lab might, perhaps, offer an answer to what to do about these gases; and the school's vault was an ideal place, in its own fetid way, to collect them. Even its geographic location helped: the dissecting room was a graceless extension on wooden piles over the muddy flats by the Charles River, and when the river rose with the estuary tides, the dissecting vaults easily flooded, sometimes to the height of a man.

"It is a good time now," Littlefield said, sizing up the river. "The tide is in, and will press the gas up."

Yes, yes, the professor agreed absently. Perhaps he'd assemble an apparatus for gathering it. But he didn't get around to it that day, or the next. There were many other cares for a professor to attend to, and the gas could wait, as it wouldn't leak away from the repaired vault. In fact, there would only be more lurking beneath the building: it was early in the semester, and soon the bodies would start piling up.

*   *   *   *

WEBSTER'S LAB was tucked into the middle of the Medical College's ground floor; flanking his lab was the dissecting room and Littlefield's family quarters. With Mrs. Littlefield's niece up from Connecticut that day to visit, the dissecting room and its vault might have been the preferable location of the two for Littlefield. It was, in any case, more truly the man's castle; for Littlefield not only saw to its maintenance, he was quietly in charge of keeping it well stocked with bodies.

The problem of obtaining cadavers had dogged Harvard for decades. Painstakingly crafted wax anatomical mannequins, imported from France, might suffice for public demonstrations, but training students in the fine points of surgical and anatomical instruction allowed no substitute. While in other cities, corpses could be had from graveyards for the price of a bottle of whiskey and a midnight bribe to the sexton, Boston's precincts of the dead were better guarded, not least because of the particular umbrage local Irish Catholics took at "resurrectionists." And that was too bad, as port cities had the best specimens; sailors were especially prized for the fine musculature they displayed under the scalpel. Harvard had some legal right to unclaimed indigent bodies but for years had quietly supplemented its supply of cadavers by buying them in bulk on the Manhattan black market. The problem was so acute that Harvard medical students paid a special five-dollar fee for access to the dissecting room, and while this collection was not labeled a grave-robbing fund, it might as well have been.

The new Medical College building opened in 1846 and was greeted in print not with acclaim but with a dime-novel shocker: *Marietta, or*

The Two Students: A Tale of the Dissecting Room and "Body Snatchers." In case there was any question about whose dissecting room was meant, the story clarified it by including a Boston street address, as well as other details whose veracity came from its author being a recent drop-out from the college.

The opening scene's taunt by one medical student to another, as they faced a beautiful young woman dead on the table, carried the hard and cold ring of experience:

"What possible harm can it do to that body—fair and delicate it is I allow—to dissect it?" the classmate asks. "Will it feel the keen edge of the knife? Will the tender limbs shrink from it, and give intimations of torture? Do you fear that those closed eyes there, will start open, and that clod-like hand will raise itself, and that still tongue will throw off the spell of death, at the first incision, and entreat you to desist? Fie! Where is your manhood?"

Marietta could be awkwardly laughed off as a fiction, right down to its unnerving scenes of bodies being electrically shocked into twitching and spasms, but events two summers later made the portrayal come uncomfortably close to the truth. In May 1848, in the New Hampshire mill town of Manchester, one Sarah Furber left her boardinghouse for the afternoon, saying she was "visiting relatives in the city." She never came back. Her fate might have joined that of many others who simply seemed to vanish from newly burgeoning cities, save for a shocking revelation weeks later in New Hampshire newspapers: "Her body was carried to Boston, where it has been found in a dissecting room, cut to pieces!"

Nobody needed to ask whose dissecting room it was. The resulting inquest, published in cheap pamphlets and hawked to the public as readily as *Marietta*, hauled Harvard before a jury to reveal the whole unsavory truth. Sarah, a young woman in whom the pamphlet found "nature was not sparing in its ornaments," had been carrying on an affair with a married forty-eight-year-old man in Manchester. Soon her housemates noticed her fashionable green-and-white

dotted dress being let out slightly; in her brasher moments, she confided that "she was going to throw off her quilted coats and join the
aristocracy." Sarah's beau had other ideas. After a failed attempt at
abortion through a laudanum overdose, she was sent to her "relative
in the city": James McNab, a doctor willing to perform procedures
for the right price.

It did not go well.

Dr. McNab, hoping still to turn his afternoon to some profit, had
coolly packed Sarah's body into a crate of straw and charcoal and taken
it with him to Boston as baggage marked GLASS. A visit to Oliver
Wendell Holmes, the medical school's dean, was quickly arranged,
and a student recalled McNab's sales pitch for "a young girl, 20 years
old, perfectly fresh. . . . He spoke of her freshness two or three times."
What was more, McNab's price was reasonable—"he said he would
sell it cheap, as it had cost him but a trifle."

Holmes needing little convincing. He sent Littlefield over to pick
up the goods from McNab's hotel, telling the doctor that if the body
was all he said it was, he had a sale.

"If I send a man with ten dollars," Holmes assured him, "there will
be no trouble about it."

But there was trouble. The body, examined on the dissecting table,
was distressingly fresh—too much so to have come from a graveyard.
Joined by Professor Ainsworth in examining the specimen with a few
incisions, Holmes found that the cause of death became readily apparent: a very clumsily pierced uterus.

"Never in my practice have I seen anything like this puncture," Professor Holmes shook his head. "I hope I never shall again."

Littlefield was sent back to McNab with a curt response: No sale.
The doctor swallowed his rising panic and asked the janitor for a
small favor.

"Bury it," he asked. "Or cut it up or put it down the vault."

Littlefield, sizing up the situation, demanded five dollars. Instead
of earning ten dollars, McNab was now taking a loss on Sarah—and,

desperate, he handed over the money, reminding the janitor to "put it where it would not be found."

But it was already too late: Holmes had sent for the police, as McNab was clearly a menace to the medical profession. So the Medical College had indeed done the right thing—eventually. Nevertheless, the scandal dragged both Holmes and Ainsworth before a jury, as well as Littlefield, and left the school firmly established in the public mind as a den of body snatchers. In that fall's newly printed Harvard catalog, the school now sheepishly promised, "No exertions are spared to obtain a supply of subjects according to the existing laws."

Just about the only person to come out ahead was the janitor. He'd kept the doctor's five dollars.

* * * *

WEBSTER'S LECTURES weren't all dry recitations; he always affected some theatricality. In his undergraduate chemistry class, he was known for pyrotechnic displays that on at least one occasion had nearly set the building afire. On another, a gas explosion shot a copper vessel across the lecture hall and demolished a seat in the back row—a seat whose usual inhabitant, fortunately, was absent that day. After being upbraided by the college president, Webster reluctantly admitted, "He said I should feel very badly indeed if I had killed one of the students. And I should." But demonstrations in animal chemistry to graduate students were a different matter; a medical school lecture required a more subtle flair. That Thursday, November 22, he retreated back down the stairs into his laboratory, doffed his lecture coat, and decided that he needed another important tool for his lectures: blood.

Blood was a splendid thing to have in the lecture hall. You could show the absorption of gases by agitating the stuff in a vial of oxygen and watching the fluid turn bright red; with some low heat you could separate out the serum, so strangely like egg whites; and if the blood came from a gout sufferer, you could cook down that serum into pink crystals that resembled cayenne pepper—uric acid, the fiery cause of all the patient's agonizing woes. Later on, when the students were more advanced, they could be shown the delicate process of the Marsh test. Webster, as a hired expert in a murder cases, often had occasion to use the test on blood. And Massachusetts General, just across the field from the laboratory, was a veritable spigot of the stuff.

"I want," he instructed Littlefield, "as much as a pint."

The shelf by the stairs to the lecture hall held a number of glass receptacles, and the janitor grabbed a larger one, about quart-sized; the extra capacity was good to have, as you never knew how much blood they'd actually drain out of a fellow.

How's this? he asked Webster.

"Yes," the professor said with a glance. "Get it full, if you can, over at the hospital."

The janitor took the jar upstairs, but he paused before continuing up to the second floor; the person he needed would be coming out of another professor's class, and the lecture was still in progress. Littlefield gently set the jar down atop a display case and waited for the inevitable swelling of noise at two p.m.: the scraping of chairs, shuffling of papers, a professor's final instructions—*Gentlemen! Remember!*—called out over the din.

Inside the anatomy lecture hall, students were emptying out as Professor Holmes gathered up his presentation aids. To most of the public, Oliver Wendell Holmes was a poet—the man Poe had praised for "Old Ironsides," written when he was just twenty-one. To Bostonians, he was a physician from one of the area's oldest families, a man whose impeccable breeding made his newfangled insistence that doctors wash their hands all the more remarkable: opponents might protest that "a gentleman's hands are clean," and what was Holmes but a gentleman? To his colleagues, he was the respectable public face of the institution, a dean still fairly new to his job, but an old friend of Emerson's and a Med Fac prankster of the Class of '29. He could be seen strolling the leafy campus, a tape measure in his pocket to measure tree trunks—he had a peculiar love of anything arboreal—and pointing out the wonders of nature to his eight-year-old boy, Oliver Jr.

Yet to the students in this lecture hall, Holmes was neither poet nor physician nor Harvard dean; he was "Professor Bones"—a sharp-eyed anatomy instructor, a man whose amiability made his precise incisions into his students' inexperience painless.

"My subject this afternoon," he'd drolly begin a lecture on female genitalia, "is one with which I trust you young gentlemen are not familiar."

Sometimes, while wandering the raked seating of the hall, hefting and weighing a disarticulated piece from one of the room's many display skeletons, he'd gaze in one direction while thrusting a bone at the surprised student to his side.

"Smith!" All at once he'd pounce, jamming a femur into fumbling hands. "Here, take the bone! What is the reason that the thigh-socket is much deeper than the arm-socket?"

Because . . . Nervous laughter from the student's classmates. *Because* . . .

"Because upon the leg rests the entire weight of the body, and it does not need much range of movement; but the arm requires to be moved in every direction, as, for example, in knocking a man thus"—Holmes mimed knocking down the hapless Smith, to laughter—"or in the oratorical gesture."

And with a flourish, his lecture would be done. Chastened students signed up to borrow one of the many skeleton boxes maintained for checkout: ten bodies, broken up into six wooden boxes apiece, that could be taken back to the dorms for further study. When it was not jovially keeping its fixed smile over a candlelit textbook, a prized cranium segment might serve as a fine companion over a late-night cigar and brandy.

Amid the swirl of students picking up boxes and gathering up their notes, Littlefield spotted the young man he was looking for. Just twenty-one years old, John Hathaway worked in the apothecary shop over at the hospital, but he was keenly ambitious for a higher station in life. Because many of the Med School faculty also served as visiting physicians and board members at the hospital, Hathaway knew them well; he'd leave the apothecary counter with alacrity to observe any surgery at the hospital, and he had been auditing all of Webster and Holmes's lectures that fall in anticipation of formally enrolling as a Harvard Medical student.

Webster's lecture needs a pint of blood, Littlefield asked. *Can you get it?*

"I think we shall bleed someone tomorrow morning," Hathaway said thoughtfully, taking the jar in the entryway. "I will save the blood."

It was a reasonable enough request. This wasn't the first time Webster had asked for blood, after all, and Littlefield's reputation as the building's middleman meant it was hardly the first time he'd relayed such a request. Who else would know where all the skeletons were in the building, or where to find a man with extra blood on his hands?

4

THE GREAT WORLD
GOES CLANGING ON

WHILE LITTLEFIELD FUSSED OVER THE OTHER LECTURERS
and labs, Webster generally retreated back to his Cambridge home
by two in the afternoon. That day the sun had broken out bright
and warm, a final reminder of Indian summer just one week before
Thanksgiving. For one of Webster's neighbors, the day was a welcome
one indeed. Emerging from long weeks of finishing *The Seaside and the
Fireside,* Henry Longfellow stepped out of his Brattle Street house,
looking the resplendent part of the local poet, with his slightly disheveled hair and subtly luxuriant clothes; but he also bore the exhaustion of a middle-aged language professor. Though he lived in one of
the finest homes in town—Craigie House, where Washington had
once headquartered—Longfellow hadn't had the time to enjoy it much
lately, as he'd raced to finish his manuscript. Over the past few days,
some of his greatest pleasure had come simply from closing his eyes
and letting his wife, Frances, read to him.

Now, at last, the manuscript was finally in the mail. Longfellow was
ready to go with Frances to "the place we have selected for ourselves"—
their future grave sites.

The wind and rain of a few days earlier, which had dotted Cambridge's potholed lanes with "porridge basins," or outfit-ruining mud
puddles, had dried enough to allow for a pleasant walk out over to
Mount Auburn. Cambridge's bucolic city of the dead had become a
place that drew picnickers and was a model for what the area's decrepit
churchyards might one day aspire to. Its creation had been an abiding
interest of the elder Professor Bigelow of the Medical College; indeed,

since handing over the professorship to his son that fall, Bigelow Sr. had turned his focus to Mount Auburn altogether, capping a lifetime of keeping patients alive with a retirement of helping them get pleasingly buried. Bigelow's Harvard colleagues already had a very permanent presence at the cemetery; there was, inevitably, a "Harvard Hill" of late professors and students, including former president Kirkland.

Longfellow had picked a spot for his own family plot away from his colleagues' resting places, Lot 580 on Indian Ridge Path. A decade earlier, after purchasing the lot, he had watched his own monument prepared "without one feeling of dread." And now, lingering over the dirt and grass that would one day become a more permanent home than Craigie House seemed to cheer Longfellow again.

"The foliage all gone," he rhapsodized over their plot, "and the sunshine falling warm and bright on all the graves"—ah, what was there not to love about such a place on an afternoon like this? An almost Puritan stoicism toward the blessing of bodily release could still be found in Longfellow's own newly written verses in *The Seaside and the Fireside*:

> *Take them, O Grave! and let them lie*
> *Folded upon thy narrow shelves,*
> *As garments by the soul laid by,*
> *And precious only to ourselves!*

Mortality had been on his mind much more of late. His first wife, Mary, was buried at Mount Auburn, and a one-year-old daughter by Fanny had died in 1848. His own father had passed away in August. It had been up to Henry to clean out the old lawyer's offices in Maine; he'd sat numbly staring at the years of unpaid bills his elderly father had been too kindly to dun his neighbors for, and was dazed to find how "again the great world goes clanging on, as if there were no dead and no mourners."

If here at Mount Auburn Longfellow and his wife could muse over their own future, the fine view atop the hill also hinted at Cambridge's; in the distance, Irish rail workers laid new steel tracks, so that the living could indeed go clanging on. Ground had been broken three weeks earlier for the Harvard Branch railway, the town's first; the terminus sat just north of Harvard Yard and a ten-minute walk from Longfellow's house. The construction moved so quickly, with the opening set for the end of the year, that the railway's board still hadn't even voted on what color to paint the station house. How its arrival would affect the town was, naturally, the subject of endless discussion. Henry and his wife had spent a pleasant meal with his colleague Louis Agassiz musing upon what it all meant; the Swiss biologist had inevitably turned the question into one of nature.

"He says," Longfellow recalled, "whenever a railway is opened in this country, there European weeds spring up." Ribwort so commonly followed development that the Algonquin Indians had dubbed it "the white man's foot."

And now the march of those feet, real and figurative, was becoming louder and faster: Cambridge's horse-drawn omnibuses only just outpaced walking the four miles into town, which made the city feel curiously distant. But the new trains, slated to begin running on Christmas Eve, would be a fraction of the cost and time. From here, atop Mount Auburn on a sunny afternoon, Cambridge could still seem like a town in a pleasant slumber, but for how much longer?

* * * *

WALKING DOWN from the hilltop cemetery to Craigie House, Longfellow was briefly free from the cares of his next book; there was even the pleasant prospect of a $1,000 check in the mail from his publisher. But Longfellow knew that as hard as he worked, he was nonetheless deeply fortunate. For he'd married well; even his lovely home was a wedding gift from his father-in-law. Had they relied solely on Harvard's pay to language instructors, Longfellow's writing would have been less an artistic necessity than a financial one. Harvard was no place for poverty, either in students or faculty: most of the instructors were Harvard men themselves, and already wealthy by birth or by marriage. A typical Harvard professor's net worth was an impressive $75,000, and they had not come by that money through teaching. Some salaries scarcely broke $1,000 per year, and for years a number of language instructors had earned a stingy $500 annually.

For all the poetic fame Longfellow brought to the post, Modern Languages was long an ailing department, and a palpable drain on the poet's energy. He'd arrived in 1836 to find that he'd inherited a team that was a "*four-in-hand* of outlandish animals, all pulling the wrong way, except one"—the Italian instructor, who eventually proved problematic as well. The department was already roiled by the past firing of a German instructor for abolitionism, an offense to the school's soberly conservative Federalism. Under Longfellow's exacting standards, the next German instructor was also fired, as was the French instructor. These decisions came to haunt him; to save money, Harvard simply piled many of their former classes into Longfellow's duties, raising his salary only slightly.

But the most troubling loss was of the one instructor he respected: Pietro Bachi, a Sicilian exile with, as Longfellow mused, "a cloud of mystery in his life." Bachi was widely believed to be a political exile, with his past station in society evident by his cultivation. He was in no rush to dispel the mystery about his person—to admit that his real name was Bartolo, for instance, or that he had actually fled an unfortunate romantic affair. Bachi's brilliance as an instructor, though, was quite real. Even their contrarian alumnus Thoreau had studied with him in every one of his years at Harvard, drinking deeply from readings in Tasso and Dante.

A penniless Catholic in a faculty of well-heeled Unitarians, Bachi eschewed the usual whitewashed Cambridge cottage and had moved into the grimy brick depths of Boston. Except for the medical faculty, where all but Webster took up urban residence near the city campus of their medical school, Harvard professors typically lived in the pleasant enclave of Cambridge. But Bachi lived in mortifyingly cheap city digs—on a stretch, one friend put it, "given up to pawnbrokers, gin-shops, and coach and omnibus offices." There he spent his evenings writing Italian and Spanish textbooks, steadily fueling himself from decanters helpfully labeled RUM, GIN, and WHISKEY. "I never drink more than is good for me—at least not while I am in good company," he explained to visitors. "The mischief is, what is a man to do by himself in the long dull hours of a New England winter evening!"

When books and the scant Harvard pay weren't enough to sustain him, Bachi took to borrowing and, a friend later recalled, became "like a horse that has once fallen on its knees—never safe from new and more disastrous troubles." Bachi had once been the president of the Boston chapter of the Italian Charitable Society, helping poor émigrés; now he was about to become a client himself. After the beleaguered Sicilian declared bankruptcy, he at least had fair reason to hope that Edward Everett, then the president of the college, might assist him.

"Mr. Everett cold! Mr. Everett haughty or indifferent!" he'd scolded a worried countryman. "Is it because he does not hug you in his arms like a Neapolitan? You must take men as they are. Reserve is the main feature of the English character; and an American, if a polished man, if a gentleman, is as stiff in his behavior as an Englishman and a half. . . . There is not one man in the world with readier sympathies or more generous impulses than Edward Everett."

And indeed, Everett did come to the rescue—of the university. Bachi was fired. Harvard, the president insisted, was "not to be trifled with."

Bachi had worked at Harvard for twenty years without a raise or promotion, even after authoring popular textbooks. The school was too circumspect to give a public reason for Bachi's departure; even years later, the university's preacher would say only that the dismissal was "not without reason." But that reason had less to do with honor, perhaps, than the embarrassing revelation that Bachi's salary was inadequate for a poor exile to support his family.

"Poor Bachi!" Longfellow wrote in his journal. He'd pleaded for Bachi's job to be saved, and even for the man to get a raise—to no avail. Since then, no further scandal had touched upon Longfellow or his colleagues. But Bachi's dismissal stood as a stark warning to the remaining instructors to remember who they were: respectable Harvard gentlemen of sufficient means. To be revealed as anything less was to end one's career.

* * * *

NIGHTTIME BROUGHT the inevitable social obligations: dinners with faculty, followed by music with the Cambridge Musical Association; Longfellow's most recent foray with the association, in fact, was at a piano and violin soiree in the parlor of Dr. Webster's house. The poet was skilled enough on the piano and flute that he sometimes found himself idly wishing that he'd taken up music as a profession instead, and his colleagues were no less passionate on the subject. Peirce had authored a treatise on the science of sound and music, while the young Dr. Bigelow played French horn and attacked the drums so enthusiastically that he sounded like a clattering army regiment.

Tonight, the distant plink of piano notes could be heard once again, this time from the music hall on the corner of Brattle Street, where the local dancing master led his seven-thirty class in the polka, the minuet, and the gallopade. But Longfellow and his wife were not staying in town, and headed onward into Boston, on a road that darkened as it wound eastward. It was here, on the stretch between campus and the bridge, that the smallness of Cambridge closed in; the town still had no streetlamps, and carriages and omnibuses plunged through a darkness only faintly relieved by the soft glow of candlelight from the faculty and student homes. The effect, as one approached the bridge and the city hove into view, was to render Boston all the more blazingly bright; it was a vision of brick and gaslight, its glow growing upon them as they crossed over the Charles River.

Of all the mansions in the city, the brightest lights shone from the

Deacon House, an immense new brick château on the corner of Washington and Worcester. It was there that the Longfellows pulled into the great courtyard, where carriages circulated around a stone perron column as if arriving at some French duchy newly declared in Boston. The poet and his wife were ushered in by liveried servants, through an immense atrium, up a grand oak staircase, and into a sumptuous billiards room, where they signed their names in a guest book. They then glided through throngs of guests in one grand room after another—a library, a drawing room, a dining room, and finally into the stately whirl and grace of the ballroom. Somewhere amid all this was Mr. Edward Preble Deacon himself, the owner of this great architectural folly; on costume nights, he was sure to be dressed in the finest outfit of all, pointedly favoring the attire of a thirteenth-century feudal lord.

Like Longfellow, he had married well. His wife's grandfather had risen from driving a country butcher's cart to become a wealthy merchant, and had built the newly married couple the finest rococo mansion money could buy. Designed by a French architect in the style of the old nobility—"a chateau as Monte-Christo might have lavished his riches upon," one newspaper mused—it had thrown its doors open just the year before to a procession of amazed patricians, who marveled at its mirrored halls, marble floors covered with animal rugs, a fountain of cologne, and rooms upholstered in pink satin. The centerpiece of the house was a boudoir, the Marie Antoinette Room, that held claim to being an exact reproduction of the original—complete with paintings of Cupid, a marble statue of Venus, and ceiling frescoes depicting, as one visitor put it, "young cherubs tumbling about in mid-air irrespective of all laws of gravity." Deacon had bought the furnishings the year before, without apparent irony, during the frantic auctions by fleeing and ransacked nobility in the Revolution of 1848—yet another paroxysm of French workers trying to throw off the very nobility Antoinette had stood for.

The mansion was wealth in the style of the Old World, but not of old Boston: making vast expenditures visible was not the local way, though acquiring the means to certainly was. Some of those who walked soberly among these halls quietly possessed fortunes that would make Deacon himself swoon. Their money was inherited, invested, and grimly held on to; their contracts were exact and binding. And yet even a thoughtful and well-provided poet like Longfellow, beholding the Gobelin tapestries on the landing and the Rubens painting in Deacon's private library, could hardly keep from admiring what an outlandish aesthete's money could indeed buy. "It haunts me like a vision," he once confessed in his journal.

The respectable men and women of Boston danced, drank Deacon's champagne, and cheerily spilled out to the courtyard; pleasantly abuzz, the Longfellows journeyed back across the river and into that looming headland where, for just a little longer, neither railway nor gaslight could penetrate the darkness. Across Cambridge, the final omnibuses for the night rattled in from the city; books were closed and candles snuffed out; the dancing studio's doors were locked; and even over in Hollis Hall, the midnight prank of rolling cannonballs down the stairs eventually had to cease, giving way to the exhausted early morning slumbers of a new Friday. And save for perhaps one man, none in the town would have the faintest premonition of what was to happen next.

Part II

* * * *

THE
VICTIM

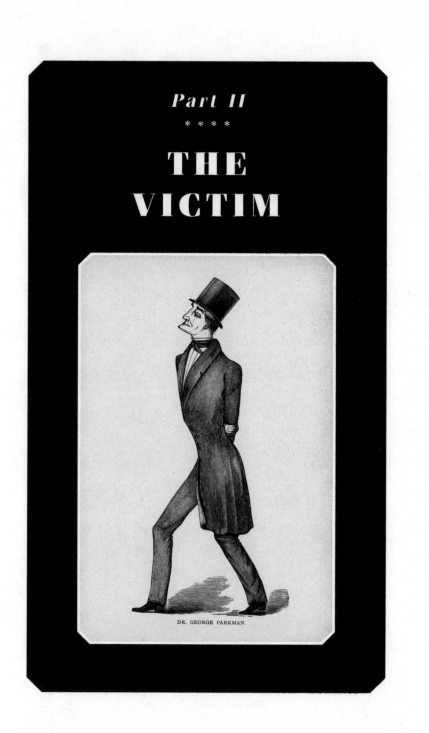

DR. GEORGE PARKMAN.

5

A BAD
BUSINESS

DR. GEORGE PARKMAN STEPPED DOWN THE LONG, VERTIGI-
nous spiral staircase, each footfall paid out precisely; the trapezoidal
steps of his home, thriftily twisting inward, demanded an economical
gait. The doctor emerged on the ground floor each morning, always at
the same time, to be placed in receipt of his breakfast from his manservant, Patrick, whose attention would be divided between Parkman's
meal and seeing callers arriving in the vestibule. Their forms were
silhouetted in the hallway under a spiderweb transom, their voices
low and respectful. The first visitor this morning, a gentleman stopping by before the clock had chimed nine, had managed to catch sight
of Parkman himself as the doctor passed between his office and the
breakfast room.

"Yes," he'd said in his usual curt manner. "I will be there at half past
one o'clock."

It was inadvisable for Patrick to inquire too deeply; there was simply
too much else to attend to, with all the duties bestowed by Parkman
upon his single manservant. With breakfast finished, it was getting
past nine, after all, and the doctor wished to go and make his business
calls; he must have his stick and his silk top hat. Thus suitably attired,
he exited into the morning sunshine of Walnut Street. He walked with
his customary stiff and impatient gait past a brief stretch of Boston
Common and up to another Beacon Hill home one block away—a Joy
Street mansion nearly as fine as his own, that of his brother-in-law,
Robert Gould Shaw.

Their neighborhood held an unusual excitement that morning, literally burbling and rushing all around them: one block past Shaw's house, the city's immense new public works building, the Beacon Hill Reservoir, opened its valves for the first time at nine o'clock. It augured a newer, greater Boston; the city's population had already more than doubled in just the last generation, and with Ireland now in the fourth year of a potato famine, city neighborhoods overflowed with new immigrants. Boston had already been drawing running water from Lake Cochituate for a year now, creating a delighted frenzy of overwatering by wealthy residents who were, as one newspaper put it, "procuring elastic pipes, by means of which they are able to sprinkle the streets, wash the sidewalks, and clean their windows." Thanks to the mania for garden hoses, they mockingly warned, "Boston will be transformed into a blueberry swamp . . . navigable only by canal-boats and skiffs." With the addition of the local reservoir, and its promise of "a perpetual supply of pure water to the citizens of Boston," dwellings in the booming city would become even more valuable to landowners like Shaw and Parkman.

As the ordinary citizenry gawped at the gush of waters into the reservoir, the two men made their pilgrimage, as was their wont, to the local bank. Much of the route was along the improbably tranquil common, an open space that became all the more precious as the city grew. The park, if anything, had only become more green and pleasant in recent years: the old wooden benches had been replaced with wrought-iron ones to discourage idlers from whittling at the slats, and the police had swept through to throw out the scruffy boys bathing in the Frog Pond, the better to protect the sensibilities of promenading Beacon Hill residents like Shaw and Parkman.

They'd been in-laws for decades, and as graying men of business, they found that their concerns now turned as often to family as to money; George had one daughter and Robert had three, all in delicate health. Robert had been sending his to a mineral spa in Vermont. "Some of the patients bathe six times a day," he'd patiently explain, ever the hopeful father. "And drink water twelve times."

This sounded rather like idleness, not to mention an unnecessary expense, given the new reservoir. In any case, the stern old doctor had his own long-standing preference, one that included keeping patients industrious and on the blandest of food. His clientele of old, it was true, had largely been unhealthy of mind rather than body, but he held that a "stimulating diet is fuel to their disease."

The vexing ailments of those around them was a cruel irony; here were two wealthy pillars of society, and one of them a doctor at that, both facing the stubborn ill health of their own families that neither money nor skill could quite cure. The two gentlemen parted by the Merchant Bank on State Street, where their fortunes, at least, remained healthy. The sums moving through their accounts—thousands, *tens* of thousands of dollars at a time—hinted, like the water coursing through the neighborhood's Cochituate pipes, at some much larger and more powerful accumulation stored up in Beacon Hill.

*   *   *   *

DR. PARKMAN walked between the imposing exterior columns of the Merchant Bank, dodging the pigeons that nestled on its marble pediment—the subject of some local amusement, as they exerted a humbling influence on the top-hatted gentlemen below. The bank had tried to scare the birds away by installing a fearsome wooden cat, only to find the winged miscreants perching atop their would-be grimalkin; finally, the hapless feline was moved inside to drolly overlook the bank's boardroom.

Not everyone found humor in their visits to the bank, least of all Parkman.

"The devil you have!" he'd snap at the clerks.

It was unwise to err with funds that were rightfully those of Dr. George S. Parkman. For much *was* rightfully his; he'd inherited a sizable fortune from his father, Samuel Parkman. The elder Parkman was an India merchant who had built a fortune on silks and indigo, and since then, his son had enlarged the family fortune through canny land deals across the West End. When the value of his riverfront land was threatened by a proposed new bridge, he lobbied against development; when the value was improved by extending a wharf, he lobbied for it. In the past year alone, he and Shaw were on record for 111 real estate transactions, and at length he'd hired his own agent, Mr. Kingsley, to deal with the sheer volume of work. That just made the occasion of a personal visit by Parkman all the more discomfiting for the bank personnel. The old doctor covered his fiscal precincts on foot, and he berated dilatory bank clerks and tenants very much in person.

Politely inquiring if a mistake had been made in his accounts did not notably improve Parkman's temper.

"I should think," he'd replied icily to one clerk, "that you might judge so, from my manner."

The doctor marched back out onto State Street, headed in his usual double time to those West End tenants and business partners who needed encouragement in paying their bills. Much had changed on this block since he'd taken over his father's estate, some two decades ago. Back then, the Merchant's Bank was still an outpost of the federal U.S. Bank; across the street from its grand columns, in a tidy allegory of power, had been the local whipping post, a brutally stout wooden beam painted a bloody red. Parkman could still recall when thieves here were also thrust into a sturdy set of stocks, to be mocked and pelted with rubbish by passersby—a punishment inaugurated by the carpenter who built them, since he was promptly clapped into his own contraption for overbilling the city for his work.

The law was not quite so harsh and unyielding now, though perhaps that was to change again. In that morning's *Daily Bee,* an editorial supporting Mayor John Bigelow lashed out against the simpering ways of Bostonian reformers. "SYMPATHY FOR MURDERERS," the headline scoffed. The mayor needn't worry: there was no danger of such softheartedness from George Parkman. Just this year he'd sent a fellow to prison for theft—his old manservant, Patrick's ill-fated predecessor, an Irishman who'd stolen $1,500 in cash, plus over $300 in checks and gold coins and silver, from the back of a closet in the mansion. Parkman noticed the loss right away, of course, but foolishly went to the police, who, instead of arresting the ungrateful servant on the spot, spent three weeks tailing him. Officer Clapp discovered that, though the servant claimed to be unmarried, he had a wife and kids secretly living in another house; they found there some china he'd stolen from the mansion, and a stolen dress, too. All very well, but the money, *the money*, had seeped away: when officers finally collared the scoundrel as he reported to work in the morning, they could scarcely recover a tenth of the cash. Being robbed was outrageous enough for Parkman, but the public revelation of it was almost worse—not to mention the newspapers blurting out that much of the money had not been recovered.

Parkman walked purposefully toward the river, to the blocks where his rents and holdings multiplied fruitfully. Prosecuting the servant had been a mistake, perhaps; Parkman's fearsome reputation came from enforcing his deals and exacting his penalties in person, eschewing the courts and meddlesome lawyers.

"Never go to law," the old doctor now held. Nobody need know the details of anyone's finances except for himself and trusted associates like Mr. Shaw. "Bad business, bad business, friend," he vowed. "*Never go to law.*"

* * * *

HEAVE.

The men and horses strained, the cart rocking tantalizingly forward, then stubbornly falling back into the mud by the corner of Fruit Street. *Heave.*

Again it rocked forward, then back. It wasn't moving. The reason why was no mystery: the cart was loaded with pig iron, now maddeningly stranded yards from its North Grove Street destination at the Fuller foundry, where it was to be smelted and refined into castings. Two horses could be expected to steadily pull a cart loaded with a ton of pig iron, but in these muddy and mercantile streets by the

Charles River, the task was becoming impossible. The streets were busy with Harvard students headed across the street to the medical school. Collegiate wits could take a certain amusement in the hauler being named Marsh, yet being defied by the sopping-wet land around him. Men from the foundry regarded the scene with detachment, and local children, racing a school late-bell in returning from their lunches, stopped for a moment to gawk at the two horses straining to dislodge their load.

Heave.

It would take a while; the horses couldn't do it on their own, and the driver at least showed enough forbearance not to whip them. The schoolboys moved on, and the ironworkers finally returned to rolling their heavy castings over for weigh-in, where foundry master Albert Fuller paused from the heat of his building to look back out into the street.

Afternoon, Doctor.

Dr. Parkman bowed to him, scarcely breaking his quick stride. Fuller knew him well enough, as did any businessman here; Parkman was one of the great landowners of this neighborhood. It was the doctor who owned the land under the foundry, after all—and who had owned the land across from the foundry, and donated it for the new Medical College building. This was a bafflingly generous act for the thrifty old man, so much so that Oliver Wendell Holmes had been promptly named to a newly created Parkman Professorship of Anatomy and Physiology.

Then again, though his business was as a landlord and developer, Dr. Parkman had taken some pains to live up to his medical title. He remained a member of the Boston Society for Medical Improvement, and he still contributed the occasional squib to the pages of its newsletter. And he'd kept the same listing in the city directory for decades: *Parkman George, physician, house 8 Walnut.* No mention of being a landlord, or of not keeping hours anymore.

Medicine had been the job he had chosen, rather than tending to the family fortune, which had chosen him; and for a great many years before he began running these neighborhood properties, doctoring had been the focus of his life. He'd suffered poor health in his own child-hood, and this had given him a sense of direction; after entering Har-vard at scarcely fifteen, and graduating in 1809, he'd turned to a career in medicine. The young Parkman scion scarcely needed the money, which was just as well; the local rate for house calls was $1.50, with an extra fifty cents to board a ship in the harbor. His doctoring was more out of a sense of noblesse oblige; he served as a medical surgeon for the Massachusetts militia, and during the city's smallpox and cholera epidemics had offered some of his many homes as field hospitals.

This neighborhood was Parkman's history writ large. Turning away from the local firms he extracted rent from, and away from the med-ical college whose grounds he had donated, and looking down North Grove Street, one simply faced another old Parkman property: a riv-erside lot he'd sold to the city, and which now had the new Suffolk County Jail rising upon it.

This, too, seemed fitting. Dr. Parkman had known a number of accused men over the years, with his expert courtroom testimony as a physician saving some and damning others. In his early years as a doc-tor, he'd been called into a trial over the death of a prostitute, Pamela Percy; her pimp was accused of beating her, but Parkman's postmortem found that she'd downed at least seven glasses of brandy before a likely tumble down some stairs. He was just as formidable when called upon by prosecutors, though. He'd attended to the first Boston policeman to die in the line of duty, Jonathan Houghton; the constable was drunk-enly assaulted on the docks while arresting a friend of the accused. Dr. Parkman testified that five of Houghton's ribs were broken, two of them piercing his lung and liver. "I have no doubt but that the deceased died in consequence," he informed the court, and his statement sent the assailant to Boston's scaffold.

But at this moment, strolling down Fruit Street, the doctor's thoughts turned instead to—groceries.

He was already carrying one small parcel, and he paused in the doorway of the local corner grocer, in the manner of all men trying to recollect what they were supposed to buy their family at the shop. His son George Jr. was in Paris, which simplified things, but there were still his wife and daughter to consider. Finally, Dr. Parkman strolled in and bowed stiffly to the storekeeper.

I require crushed sugar, Mr. Holland.

The expensive white variety—some thirty-two pounds of it, enough for the teas and sweetmeats of many a visitor on business. The grocer fussed over finding a receptacle for so much sugar; the doctor calmly pointed to a bucket, and watched carefully as it was weighed two, then three times, so as to subtract the receptacle's tare weight. Some grocers were known for including the weight of bags, buckets, and thumbs in the weighing out of sugar, and Dr. Parkman was not a man to be taken in by humbug. He then directed the grocer to cut off a six-pound portion from a firkin of butter, and to have both sent over to his mansion on Walnut Street, "any time in the afternoon," he added.

As the grocer worked away under the doctor's watchful eye, the inevitable bothersome neighbor used the pause to accost them for pleasantries.

Fine weather today, Doctor.

Dr. Parkman was not a man given to small talk; but for a moment, regarding the sunny November day outside, he almost seemed to find cause for cheerfulness.

"We cannot find fault with such weather as this," he finally admitted.

Parkman took up his stick and hat to leave, and paused once again in the doorway; he was still carrying a closed-up paper bag from another shop. He leaned over the counter to Mr. Holland.

Might I leave this with you for five minutes?

Of course the venerable doctor might; the grocer gingerly placed it behind his counter. And with that, Dr. George Parkman walked out of the shop and into a faultless Boston afternoon.

Holland followed soon after, off to take his lunch; when he returned, he was surprised to find the bag still there. Not too surprised, mind you: customers left all sorts of unaccountable things in shops. And so there it remained behind the counter for the rest of the afternoon, until, as the early November dusk stole over the neighborhood, the grocer finally peeked inside the bag.

Lettuce. That was it: one head of lettuce. It was a greenhouse delicacy this late in the season, and just the sort of bland stuff Dr. Parkman would buy for his sickly daughter. Well, he'd remember and be back for it on the morrow. Or perhaps not; some of these old fellows would forget their own heads if they weren't fastened to their bodies.

6

A GENTLEMAN
UNKNOWN

It was all most irregular. In thirteen years of working for George Parkman, Charles Kingsley had scarcely ever known his employer to be late for anything—particularly his mealtimes at home. Nor were there many days in which the old man did not consult him on running his properties. And so Kingsley had come by at three p.m. on Friday, his customary half hour into Parkman's late lunch, when the doctor would be ready to lean back from his meal and dictate filings and lease decisions to him. Except the doctor wasn't in, and his baffled manservant seemed unable to account for the absence. Stopping by again on Friday at dinnertime had not helped either; Dr. Parkman was still out.

And that was what brought Kingsley back at seven forty-five on Saturday morning. The agent's breath hung in the early morning air as he waited in front of the grand entrance of the mansion. The door swung open, and he stepped into the atrium, which the manservant kept as ready as ever for its daily procession of tenants and business partners. But there was an unaccustomed silence in the house; the doctor's impatient footfall did not answer him, and the worried expression on Mrs. Parkman's face told Kingsley everything.

He's not been back, she fretted.

The house was lonely—alarmingly so—with George Jr. off in Paris, and now Dr. Parkman not home for the night; there was only Mrs. Parkman and their ailing daughter left. It was simply not like him to leave them like that.

Word was sent a block over to Robert Gould Shaw to come quickly to his brother-in-law's house. Together, they pieced together Parkman's Friday schedule. He'd gone out to the bank with Shaw, briefly stopped back at the house again around noon, and then went on to make his usual rounds. He'd had some sort of appointment at one-thirty p.m., though the manservant couldn't remember the morning caller who had made it; Shaw couldn't recall Parkman mentioning it, either.

And that was it: he'd been due back at the house at two-thirty p.m., and none of them had seen or heard from him since noon of that day. With as much gentle reassurance as they could muster to Mrs. Parkman—why, any number of things could detain a busy man like her husband!—Shaw left Kingsley in charge of matters at the mansion and walked out into the brightening morning to make inquiries.

With each block he covered, though, the matter only darkened. There was no sight of the doctor quickly marching home, his chin up in the air, no hint of his unmistakable silhouette on the common, cutting through the morning fog in anger at having been detained so unforgivably late across town. There was, quite simply, no Dr. Parkman to be seen at all.

Shaw made his way to Bowdoin Square, where the Reverend Francis Parkman kept a household as distinguished as that of his younger brother, if less mercantile. He had not seen George, either. As no Parkman or Shaw would want to admit police into the matter, there was no question of whom they should consult next. The two men promptly walked over to Court Street, just out of the shadows of city hall, and into the offices of James Blake.

Any unexpected pleasure in a morning visit—*Why, Uncle Francis!*—was quickly dampened.

Blake was the doctor and the reverend's nephew, but more importantly, he was the closest tie the family had to Boston's constabulary. Blake, Shaw, and the Reverend Parkman were all Harvard men, but only Blake had ever had occasion to wield a billy club. Though now in the railway shipping business, until a few years ago Blake had served as city marshal, a rather genteel head of the city's police force. Sitting in his office that morning—the brother, brother-in-law, and nephew of the missing man—they recognized that their fears were immediate and blunt. There was just one suspicious character in recent memory with abundantly clear motive to detain and possibly hurt the doctor.

It's that Irish servant he sent to prison, they nodded. *He's to blame somehow.*

Now a private and very upstanding search party of three, they marched down to the office of John C. Park, Esq., the walk taking Shaw past the same blocks he had strolled with Parkman just a day earlier. The lawyer ushered the men into his office; he was busy, but it was not often he had such distinguished visitors.

The problem, they explained to him, was with one of his clients.

That was understandable: Park represented a great many problematic fellows. Just yesterday he'd added four counterfeiters to his rolls, a local butcher and his friends, all accused of passing on two-dollar bills altered to resemble one-hundred-dollar notes. In another of his cases, he'd been the defense counsel in an assault case between two stage actors whose offstage bickering had moved onstage with a very real "fight scene" in full costume, to the slowly dawning realization of the audience. But though he represented every sort of rascal, Park was a respectable man himself, one who'd been on the city council and had served side by side with Blake in the local militia.

It's that crook Patten, they said. The doctor had suddenly gone missing on his rounds—surely Park could see that the doctor's former servant was behind it?

At North End Church, where the Reverend Parkman had just retired from preaching that year, the bells tolled ten o'clock; they were losing precious time.

Impossible, the lawyer replied.

His client was still firmly locked away in prison—he wouldn't be out for another fourteen months—and as for the witnesses he'd brought to vouch for him during the trial, they were either out of town or not the vengeful sort. And what had they to be vengeful for, anyway? Dr.

Parkman never did get most of his money back from that crowd. He was, one might say, their great benefactor. No, Robert Patten was not the man they wanted.

It was a painfully logical point, and all the more so because Park was clearly right. They were wasting their time here; the man they really needed was over in the city marshal's office. Park had known the marshal for a long time—perhaps longer than these gentlemen realized, and there was no getting around seeing him now. Private inquiries could get them only so far; now they'd have to take it to city hall.

* * * *

To FATHOM what kind of fellow Boston's police chief was, a visitor needed only to glimpse one of his prize possessions: not a signed proclamation, or an ornate mace of office, or an golden epaulet for his uniform, but what appeared at first glance to be a simple silver jug. Pick it up and examine it though, and one would find that it had a singular inscription on its side: "Presented by the Dry Good Merchants of Boston, to Francis Tukey, Esq., City Marshal, for his noble and humane assistance in rescuing Charles Pierce from the ruins of the Dearborn block, Federal Street, July 24, 1848."

It was an event Bostonians knew well: the dramatic collapse the summer before of a brick merchant's building—precipitated, it was thought, by one of its pillars plunging into an ancient, disused sewer. The proprietor's younger brother suddenly tumbled below an immense pile of rubble, under which he could be heard calling weakly for help. Arriving firemen and police chose Tukey on the spot to lead a rescue operation deep into the night, even as a remaining three-story brick wall leaned ominously over them. Not only had Tukey saved his man but, almost as soon as Pierce was carried out, the last wall fell with a dramatic crash, obliterating the spot where the victim and rescuers had stood just moments before.

It had been only a few weeks before, come to think of it, that Tukey had also carried a printer's apprentice out of a burning building where a fire roared so ferociously that the man was spattered in molten type. He, too, had survived.

There was not a man in Boston—nor a building—that could deter Francis Tukey. At only thirty-five years old, the marshal possessed what one reporter described as "a voice of cast-iron" and the lean form and dark and piercing eyes of a stage actor, a profession it was rumored he'd worked in his youth. Now, as the city's top policeman, he had all Boston as his stage. That week he'd collared counterfeiters, pickpockets, umbrella snatchers, and one Madam Hufeland, an abortionist whose office doubled as a fence for melting down stolen flatware. His inscribed silver pitcher, as it happened, would have been a fine haul for her.

Gentlemen?

The trio had the marshal's full attention; they were a respite from the usual run of rascals coming through his station. And for James Blake to be visiting with them was a peculiar honor indeed: Blake, the former city marshal, the man who the previous summer had petitioned the city council to throw Tukey out and give him his old job back—and failed! James Blake, whose signal achievement had been a dog-collar law! James Blake, who local criminals feared so little that his house had had its linens burgled from it a few months ago!

But let it pass: they were both Harvard Law alumni, and there were certain courtesies to be considered.

Shaw, Blake, and the Reverend Parkman laid out their worries to the marshal: Parkman's schedule, his usual route, his mysterious absence overnight. Tukey pondered the situation; Dr. Parkman was a busy man with many business affairs, so might he not have simply been called out of town? The mere mislaying of a letter directed back to Walnut Street, announcing his absence or calling for his trunk to be sent onward, might explain the entire matter. Yet there was the real possibility of imperilment—a fit of apoplexy or a fall down the stairs while examining one of his vacant properties. He was a man on the verge of turning sixty, after all. And there were worse possibilities: he was a respectable citizen of well-known habits, identified by local scandal writers as possessing an estate of at least $500,000—Mr. Shaw, appraised at an astounding $1 million, was one of his few rivals—and the doctor was known to carry large sums of money on his person. He might, perhaps, have been lured into a dark cellar and robbed.

A number of out-of-town trains would be arriving by two p.m.; one of the first matters would be see to see if he was on board one of them. If so, the whole matter could become a fine story for next week's Thanksgiving dinner—*The thought of a den of thieves trying to tangle with you! Ha-ha!*—a comical misunderstanding that might make even the stern Dr. Parkman crack a thin smile. In the meanwhile, the half dozen police officers who worked the West End would be sent around to Parkman's properties to inquire discreetly—no alarm would be raised, nor any word breathed of a man being missing. Instead, they would knock on doors and claim to be responding to a local complaint, perhaps of a drain flooding into the street. Thanks to Tukey's reputation for fining Bostonians for everything from improper ash disposal to insufficient snow removal from sidewalks, it was a credible cover story for entering a house and poking around.

They would also prepare a notice just in time for it to be typeset for the evening papers, the *Boston Daily Journal* and the *Boston Daily Evening Transcript*. Tukey drew up an ad and waited as the three men fussed over minor corrections.

☞ **DR. GEORGE PARKMAN**, one of our most respectable citizens, left his dwelling house yesterday at about one o'clock in the afternoon, to keep some appointment at about half past one o'clock, made with a gentleman unknown, who called upon him in the morning; and Dr. Parkman has not since been seen by his family.

Any one who can give information respecting him, or saw him after one o'clock yesterday, will confer a great favor by communicating with the City Marshal.

Saturday, Nov 24.

They did not bother with a physical description, any more than they would bother giving the marshal's address: Bostonians knew both well. Dr. Parkman's rapid walk and his curious bearing—prominent chin high up in the air—were recognizable even at a distance.

When the bells in the church nearby finally rang two o'clock, the report soon came back from the train station: Dr. Parkman was nowhere to be found. Tukey called in a *Journal* reporter who had been loitering nearby in the city hall's suite of offices and handed over the ad, saying, *Run this on the front page of the evening edition.*

The time for discretion had passed. The police now had themselves a missing persons case.

* * * *

CHARLES KINGSLEY waited at Dr. Parkman's mansion, serving as the dutiful assistant to his missing boss by reassuring the women of the house. With the report from the train station, though, the real estate agent quickly excused himself and left. He knew better than anyone where George Parkman's properties and daily circuits took him, and he purposefully set out to walk the old man's rounds.

Kingsley roamed the streets around Beacon Hill, moving toward downtown, asking shopkeepers and acquaintances along the route if they'd seen the doctor the afternoon before. He picked up the doctor's trail on Bromfield Street, a sleepy stretch of two blocks favored by furniture dealers and such arcane trades as feather selling and shade painting. Kingsley doggedly followed Parkman's track from block to block, plotting out his walk: the doctor had turned up Washington Street, then proceeded through a stone archway and down an alley, emerging by Joy's Building; he'd moved past Paine & Newcomb's Fruit and Refreshments Room and continued beyond the People's Daguerreotype Room. His route then confoundingly circled around the Old State House and turned back down Washington Street again, before heading north in a double loop, steering out of the downtown altogether, and arcing back into the heart of the West End. From there the agent followed his boss's trail all the way back to Blossom Street—and into a stunning realization.

Kingsley was at his own house.

It was if the very search was mocking him: he'd just made an absurd day-long circuit through Parkman's home and half of downtown Boston to wind up where he himself had woken up that morning. But the absurdity held a hint of unease: the doctor habitually stopped at Kingsley's when in the neighborhood, and, indeed, many of the surrounding houses were also the doctor's own properties. If Dr. Parkman had walked right through Blossom Street, what had kept him from knocking on Kingsley's door?

Kingsley hadn't been the only one to trace the doctor's route here. Half a dozen police officers were walking the same blocks, questioning neighbors. As the sun set and the evening papers came out, word spread around the neighborhood. Locals joined in, with everyone quickly focusing on the doctor's own vacant properties in the neighborhood, their calls reverberating down hallways and into attics, across empty backyards, the men holding lanterns aloft and peering intently as they descended into one damp cellar after another.

Parkman had last been seen along North Grove Street, and then perhaps on Fruit Street by the Medical College, around one-thirty in the afternoon. For night policemen, hunting down clues along that stretch was strangely familiar from a murder just three weeks earlier. The Grove Street Murder, as the newspapers immediately dubbed it, had begun with two black freedmen arguing over a woman. It was the old story: one beau scoffed, "Old fellow, are you following me?" and knocked off his rival's top hat; the other suitor responded by stabbing the first twice in the throat. There had been much notoriety to that murder, but little mystery: the local barber languishing miserably in the city jail had numerous witnesses to his crime. But now one of the city's most respectable men had simply walked down these same streets and—disappeared.

Kingsley, accompanying the police in their house searches, was baffled. Despite the faint leads around the college—where Parkman had been spotted by neighbors partway down the block, though none had talked with him—the last unequivocal sighting of the man had been in the corner grocery, where Dr. Parkman had ordered sugar and butter to go to his house and asked the clerk to hold on to a paper bag for five minutes. His lettuce was still sitting there forlornly behind the counter, those five minutes having now stretched into well over a day. But nobody could tell Kingsley *where* his boss was to be going for those five minutes.

Wait, a grocer's clerk said before Kingsley left.

Yes?

It was a mere boy working in the store—but sometimes they were the ones who noticed the most important clues of all. Finally, the lad spoke.

Can you take the lettuce with you?

Kingsley pushed open the door, looked down the darkened streets, and walked out into the deepening November night.

7

THE
YELLOW ENVELOPE

AT EIGHT O'CLOCK, JUST LIKE EVERY MORNING, THE DAY CON-
stable roster was called out at the police headquarters in city hall.

Derastus Clapp . . . Lucian Drury . . . Lysander Ripley . . .

This was the Sabbath, though—normally a day off, save for the
small special contingent of Sunday police. But with the disappearance
of Dr. Parkman, the city marshal had turned out his entire force.

Marshal Tukey always stayed out of sight, behind his closed office
door, his plans shadowy, so that, as one constable drily observed, "the
Police were not usually overstocked with information in relation to his
intended movements." Whenever his door swung open and his brood-
ing visage fell upon his men, nobody dared interrupt the low voice
that sent them afoot for the day. Some days they had gambling dens
to raid or unlicensed cabdrivers to harry; and still others, they were
sent on inexplicable variations of their usual rounds. "Officers north of
City Hall," he would announce, "will pass the north end of the Court
House every hour while on duty; officers south, will pass through
School Street same, no questions asked or answered." Then he would
disappear. Only later, perhaps, would they find that they were foiling
robberies that had not yet occurred or safeguarding shipments or prisoner transfers still unknown, the dangers of which had been whispered
up into city hall through the marshal's network of informers.

This morning, as usual, they could not guess his plans—but they
could already assume whom they'd be centered upon.

Ebenezer Shute . . . the roll call continued. *Archibald Towle . . . Willard Whiting . . .*

The marshal, it seemed, had plans for all of them today.

The police fanned out. A number of men were to take to the rails, spreading fifty to sixty miles in every direction to nail up handbills reporting Dr. Parkman's disappearance. For some pious Bostonians, this traveling by train on a Sunday was almost as shocking as the disappearance; in fact, legislation had been proposed to ban the pernicious modern practice. Tukey and his force had no such misgivings. Those not sent out to the railway stations were to instead go back to the West End, where they would be joined by Kingsley and concerned neighbors; even Littlefield, the Medical College janitor, dropped his Sunday chores to join in. Overnight, the revelation of the doctor's disappearance had become the talk of Boston.

"The general enquiry," one reporter noted, "is, 'Have you heard from Dr. Parkman?'"

The search parties converged on Parkman's houses and vacant lots, sweeping over the half-constructed new jail by the riverside, where they broke the Sunday quiet of the waterlogged site by crawling over its lumber stacks and dirt piles. As morning passed into afternoon, the weather began to turn; after a week of unseasonably warm days, the cold was creeping back in, and those who had left their coats at home regretted the decision.

Pocket watches ticked toward four o'clock, tensing searchers with the knowledge that an early winter nightfall would soon arrive. Ephraim Littlefield rested from the search in front of the medical school and gazed wonderingly around North Grove Street, only to see the familiar form of one of his employers some twenty paces off. Dr. Webster, caught out in the gathering gloom, lacked an overcoat in the plunging cold, but he'd remembered his stylish cane.

"There comes one of our professors now," Littlefield said, pointing him out to another searcher.

The chemistry professor seemed animated, his gaze scrutinizing the ground, as if seeking the doctor's footprints. Like seemingly everyone else in the West End, one question was foremost in his mind this afternoon.

"Mr. Littlefield," he blurted out, "did you see Dr. Parkman, the latter part of last week?"

Indeed the janitor had—not much went on around the college without him seeing it. Everyone had now heard that there had been a mysterious morning caller to Parkman's and that the local foundry men had seen the missing doctor marching toward the medical school. But were that morning caller and the school connected?

"*Where* did you see him?" Webster asked.

"About this spot." Littlefield indicated where they were standing. He'd been sweeping inside the college and had stopped at the front door for a moment and seen Parkman approaching. But he'd witnessed nothing further, because then he'd gone to lie down on a settee in an empty professor's office.

"At what time?"

"About half-past one."

"That is the exact time," Webster banged his cane on the ground, "that I paid him $483."

And in a moment, one of the great puzzles in Parkman's disappearance became clear: the identity of the mysterious morning caller and, hence, Parkman's destination that afternoon.

"I never knew that Dr. Parkman had disappeared until I read it in the *Transcript*," Dr. Webster announced to the startled janitor. "*I* am the unknown gentleman referred to."

* * * *

IT WAS all an ordinary enough transaction, Dr. Webster explained. Like seemingly half of the West End, he had a payment to make to Dr. Parkman—in his case, a mortgage for $483.

"I counted the money down to him, on my lecture room table. He grabbed the money up, as fast as he could, and ran up two steps at a time." As ever, Parkman had moved with impatience. "Dr. Parkman said he would go and discharge the mortgage."

Dr. Webster had just been to the Reverend Parkman to explain all of this to him. As for where Dr. Parkman went next, well, most likely it was over the Craigie Bridge into East Cambridge, where the mortgage had been held.

"But," the chemistry professor added, "I have not been over to the Registry of Deeds to see."

For Littlefield, having already sunk much of his Sunday into the search, this piece of information made his next destination immediately apparent: he needed to walk along the Craigie Bridge. The span was just north of the medical school, and the point at which it crossed over to East Cambridge made it the logical route for a man headed to the Registry of Deeds. Littlefield fell in with a crony from the local customhouse, and their footsteps on the bridge crunched loudly together in the cold sunset; the Craigie was unusual in having gravel spread over its planking, and even more unusual in having a branch bridge extending out from its center, going to the state prison. Every walker who crossed the bridge from Boston faced, as they paid their toll, two paths diverging before them: one to the prison, and the other toward Harvard.

The two came up to the midbridge tollhouse in the fading light and peered in through the window of the tollkeeper's station. Feeling generous, Littlefield paid both their fares.

Seen Dr. Parkman? he asked, handing over the coins.

Indeed a tollkeeper had. Maybe within an hour of the sightings near the Medical College, their Friday afternoon shift had seen Dr. Parkman walking over the bridge with a shabbily dressed Irishman, and what was more, the Irishman had paid their toll. It was an intriguing hint, because police returning from East Cambridge reported that Parkman *hadn't* arrived at the Registry of Deeds over there. It was as if, rather ominously, Dr. Parkman had simply vanished off the Craigie Bridge. As night fell and the temperature sank further, men took to searching around the docks on either side of the river, gazing into the black and frigid waters. They found nothing.

The neighborhood men finally turned in for the evening, and Tukey's force returned to city hall empty-handed. Clues had been pouring into the central office, though: one short-lived rumor placed Dr. Parkman in Salem, while other witnesses recalled having seen Parkman back in downtown Boston at different points along Washington Street, and in at least one case with the same mysterious and shabby companion. Another report pondered the rapid departure from Boston of two disreputable men with skulking looks, driving a carriage in haste across the South Boston Bridge and out of the city. Their descriptions— "Both had on green pants—one, a glazed cap, black whiskers, black coat—the other, brown overcoat, light goatee, black hat, and yellow vest spotted with red"—were almost as good as any the police had of Parkman himself.

So it now seemed that Dr. Parkman had walked out of the medical school and into the streets of Boston with nearly $500 in his pocket and had perhaps been spied later that afternoon with a rough-looking gentleman or two. And no witness—in any part of the city—had seen him since.

*   *   *   *

FRANCIS TUKEY awoke the next morning inside a murder scene.

He had, in fact, been waking up *every* morning inside a murder scene, for years now; perhaps few but the city marshal had the bravado to knowingly live in such a place. All of 48 South Russell Street—from the ceiling he stared up at upon waking, down to the cellar, where he stored his coal, and out to the parlor, where he thoughtfully considered his cases—was reputed to be haunted. And that assessment was fair enough, considering that just that last week he'd hosted a friend's funeral there. But even before then, there'd been a very good reason for that reputation: some twenty-nine years earlier, what was now Tukey's home had been the scene of an ax murder.

Old-timers still remembered the case well. In 1820, Michael Powers had been a hardworking Irish laborer who, in a regrettable moment of generosity, loaned money to four cousins so that they might follow him to America. Once in Boston, they denied the loans, and cannily dodged Powers in court because he, an illiterate man, hadn't committed anything to writing. In defeat, he made a point of reconciling with them—they were family, after all—until one of his cousins was observed entering his house but never seen to reemerge. Local police officers, growing suspicious, broke in to find that neither Powers nor his cousin were anywhere to be seen. But a newly cleaned ax with hair still stuck in a crack, and some recently disturbed earth under a basement woodpile, augured what they'd find next: the cousin's horribly mangled body, in a grave scarcely eighteen inches deep. The man had, in the end, repaid his bad loan with considerable penalties. Along with three savage blows to the back of the skull—the coroner found the wounds "large enough to pass his finger into"—the man's face and hands were burned. The victim, the officers surmised, had been caught unawares while warming himself in front of Powers's hearth, and struck so hard in the head that he'd pitched face-first into the fire.

Powers was apprehended just as he was booking a passage back to Dublin, carrying a trunk containing his victim's clothes and wallet. Yet the suspect was curiously convinced that he couldn't be prosecuted. "The most he could say," one chronicler noted, "was, 'no one could say *I saw him do it.*'" Powers discovered, to his great disappointment, that circumstantial evidence was indeed enough to send him to the scaffold.

Tukey's new case was baffling, though; if only they could all be as simple as the murder in his basement! He'd have been perfect for that investigation—some of the marshal's fame had come, after all, from a terrier-like knack for knowing where to dig. It was how he'd saved his man in the Dearborn Block collapse; it was how, not long before that, he'd dramatically unearthed a sum of over $1,000 buried on Boston Common, the plunder of a jewelry store robbery. Even one of his failures—digging in the basement of another house reputed to be haunted, but of which he had more earthly suspicions—had proved nearly right. He'd accidentally struck through a few beams buried in the dirt before giving up. A few weeks later, the cellar collapsed into a subterranean lair furnished with zinc blanks and a keg of suspicious looking half-dollars. The house's "ghosts" had been counterfeiters, and Tukey had very nearly dug right in through their ceiling.

But this time Tukey was running out of places to dig. He left his house that Monday morning and had his men walk over the same grounds again and again, straining for any clues they'd missed. The cellars of Parkman's properties turned up nothing but cold, damp earth. Charles Kingsley, still loyally searching for his boss, joined the officers and doggedly made inquiries all up and down Leverett Street, where Parkman must have walked to reach the Craigie Bridge. Nobody else could verify the tollkeeper's story. All the other leads from later in the afternoon along Washington Street still suffered from one maddening flaw: sightings by just one person, with no other witnesses.

The last place everyone agreed Parkman had been seen was the Medical College, and so Kingsley and a couple of policemen duly trudged back and called upon Littlefield.

"We want to look around this college," Kingsley said wearily to the janitor, who quickly motioned to Dr. Holmes to come help, "for we can't trace the doctor anywhere but here."

Holmes, more college dean than concerned citizen, gently remonstrated with them; of course he wanted to help find their school's great benefactor, but the building was in fact *full* of dead bodies— and always had been. The memory of last year's abortion and body-snatching scandal with Sarah Furber still stung, and though Harvard now tried rather painstakingly to acquire its cadavers legitimately, and kept them carefully on ice, the prospect of breaking them all out was not a pleasant one.

"You don't want to haul all our subjects out of the chest, do you?" Holmes asked worriedly.

"No," Kingsley assured him, "we want to look about the attics, and . . ." He vaguely indicated the larger building about them.

"Take them up and show them all around," the dean told Littlefield.

They briskly searched nearly every corner of the school, from the attic down to the lecture halls, from the cellar up to Dr. Webster's laboratory, where the professor absently let them in without so much as a word of greeting. Nothing: nothing in the school, nothing anywhere else. Officer after officer brought the same report back to the marshal. Parkman had, it seemed, vanished as completely as the vapors from one of the chemistry laboratory's glass beakers.

Tukey returned to city hall, where the usual run of the day's crimes washed in on their ceaseless tide of human flotsam: drunk and disorderlies, pickpockets, and the always popular crime of stealing pocket watches. Just that evening they got a report from the docks of a ship stealthily boarded and a fifteen-dollar French silver watch stolen; and then, on land, a house break-in with two more watches taken. The timepieces were easy to spirit away and sell, which was more than one could say of the entire bale of waxed twine for candlewicks also brazenly lifted from in front of a store on Milk Street. The newspaper reporters who waited around for the day's police reports devised a fine headline for that one: "A WICK-ED CRIME."

Yet the marshal's attentions remained on the Parkman case as the day's paperwork and correspondence came in. Among his letters was a grubby yellow envelope addressed to *Francis Tukey, City Marshal*. The marshal opened it carefully, and stared at the message scrawled inside:

Dr Sir—

    You will find Dr Parkman
    murdered on brooklynt
    heights. yours, M.—

Captain of the Dart.

8

SOME ABERRATION OF MIND

DR. PARKMAN WAS NOT FOUND MURDERED ON "BROOKLYNT Heights." Nor was he found murdered on Brooklyn Heights, or murdered on Brook*line* Heights, or murdered in any other Brook or Heights of any variety at all. Perhaps inevitably, Tukey was now receiving crank letters. Not only was much of the information coming into his office false, but some of the facts emerging about Dr. Parkman were a little too uncomfortably true.

"The supposition of those who know him best," revealed the *Boston Courier*, "is, that he is laboring under some aberration of mind, and that he is wandering through woods in some adjacent town. We understand that he has occasionally been affected with slight mental derangement, during which it has been his custom to seek seclusion."

This was news indeed to many: the Parkman family had primly left any "aberration" unmentioned in its blizzard of thousands of handbills. Now their infirmities had been thrown open to the world. Though some Boston newspapers, like the *Herald*, took a crusading zeal in exposés, and even engaged in subtle blackmail to withhold the publication of damaging stories, most papers kept at least some respectable distance from such revelations. But the papers of late had been feeling their influence in the city—just that day, the *Transcript* reported, the recently formed Independent Order of Boston Reporters had successfully lobbied for new furnishings to replace the shabby arrangements for the courtroom press. And now, with the report of Parkman's "derangement" in the *Courier*, local reporters would slowly reveal, newspaper by newspaper, this painful fact.

The Parkmans did not try to deny it; there was no point now. "Brain troubles" had exacted a terrible toll across their family, not least on the doctor's older brother, the Reverend Francis Parkman. He was, as one colleague later mused, "subject to depression, as men of mercurial and humorous disposition are apt to be," and he'd had a full-blown breakdown for a substantial part of 1844 and 1845. Nor had his namesake son, Francis Jr., escaped the curse. Just twenty-six, the young man was surpassing his father's fame with his newly published account, *The Oregon Trail*. One of his driving motives for traveling out west in the first place, though, had been to try to cure what he privately termed his "conditions of the nervous system abnormal . . . since infancy." He'd begged his friends to warn him if, like his father and his uncle George, he began showing signs of incipient insanity in his correspondence.

Like many sufferers, Dr. George Parkman's way of grappling with his own disordered mind had been to take up the study of the field itself. As a young scion to the family fortune, he'd toured Europe—but not to simply dawdle among nobility or the great sights. Instead, he'd visited insane asylums in Britain and Switzerland, and spent months in a women's asylum in Paris. A week after graduating from the Medical College in 1814, Dr. Parkman had published a remarkably forward-thinking booklet, *Proposals for Establishing a Retreat for the Insane*. The insane, he argued, did not benefit from shackling and solitary confinement; they needed "salutary exercise and employments." Nor did they deserve censure for their mad acts; these came from palpable physical alterations of the brain itself and required treatment by doctors. Parkman helped lead the creation of the Massachusetts Lunatic Asylum and exerted care in its every detail, down to the design of its beds and bolted-down furniture. The facility was advertised as an institution for the well-to-do, "a mile from Boston, on a gravelly eminence, commanding an extensive amphitheater of prospect."

Even as his career eventually turned away from medicine and to

expanding the family fortune, Dr. Parkman's ruthless property development hid a lingering tenderness for the plight of the insane. He still
testified as an expert in murder trials, a lonely voice of caution in a
world that bundled off homicidal madmen to the scaffold. Derangement was a vulnerability whose origin, Parkman explained, was no
more one's fault than the color of one's eyes or the line of one's nose:
"Temperaments, features, humors, are transmitted; ferocity by tigers
and leopards, mildness by sheep and doves."

This was also true of suicidal impulses, which could grab even the
healthiest of men. "Almost everybody is occasionally indifferent to
life," Dr. Parkman mused. "People on an eminence feel a strong pro-
pensity to leap down."

And now, as his trail went cold, his family had to consider the painful possibility that Dr. Parkman—perhaps from the Craigie Bridge,
perhaps from the Medical College's riverside grounds—had finally
made that leap, and drowned in the frigid Charles River. Just as much
as the fabled Parkman wealth, George had inherited the family's frail-
ties; and in thousands of handbills to be printed and posted across the
city, the family now revealed both.

SPECIAL NOTICE!
$3000 REWARD.

Dr. George Parkman, a well known citizen of Boston, left his residence, No. 8 Walnut Street, on Friday last; he is 60 years of age,
about 5 feet 9 inches high, grey hair, thin face, with a scar under his
chin, light complexion, and usually walks very fast. He was dressed
in a dark frock coat, dark pantaloons, purple silk vest, with dark
figured black stock and black hat.

As he may have wandered from home in consequence of some sudden aberration of mind, being perfectly well when he left his house;
or, as he had with him a large sum of money, he may have been foully
dealt with; the above reward will be paid for information which will

lead to his discovery if alive; or for the detection and conviction of the perpetrators of any injury that may have been done him.

A suitable reward will be paid for the discovery of his body.

Information may be given to the City Marshal.
ROBERT G. SHAW

Three thousand dollars. It was a staggering amount—as much as one of the city's detectives earned in five years. What had been a local mystery occupying the police and concerned citizens now became a frenzied all-out search of house, riverbank, and woodland.

* * * *

THE CLUES kept coming into Tukey's office.

I saw him at six o'clock that evening, a freedman insisted. *It was over by the Harrison Avenue church.* This man was a better witness than most: he'd once been a messenger for the Registry of Deeds and knew the city's landlords by sight.

In all these sightings from later that Friday afternoon, though, Parkman never spoke, and that left the leads open to mistaken identity. Then again, perhaps such silence hinted at the nature of his disappearance. Searches for missing persons generally fell into one of three categories: they didn't want to be found, they did want to be found, or they were too distraught to know what they wanted at all. Each type dictated a different kind of search.

Escaped slaves didn't want to be found; neither did escaped apprentices. Debtors didn't want to be found; indeed, the recently lamented Edgar Allan Poe, in his reckless youth, had fled Virginia creditors by living among Boston's docks as one "Henri Le Rennet." Runaway young men didn't want to be found. Tukey had recently had a case involving a sixteen-year-old boy who vanished between home and school one morning; the lad was found in New York, trying to book a passage to California to hit it rich in the gold fields. And young runaway girls? Some stealthily left to obtain a midwife or an abortion and never made it home, as the sad case at Harvard the previous summer had shown. Newspaper notices for missing sixteen-year-olds that concluded with the phrase "her friends feel much alarmed" hinted, without ever saying it frankly, of such sorrows. But sometimes it was simply elopement: Tukey once found a sixteen-year-old girl by going to the house of her beau, a forty-year-old widower who boasted that he'd hidden her perfectly. Tukey promptly broke into the fellow's house to find the girl in his front room. She was sent on her way home that same evening.

Newspaper ads and ship's manifests had long been essential tools in tracking down errant souls. But these days, ticket masters at railroads were also the eyes of public watchfulness—it seemed as if all the population passed under their gaze at some point—and thanks to the telegraph, the stations could be alerted instantly.

There were also those who *wanted* to be found: the very young, the very elderly, and the very drunk, all of whom were prone to wandering off into trouble. In a seaport like Boston, the immediate danger was drowning, and in those cases, the search party was best. Sometimes these arrived in time, and sometimes, as with a drunken carpenter recently found floating facedown in an F Street quarry, they most certainly did not.

And then there were the robbed, who if still alive also wanted to be found. Here the tip-off was the carrying of cash. If the missing fellow was a deliveryman or messenger, a landlord or a jeweler—especially if the newspaper ads for him noted that he had been carrying $100, $500, even $1,000 or more—then the odds turned grim. The happiest result in such cases was that the man had run off with the money himself or had stopped off in a tavern and drunk it all. That fall, the city had seen a circus around the disappearance of a deliveryman, whose desperate friends even consulted mesmerists. One seer gravely announced that the fellow had been killed and buried in a stable on Sudbury

Street; men spent two days shoveling out horse manure and digging down into the fragrant dirt floors before giving up. No, scoffed another mesmerist, the missing man was a raving lunatic and had locked himself into the run-down Howard's Hotel in New York City. That city's police, alerted by telegraph, had no more luck than the manure shovelers. When the deliveryman finally turned up, it was in neither of these places but on a steamboat bound for Albany—much confused, and with his cargo perhaps distilled into a heavy hangover.

But it was the cases involving "aberration of mind," and particularly suicidal despair, that were the hardest to grapple with. Families were reluctant to talk about them. Moreover, a determined man or woman could reach heavily wooded land within the space of an hour from Boston and, in the throes of brain trouble, might lose themselves so thoroughly that they couldn't reemerge even if they wanted to. There was still the open case of Franklin Taylor, lost that June, who had been miserable with delirium tremens; he'd last been seen wandering on a country road out past Concord, and search parties had failed to find him ever since. If he'd hung himself in the denser stretches of those woods, his body might not become visible until midwinter had stripped all the leaves from the trees.

But that answer—suicide—just didn't make sense this time.

I saw Dr. Parkman, the old Registry of Deeds messenger insisted.

Was it light out? Did you speak to him?

No, but . . .

The lead would probably go nowhere; most proved useless.

Tukey had his own suspicions about Parkman, and they didn't involve wandering moodily around lonely woodlands or empty churches. The doctor's mental ailments might have explained a disappearance at other points in his life, but his actions that day, just before the last reliable sighting outside the Medical College, didn't sound like those of a man about to go hang or drown himself. He'd still been collecting his rents; he'd bought a head of lettuce that he was to return for in a few minutes. Another new lead showed that he'd stopped by

the offices of a religious newspaper on some minor business and told
the proprietor he'd be back the next day. And, well, the man had just
had his dentures fixed. Why would he have bothered, if he'd known
they were to end up at the bottom of Charles River?

*   *   *   *

DERASTUS CLAPP was almost embarrassed to be leading three fellow detectives up the steps of the medical school again that Tuesday.
He'd been on the force for some twenty years, and he knew when
his time was being wasted. The only person with much enthusiasm
for going over the grounds again was Kingsley, Parkman's nettlesome
underling. The property agent had, as ever, tenaciously attached himself to their search.

Clapp wearily knocked on the side door to the janitor's apartment,
and a surprised Littlefield peered out. Yes, they informed him, they
were here to search the building again.

Dr. Bigelow was nearby, and the janitor looked to him for guidance.
But the busy young doctor had his own problems. Phineas Gage, the
marvelous man brained by an iron rod, had proven about as unstable
as—well, a man brained with an iron rod. Rumors had him begging
on nearby blocks, which, if true, was an embarrassment to the school.

"Show them everything," Dr. Bigelow replied, dismissing the question. One more police search would hardly make a difference to their
week now.

The officers humored Kingsley in his insistence on thoroughness.
They began in the janitor's apartment, where they looked for a body
under Littlefield's bed, *in* Littlefield's bed, and then—in the kitchen
crockery. This was ostensibly to find any belongings of Parkman's, but
Kingsley thought he could hear the officers snickering at him.

"Let us go into Dr. Webster's apartments," one of the detectives
announced drily. It took several knocks, then pounding, to roust the
absentminded Dr. Webster; he let them in and showed them once
again through his lecture hall and his chemistry lab, just as he had

the previous day. The officers, under pointless orders to search again, scarcely tried to hide their discontent.

"We can't believe, for a moment, Sir, that it is necessary to search your apartments," one of them finally blurted out.

The rooms about Webster's lab were scattered with the thick grape-vines and leather he'd been using in commercial experiments; nearby was a reused tea chest where he'd absently left some minerals heaped up. Clapp walked about, observed the laboratory equipment in respect-ful incomprehension, then paused before the door of a storeroom; it looked like it served some special purpose. What, he wanted to know, was the room for?

"There's where I keep my dangerous articles," Webster explained.

The old officer pulled a face and thrust his head in to make a very brisk inspection of the shelves. Clapp then pointed to the next door, an unprepossessing portal with a pane of frosted glass set in it.

"What place is this?"

"That is Dr. Webster's private privy," the janitor explained. This pre-sented an even less appealing investigatory prospect than the roomful of chemicals had.

"Gentlemen," Dr. Webster added, leading them to the front of the lab's storage areas, "here is another room that you have not looked into."

But there were not many places left to find a missing man except for the obvious: the various crawl spaces under the building. Littlefield, who possessed the one key to the dissecting receptacle, threw open the floor hatch for the officers; they peered inside its foul recesses with a lantern until their curiosity was satisfied. The officers then followed the janitor through a trap door and down onto the dirt cellar, and as the ceiling progressively lowered, just one hardy detective stuck with the janitor as he navigated the muddy perimeter where the river water washed in. After they emerged, old Detective Clapp was to be found chatting with Webster at the laboratory bench, their forms framed by the window that looked out toward the hospital.

Derastus tried to put the best light he could on their investigation. "If we search the college first," he explained, "people round here will not object to our searching *their* houses." But it had clearly been a waste of time. Thanksgiving was a couple of days off. Three-thousand-dollar reward or not, soon they'd find better rewards at home than in crawling around cellars.

* * * *

THE DETECTIVES returned to city hall to find Tukey's office cluttered with an improbable array of patent-office contraptions. A thief they'd arrested the night before, for breaking into a local brush factory and raiding its cashbox, was an ex-con whose efforts to go straight had repeatedly been thwarted by his habit of sawing through walls and floors to burglarize adjoining businesses. After two seven-year stretches in prison, the accused was now trying to invent new machinery for brick manufacturing, but he needed capital—so he'd merely gone to the nearest available source. From his cell, the would-be inventor had piteously asked for his patent models to be sent to Tukey, the better to plead for leniency. And here they sat, a mute testament to how a clever man might still stumble onto a path toward prison.

He'd likely get another seven years, and then, like as not, he'd be caught stealing again.

Theft was the simplest and most elemental of misdeeds; its flows of goods were the visible ripples that played across the surface where many other submerged crimes lurked. With Parkman's search parties again turning up nothing, that Tuesday night Tukey reached for his last lure: the love of Boston thieves for selling watches. If Parkman had been killed for his money, only a truly disciplined thief would stop at the man's wallet. A gold watch, readily convertible to cash, would simply be too good to pass up. While a murderer might not rise to the bait of a reward, an unwitting fence for the watch might. The key was to offer a much higher markup than the usual resale on the item, but not so much as to make someone suspicious of the ad's true import.

The Boston police knew their stolen goods. As a young man, Derastus Clapp had worked for years as an auctioneer, and even before joining the force he had shown a penchant for personally tracking down auction room swindlers. And so, as the officers wrote up their ad, they knew just the right amount to offer.

$100 REWARD will be paid for Information which leads to the recovery of a gold double-bottomed lepine turned case-watch, ladies' size, full plate, four-holed jeweled, gold dial, black figures, steel hands, no second hands, no cap.

Marked, F. B. Adams & Sons, St. John street, London. No. 61,351.

FRANCIS TUKEY, *City Marshal,*
Police Office, City Hall.
Boston, November 27th.

Parkman's peculiar timepiece made it the perfect ploy, as no newspaper reader would suspect that the ad was related to his case. Everyone knew that doctors carried masculine watches with a sweep hand, in order to take pulses. But Parkman, indifferent to style and long out of clinical practice, carried a ladies' model with no second hand.

The usual arrests of a Tuesday evening rolled in, along with more unconfirmed leads in the case: the doctor had been seen in Lynn, he'd been spotted grabbing a traveler's horse by the reins on the Salem road, and so forth. The most intriguing visitor that evening was a Cambridge merchant who recalled crossing a bridge at four in the morning the previous Saturday; he'd seen a suspicious character carrying a very heavy parcel across the spans—and "so disliked the looks of the man, that he shunned him by crossing to the opposite side of the street, and started immediately for his residence."

But even as the hours on the city marshal's own watch ticked onward after the ad ran, still there was no discovery of the living doctor, no finding of a body, and no response about Adams & Sons watch No. 61,351. Tukey went home in defeat. Dr. Parkman had now been missing for over a hundred hours. The doctor's gold case watch, if not rewound, had long since stopped.

Part III

THE
SUSPECT

PROF. JOHN W. WEBSTER.

9

THANKSGIVING
BY THE FIRE

THE MORNING OF WEDNESDAY, NOVEMBER 28, WAS A COLD and sober one. As Bostonians arose and clutched their nightgowns against the chill, at least some lacked their customary hangovers. Back in the summer, the temperance minister Father Mathew had thundered through Massachusetts, inveighing against the evils of alcohol to a crowd of twelve thousand on Boston Common, and converting half the inmates of the Cambridge Jail. And so now even the Medical College's janitor—fond as he was of staying up late, dancing, and the crackling shuffle of a new deck of cards—had, like so many local husbands, found himself rather confoundedly spending his evenings at the Sons of Temperance hall.

But whether Ephraim was sober or not, Mrs. Littlefield still could not persuade him to ever like getting up in the morning.

Though his family's quarters in the basement of the Medical College at least made the walk to work a short one, Ephraim's acknowledgment of the new day was grudging. His building duties required that he rise in the early hours to stoke the stoves, not least for his basement neighbor. Earlier that season they'd stowed a load of soft coal in a bin between the lab stairs and the privy, and another load of hard coal near the assay furnace, where it would see slow but steady use well into the spring. Perhaps some professors liked the crisp, cold air of November, but the weather simply chilled Dr. Webster, who always needed to stay warm; the chemistry professor was, as Ephraim put it, "a cold-feeling kind of man."

One might have hoped that Wednesday, being the day before

Thanksgiving, would see professors arriving late, if they came in at all. But a footfall upon the back steps announced Professor Webster's arrival—not just on time but *early*. Lately Ephraim had been freed from firing Webster's stoves in the morning; it seemed there were experiments the doctor didn't want disturbed. Still, perhaps Professor Webster would change his mind, it being so early and the room so cold. Littlefield dressed, shuffled out into the basement hallway between his apartment and the academic rooms, and turned the knob on the lab door.

It wouldn't budge.

This was vexing for the janitor. The doctor had taken to locking his doors, and while theft was always a concern, it made cleaning and maintaining the college rooms a nuisance. The door wouldn't open, and Ephraim could *hear* the doctor inside. What was Webster doing that made him oblivious to knocks and the rattling of the doorknob? What *were* his experiments?

Quietly, Ephraim bent down and placed his eye at the keyhole.

Still nothing: the lowered latch inside the door covered the keyhole. A disappointment, but one for which no janitor worth his salt would be unprepared. Ephraim had a trusty utility knife, and the door possessed a thin section of partitioning that could be pried up by the workings of a blade. The task would hardly excite the attention of anyone who should pass by; what sight in a building was more unremarkable than grounds staff fiddling about with a door repair?

He maneuvered the knife noiselessly at first, pausing periodically to listen to Dr. Webster at work within the lab. And then a small sliver of the wood detached with a loud *crack*. The movements inside the lab stopped.

Ephraim froze in place; he had been heard. Also, he had been *seen*—by his wife. On the cellar stairs behind him, Mrs. Littlefield stood unamused, watching his goings-on.

Come back! she hissed.

Ephraim slid away from the door and back into their basement kitchen, as chastened as any of their children. What was the point of rising early if you were locked out of work, and also forbidden to play?

But with the children and her visiting niece also occupying Mrs. Littlefield's attention, it was not long before Ephraim found a chance to step back out into the passage between his home and Webster's lab. He crept up to the entrance, and this time he softly lay down on the cold brick floor, in the grit and dust his broom had missed. A glimmer of light shone out from under the door, and the janitor silently moved his head closer to peek through the gap.

He could see inside—just a little.

Before him stretched the expanse of the lab floor, the legs of tables, the cold metal of an unused furnace, and then, entering into his line of sight, the shoes and pant legs of Dr. Webster. Only the professor's legs were visible, sometimes drawing near to the door, sometimes farther away, sometimes nearer again. *If he should find me here . . .*

The legs stopped in their movements; and then a scraping and dragging sound tore through the air. A pause, then another scrape. Then another: Ephraim could see Webster's hand dragging a coal bucket used to feed the laboratory furnace. A hand and a sleeve reached down again and brought the bucket to rest near the assay furnace, by the lab's privy. The doctor now lingered in that corner of the room, but whether in an absent professorial reverie or hard at work, there was no way to tell; the motions of his hands were hidden from sight.

Dr. Webster was as far away from the lab door as he would get; and having lain there for five minutes, Ephraim could count on soon being missed back in his home. He quietly drew himself up off the floor and padded back through the basement passage and into the warmth of his kitchen.

*   *   *

As always, there was work for Ephraim around the building; but it being the day before Thanksgiving, there also was shopping to do with Mrs. Littlefield. Their largest task had been made unexpectedly easier the day before when, in a fit of generosity, Dr. Webster had told him to go to a local provisioner—*Do you know where Mr. Foster's is, by the Howard Athenaeum?* The place was a bit out of the way, actually, but the janitor could scarcely complain after Webster had jotted an order on a piece of paper and handed it to him, saying, "Take that order, and get you a nice turkey." So now Ephraim and his wife searched past offices of lawyers and architects, past the corner police watch box and the plasterings of reward notices for Dr. Parkman, and down Howard Street, looking for the sign announcing A. A. FOSTER & CO.

It was hard to miss: the shop was right next to the Howard Athenaeum, a Gothic building that looked more like a church than a theater. That was fitting; the site had previously been occupied by the Millerite end-of-times sect, which had chosen the plot for the imminent rapture; the parishioners had raised their building haphazardly, with the front wall leaning out worryingly, explaining that "it made but little difference as the world itself would last but a few days at the most." Instead of the Second Coming of Christ, today the site, with a new and more stable structure, was to host a farce titled *The Irish Secretary.* There might be some Harvard students there, and not just in the seventy-five-cent box seats but onstage. Lately some had taken to low jaunts over to the theater to serve as extras, cavorting around as Roman centurions or, for tonight, donning the costume of liveried servants.

But there would be no plays today for Ephraim. He and Caroline stepped into Foster's, where the white-coated staff was busy wrapping up parcels of lard, pork, butter, and turkey for the onrush of Thanksgiving buyers. Mr. Foster read over the order—*Please deliver Mr. Littlefield a nice turkey, weighing eight or nine pounds, and charge the same to me.—Dr. Webster*—and opened his remaining stock to inspection. A. A. Foster's, he liked to claim, sold the best poultry in town.

Pick whichever turkey you like, the grocer said.

There was also an order for a bushel of sweet potatoes to be sent to Dr. Webster's house; clearly the doctor was putting on a large Thanksgiving meal, and he was not a man known for frugality in his dinners and salons. Dr. Webster had always been one to lay in orders for everything from claret to the latest sheet music; his deliveryman, Mr. Sawin, had probably made the run out to Cambridge hundreds of times.

One of the biggest tasks for Ephraim that day was not, in fact, placing orders with the provisioner at all, but acquiring a chunk of alkaline quicklime from a supplier on the local docks. This was the same order he had to pick up for the doctor's chemistry experiments every winter—*I want a piece about as big as your head,* Webster would always say. Going to Foster's had taken Ephraim too far out of the way already; the task would have to wait. This meant that he'd go out again on Thanksgiving Day itself, improbably in search of a burning caustic, but that was the nature of working in the Medical College building. He and Caroline were readying, after all, for a Thanksgiving dinner to be held just a few rooms away from the dissecting tables—where, in the cold November moonlight, a cold jar of blood waited as red as any cranberries.

* * * *

IT WAS afternoon by the time the couple returned home and set down their purchases. The medical school had that sepulchral quiet that settles over academic buildings before a holiday; the day's lectures were done, and no sounds came from the chemistry lab anymore. Ephraim still had chores around the building to do, and as he passed through the entryway into the dissecting room, he paused as he felt a curious warmth come over his body. He turned to the opposite wall in the entryway, the one shared with the lab—and, puzzled, set his fingers upon the plaster.

He jerked his hand back—the wall was *hot,* almost unbearably so. *The building is on fire. It has to be.*

The janitor dashed around the halls, banging on the lab door to no avail, and then ran into the chemistry lecture hall. He pulled on the door to Webster's private stairs down to the basement lab. It, too, was locked. Littlefield thrust his head outside, half-expecting to see crackling and roaring flames leaping out the lab windows. Instead, he found dead silence.

The river had receded enough from the muddy tidal flats for Littlefield to pad behind the rear of the building. He pulled himself up on the back wall and looked inside one of the double windows to the lab. There didn't appear to be anyone inside, nor the least hint of a fire. Puzzled, he glanced about, then hoisted himself up onto the sill and surreptitiously tried the window. It gave way under his hand; the doctor had left it unlocked. The janitor pushed it up and, with effort, pulled himself through the window and dropped catlike onto the floor.

He was alone.

In all his years at the Medical College, Littlefield had never broken into his own workplace before, and he moved about cautiously in the silent laboratory. Something was missing: the pile of pitch pine kindling he'd brought in on Friday was used up. The reason why was immediately apparent: near the privy, the assay furnace was out but still radiated heat, as did the bricks below and the flue running up the wall behind it. A heavy soapstone covered the top of the furnace, along with an iron crucible and some scatterings of minerals; perhaps Webster had been experimenting with raising them to a white heat. The furnace must have been fiercely stoked to make the very stones in the walls hot to the touch, and it was hard to imagine what beyond the laboratory's two full sixty-three-gallon hogsheads of water could have kept the building itself from catching fire. Littlefield hefted a broom from the corner of the coal pen and thrust the handle into the giant water barrels: one was empty, the other nearly so. Not only had Webster used a pile of kindling, he'd gone through about one hundred gallons of water.

Littlefield walked up the back stairs to the lecture hall, to the other side of the door he'd been unable to open earlier. Looking down, he saw curious dark brown stains on the hard pine steps.

Blood?

Hardly unusual in the medical building, perhaps. Nevertheless, Littlefield bent down and dabbed his fingers into the stains, then cautiously tasted his fingertips: the substance was acidic. Had it been used to clean away something underneath, or was it the mere splashings of the jittery professor and his chemicals? Indeed, the state of the beakers and retorts in the room were something of an exasperation for Littlefield himself; with the door locked so much, it had been days since he'd washed any glassware for Webster. Still, he couldn't do that now; he didn't dare leave a hint that he'd been inside. His presence in the locked laboratory—and he'd been there for perhaps fifteen minutes or more now—was going to be hard enough to explain if the doctor returned.

The janitor slid back out over the sill, pulled the window shut behind himself, and dropped down to the muddy earth. Out on the river, men were still probing the frigid and murky water with grappling hooks, dragging the bottom for their missing man.

10

THE
FINAL REWARD

HELLO.

The servant froze in mortification. Dr. Webster had returned unexpectedly.

The doctor was miles from the Medical College, back in his house in Cambridge—and as a new maid, Anne simply had to accustom herself to Webster's unexpected comings and goings. She'd been working in the Garden Street home for only two weeks, and it seemed a respectable if queer placement. The doctor maintained a fine house—two parlors, six bedrooms, sumptuous carpeting and easy chairs throughout—and yet did so with a curiously minimal staff. Indeed, it was just Anne; for instead of employing a housekeeper, Mrs. Webster and her three daughters still in residence would get up every morning at five o'clock and go about the house dusting, polishing, and trimming the lamp wicks. And then there was the furnace to maintain, always the furnace: the Websters kept their house stoked so warm that, had the doctor brought home the thermometers from his lab, they might have registered eighty degrees inside.

The doctor was not, thankfully, in the kitchen to ask for his afternoon tea—which was a good thing, as Anne hadn't readied it yet.

He instead passed briskly into the living room to check on his daughter Marianne and to remark on the book she was perusing. Of late they'd been discussing yet another new purchase of his for the family library—an illustrated edition of Milton's pastoral "L'Allegro." The voice that sometimes struggled above the lecture hall could easily fill the parlor with the blind poet's stanzas:

To hear the Lark begin his flight,
And singing startle the dull night,
From his watch-towre in the skies,
Till the dappled dawn doth rise;
Then to com in spight of sorrow,
And at my window bid good morrow,
Through the Sweet-Briar, or the Vine,
Or the twisted Eglantine.

It was indeed the vine the doctor had really come home for, not the poetry. He drew up the long, sharp knife he favored for pruning and went behind the house to one of his great comforts: his garden. While Webster's daughters had their own talents and pastimes to retreat into—Hattie had even built herself a little studio in the garret of the house—none shared the doctor's enthusiasm for weeding, trimming, and the patient espaliering of vines. Like the laboratory, his garden was a place where he could labor and cogitate alone. He certainly needed the fresh air and physical labor. Now that he was fifty-six years old, his short frame had become stout with encroaching age; and though still energetic, Webster was no longer the youthful doctor of two decades earlier, when he'd installed an open-air gym on Harvard's grounds. Back then, he'd led the undergraduates in pole vaults and parallel bar exercises before dinner; now, a quiet afternoon in the garden with a pruning knife was what he liked best.

It was a fine, clear day, and his plants were waiting for him—nectarines, pears, currants, and bare tangles of grapevines. Cambridge families took a great pride in their abundant gardens; it was the highest of crimes to pilfer produce from over the town's picket fences. Over the years, Webster had provided fruit and floral displays to the local horticultural society, and the doctor had a scientific interest in the plants as well: he shipped carefully packed boxes of precious bulbs and cuttings to his in-laws in the Azores, to better spread and trade new varieties.

One by one, Webster took to cutting the dense, fibrous old grapevines in his back garden. It was pleasant work, interrupted occasionally by the honking of geese; they'd been flying in formations overhead for days, escaping the chilly north. Webster was collecting thick vines for staining—for, as he patiently explained, grape was "a very porous wood." By soaking it in dye and cutting it into cross sections, he could get the vessels of the wood to reveal themselves in blue and purple, a marvel to be passed around the lecture hall by his students; and then too, with such dyeing, the plant's xylem and phloem showed even more dramatically under a microscope.

Webster had other experiments on his mind as well, of course—he'd been toying with a new method of tanning leather and had long known that extracts of chestnut bark had shown particular promise in that process. A man of talents in plant chemistry might make a fortune in this industrial era. Webster's work a few years earlier had narrowly missed the rush of the gutta-percha trade, when everything from telegraph-wire insulators to shoe soles and stethoscope tubes was being made from the rubbery plant sap. He could scarcely afford to keep failing to capitalize on such opportunities.

Webster cut carefully; he could become abstracted in thought when gardening. Just a couple of weeks earlier, his knife had slipped and gashed his hand, blood welling up onto the blade. The doctor had to be careful—much more careful.

* * * *

HALF THE Webster clan boarded the six-twenty p.m. omnibus into Boston, bound for a family party at the widow Cunningham's. Mrs. Webster and daughter Hattie both stayed home, which was no surprise; Hattie had recently become engaged to a cousin, and now had rather less need of meeting other dashing, distant relatives. Nor was Sarah present, as she was already married and living in the Azores. It was Sarah and Hattie who took after their father—and so now, dressed for the party, daughters Catherine and Marianne were rather like ambassadors for their mother's Hickling branch of the family.

The full moon was rising over a lovely and clear November night, a fine evening for a party. The doctor and his daughters disembarked from the omnibus and made their way up to Mrs. Cunningham's house on Vine Street. The residence was scarcely a block from the Medical College—though the Websters could have continued to any other house farther down in Beacon Hill, so intertwined were the families in this neighborhood. Webster had married up into a tangle of maritime trading clans—the Hicklings, the Dabneys, the Prescotts, the Cunninghams—all of them interlocked and partnering in the merchant trade since before the Revolution.

The Cunninghams were a spartan, thrifty side of the family— "dignified and severely polite," as one acquaintance explained. It was widely rumored that the patriarchs Andrew and Charles sat atop fortunes of $100,000 apiece, though one could hardly tell from the unremitting labor of the old men. They still kept offices on the docks, where they arrived promptly at seven in the morning; and there, through a hole cut into their counting room window, the brothers placed a spyglass to keep a watchful eye over their incoming and outbound clippers. Mrs. Cunningham, as a well-provided daughter-in-law, maintained a house whose hospitality to relatives was worthy of the old Puritan days: generous but plain, with little economies visible in every linen and lamp, every cupboard and closet.

Her recently married son, Charles, at least, could keep things lively, for though a Cunningham, he had an inordinate love of Italian opera, the latest fashion for Bostonians. And since his home bordered the theater district, it was a passion he could indulge in easily.

Mr. Barnum, the local chatter ran, *is trying to bring over Jenny Lind to America. Guaranteed her a thousand dollars a night!*

It sounded like a scandalous sum, but Barnum was no fool. The tickets would sell. The Cunninghams understood the verities of business: Barnum imported Swedish sopranos and Fiji mermaids, and the Cunninghams imported Sicilian lemons and Portuguese Madeira. It was all perishable goods, all calculated risk, all the careful laying away of insurance and reserves for loss and spoilage. The doctor and his two remaining unmarried daughters were not impressed, though, by such business-mindedness.

"They think only professional men are worth noticing," the doctor's sister-in-law sniffed.

That disdain had not kept Dr. Webster himself from marrying into the Hicklings, even as he chose a Harvard appointment over the dockside counting rooms; nor had it kept his daughter Sarah from marrying into the Dabney branch. Nor, for that matter, had it kept young Hattie, back home this evening, from becoming engaged to yet another Dabney brother. The Websters liked the starched civility of old Boston money, even if they did not much like the grimy particulars of how it was made.

Still, there was another, less mercantile matter for the party to consider. Mrs. Cunningham's house was near Holland's grocery, and her block, like every other in the neighborhood, had been mobilized for searches into basements and attics for the missing George Parkman. The widow's windows looked out upon streets covered with reward bills. The very doors and sheds of the college itself had been plastered with them. The almost painful politeness of the Cunningham family was not quite enough to keep one guest from blurting out her thoughts that evening.

"So, Doctor," she asked Webster, "you were the last person who saw Dr. Parkman. What if *you* should be suspected?"

The doctor scarcely interrupted his intellectual disquisitions to the other partygoers.

"What do you think?" he answered drolly. "Do I *look* like a murderer?"

* * * *

THE WEBSTERS left at ten-thirty p.m. Although the toll bridge was only a few blocks away, the eleven o'clock omnibus was a busy one—the theater omnibus, it was called—and they would need to make sure they could find seats among the press of people returning from plays and moving-panorama shows. All the omnibuses and trains had been busy, though, with Bostonians making Thanksgiving pilgrimages out to Concord, Salem, and far-flung hamlets, while country cousins, conversely, poured into the great metropolis. The new laying of rails around the state had changed the nature of the holiday; with travel between distant towns now so readily done in the space of a day or two, Thanksgiving was evolving into a grand occasion for family reunions. This year, one local observed, "livery stable keepers, omnibus proprietors, and railroad companies found handsome sums in profits."

The collectors in the busy tollhouse were a good source of gossip; that day's story was how two men, confounded by a one-cent toll "per foot passenger," promptly piggybacked up to the tollbooth, demanding to pay only a penny. It was a story about Irishmen, of course; local tales about such antics generally were, and the latest account fit neatly alongside the one about the Irishman trying to pay his penny toll with a twenty-dollar bill.

What is that?

Short as Dr. Webster was, his girls were even shorter, and they were craning to look up at yet another new handbill posted that very evening. The father peered through his spectacles at the note and read it aloud to them.

$1000 REWARD.

Whereas no satisfactory information has been obtained respecting **DR. GEORGE PARKMAN**, since the afternoon of Friday last, and fears are entertained that he has been murdered,—the above Reward will be paid for information which leads to the recovery of his body.

ROBERT G. SHAW

BOSTON, November 28th, 1849.

On the banks below the bridge, the rivermen had hung up their empty hooks for the night. The family's reward seemed to be simply a final, dignified gesture of propriety in the face of a hopeless loss.

The omnibus lurched forward and into the night. It was still possible in these waning days of 1849 to feel that one could leave the city and its mysteries behind. The railroad to Cambridge would not be ready until the New Year, and the doctor and his daughters arrived at the Harvard Square stop not with a steam whistle and the hiss of a boiler but with the subdued snorting of horses and their languid clatter upon the road. The walk up Garden Street was a quiet one, even for Cambridge; true to its name, the street held stretches under tillage, the remains of the old Cow Common, and the placid expanse of the small local reservoir for fires.

Behind them, a stealthier step might be heard in the shadows. Mr. Sanderson, the town's night policeman, made a habit of quietly trailing those returning home from the theater omnibus. In this peaceful part of town, it was as much to protect revelers from themselves as from anyone else.

The door swung inward to a home largely darkened with sleep; Hattie hadn't stayed up. It was getting late. But the doctor, a devotee of the *Evening Transcript*, shifted into his nightgown and stayed up to read the paper as midnight approached. A strange Thanksgiving, this one: the California gold rush of 1849 had diminished many family gatherings.

"How many circles have been thinned by the allurements which the golden prospects of California have held out!" the evening's paper mourned. "The young and middle-aged have left us, not by hundreds merely, but by thousands, and many a Thanksgiving board will miss their genial presence."

The rest of the paper consisted of the usual announcements: a train conductor had slipped that morning on the tracks by Fresh Pond and lost his legs; yet another water-system reservoir had been opened by the mayor, this one in South Boston; and for Thanksgiving Day, the post offices would close at noon, and there'd be no Thanksgiving edition of the *Evening Transcript*. They'd all be rising on the morrow to roast turkeys, to bake plum puddings, to spoon out bowls of squash and potatoes and oyster sauce, and to enjoy a day without news, a day too sleepy and homebound to warrant it.

11

WICKEDNESS
TAKES ELEVEN

THANKSGIVING WAS GLORIOUS: GENTLE AND STILL AUTUM-
nal, it spared Bostonians for just a little longer from the season's usual
lashings of cold. "What a contrast," one local rhapsodized, "to those
occasions when it has appeared, muffled in buffalo skins, amid snow
and ice!" For Marshal Tukey, that was exactly the problem. The holiday
meant men at home, and men at home meant feasting, and feasting
meant drinking, and mild weather meant going outside. And Boston
men at home feasting and drinking and then going outside meant one
thing: it was time for a riot.

They didn't need much of a reason to get started; with enough rum
about, reason was altogether excused from the matter. Rioting was an
honored local pastime, and even back in Tukey's first days on the job,
one had broken out because—well, nobody was quite sure why. Something to do one with one man upbraiding another's son for misbehav-
ing, claimed one account. There may not have been a father or son at
all, in retrospect; but there was rum, and there was fighting, and by the
time Tukey and his men had arrived, the crowd was a roaring, swing-
ing, kicking mass spilling down Hamilton Street. The officers were
trampled—and Tukey, in the droll parlance of a colleague, took a comprehensive set of knockings to "his knowledge-box." In the three years
since, he had suffered and dodged plenty more along the same streets.

It was also a great curiosity of Tukey's career that, at one time in his
life, he had also delivered some of those punches himself—and had
supplied the often illegal rum sales that fueled them.

The marshal's path to his job was nothing short of incredible. In the 1830s, after a youthful stint running a bakery in Salem, Francis Tukey moved to Boston and quickly fell afoul of the law. Suspected of plying the illegal liquor trade, he was hauled before a judge for viciously kicking, punching, and then tarring and feathering a police informer. A few months later, he declared himself insolvent. His next rum-selling venture netted a new charge of selling liquor without a license; a month later, Tukey was hauled in for yet another assault.

It was at around this time that he decided he was Harvard material.

Just how Marshal Tukey got out of his assault charge with a fifty-dollar fine was something, the *Boston Herald* later marveled, that "nobody, probably, but Tukey and the county attorney can tell." Yet by *some* means Tukey not only averted prison but managed to gain admission to Harvard Law School. He passed the bar in 1844, and when he successfully applied for the city marshal job in 1846, his previous hometown paper, the *Salem Register,* could scarcely contain its bewilderment. Tukey was, its reporter noted, "a more promising candidate for a police court than a candidate for a police officer." The *Herald,* always fond of a good scandal, vehemently attacked Tukey, issuing a pamphlet that declared him an embezzler, a necrophiliac, and a seducer of Sunday school teachers. Tukey's second assault victim, the pamphlet claimed, had in fact later died of his injuries. The city marshal was "a three-cent rumseller, a homicide, a thief, and a suborner in perjury," the newspaper declared. "A riper gallows apple never dangled between two uprights than this same lawbreaker."

Or perhaps he was a reformed man—a true Harvard success story. But some old habits died hard, for a year after becoming city marshal, Tukey declared insolvency again. By the *Herald's* account, the marshal had stocked up on groceries and two new suits the day before announcing himself broke. When the grocer tried to collect on the bill, the *Herald* claimed, Tukey told him "that he might go to hell, or wherever he pleased for it."

For better or worse, it was on this officer of the law that the peace of Boston, and the fate of Dr. Parkman, now depended.

* * * *

AND SO the Thanksgiving riot began. The day's pugilistic festivities commenced on India Street. Walking his beat, Officer Burnham overheard something other than the usual singing and toasting from the tenements. It turned out to be the sound of rather inexpert breaking and entering, from the vicinity of Mr. Hobbs's shop. Burnham paused and watched patiently as two men in an alleyway forced the closed wooden shutters and the first of them lofted himself inside the store. Burnham strolled up; the lookout promptly fled, and the officer peered triumphantly in through the window.

What's this then?

It was a clean collar—or it should have been. As Burnham marched the young Irishman out into the street, a crowd swirled up around them. Fists materialized, and boots; then more officers. And that's when Burnham was clobbered with a brick.

Some of the crime that day was of a blessedly tidier, more professional variety. With many Bostonians away visiting relatives, it was a fine day for housebreaking. One home on Fourth Street had a window pried open and some $700 in goods carried off—a silver plate, promissory notes, a vial of California gold dust, and nearly every stitch of linen and clothing in the house, from the mother's and father's right down to their children's garments. But drink and a day off had largely brought out the amateurs. One would-be gang picked a house on Lexington Street that, once the would-be burglars tumbled inside, proved to have little worth stealing; they were so indignant that they tore open the home's straw mattresses and set them afire. Another fellow, caught stealing pantaloons, appealed to his recent military service. "I fought in Mexico," the suspect explained stiffly, "and am an honest man." He was bundled into jail with the rest of the day's catch.

And, as on every day for the past week, there was the matter of the missing doctor. Some men were spending the holiday still trying their luck at dragging the river, spurred on by yet another rumor—someone had been spotted dumping a package off a bridge—and by the Parkman family's promise of $1,000 for even a dead body. Telegraph lines clicked insistently with sightings in other towns of eccentric wanderers who might or might not be Parkman. One of the more frequent reports—of shadowy appearances in the woods around Milton—did turn out to be a missing Bostonian: Benjamin Talbot, an insane man who'd gone missing not long after Parkman had. Another fellow, this one down in Braintree, proved too incoherent to identify at all; the police spared him the indignity of a holiday in jail and booked their ward into a hotel, waiting to figure out his name. But he did not, alas, appear to be Dr. Parkman.

Another fretful message came into Marshal Tukey's office: there was an unbalanced older man answering Parkman's description in the village of Lynn. *Inquire into the matter*, Officer Rice was ordered. Rice trudged back later with an explanation: the fellow was nothing more than "an honest old cobbler" whose alarming evidence of madness had been to inquire whether a local school admitted poor children.

"This," a report marveled, "was considered proof of insanity!"

* * * *

Dr. Parkman's disappearance also cast a strange unease over the Littlefields' holiday in the Medical College building. Their turkey sat uneaten. It seemed a waste, as they'd had turkey every Thanksgiving; the one they'd picked up from Mr. Foster was a fine beast. But Ephraim Littlefield couldn't shake off his sense that something was wrong. That morning, the janitor had pulled his wife aside to the bedroom, away from the children, to whisper his suspicion.

Just as much as I am standing here, he'd confided, *that doctor's involved in Parkman's disappearance.*

"What makes you think so?" his wife rebuked him. "For mercy's sake, never mention it again. If the Professor should get hold of it—" She hardly needed to explain. Not just their livelihood but their very living quarters depended on the Medical College job. "It would make *trouble,*" she finished. Anyway, Littlefield had work to get done: the grapevines delivered to the lab by Mr. Sawin had been sitting out in the cellar, and the children had been scattering them all over the house and making a nuisance. Why on earth hadn't they been stowed correctly in the lab?

He marched with her down the hallway and over to the lab door. The diminishing bundle of grapevines still sat in the corridor, along with three small pine boxes marked, in red chalk, J. W. WEBSTER, CAMBRIDGE. The various deliveries of the week were simply piling up outside the lab. Littlefield turned the doorknob, then tugged on the locked door.

"You see?" he snapped. "Fastened."

The two returned to their quarters, where the promise of a day's cooking awaited. But the turkey in their larder weighed on them. Why had they been given it? In all Littlefield's years of custodial service at the college, Dr. Webster had never shown any kindness at the holidays.

"He never gave me a present before this time," he reasoned, "not even to the value of a cent."

Nor had Webster, as was his usual wont, had these purchases delivered. No, he'd sent the Littlefields themselves out to a provisioner—a fine one, but many blocks away—to pick out a bird at the height of the holiday rush. It was as if the doctor had been trying to get them away from the building. And in that building, there was only one place that still hadn't been searched at all.

So Littlefield didn't want the turkey. He had a better plan for how he was going to spend the holiday.

I'm going to break in, he announced.

He'd had a sledgehammer lying unused in the cellar ever since the building was unveiled—the stonemasons had probably left it behind—but, of course, now that he needed it, he couldn't find it. The local hardware stores would be closed today; and so, Littlefield had to make do with whatever he could procure: namely, a hammer, a hatchet, and a mortising chisel.

Here, he said, pressing the hammer upon his dubious wife. *If you see Dr. Webster coming, hammer on the floor four times.* It was a shame, really. He needed that hammer, but he couldn't very well have her hitting the floor with a hatchet. So Littlefield lit a lamp, grabbed the hatchet and chisel, and, with his wife watching worriedly, slid down the trap door.

The medical school's crawl space was as he'd left it two days earlier, when he'd shown Officer Fuller around. He made his way to the back of the building, the space narrowing lower and lower, to crouching and then crawling height. The damp and cold of the river surrounded Littlefield; somewhere, a few feet over his head and a house or two away, his neighbors were probably enjoying some coffee and pumpkin pie right about now. That was how any sensible person would be spending Thanksgiving afternoon. Yet here he was: stooped over, cold and alone, a hatchet in his hand. Before him, a thick layer of brickwork extended to either side, disappearing into the darkness of the crawl space. He set the chisel into the mortar between two bricks and reached for the hatchet.

He swung the flat of the hatchet hard, and again and again, the racket rebounding off the brick and the floorboards above. Bits of mortar smashed and crumbled into the dirt, scattering into the plot of land Dr. Parkman had once owned, the soil he'd given over to this very school. Still there was no sign from upstairs; Caroline hadn't struck the floor with her hammer. It was probably safe—why would the doctor come in on a holiday? But if he did, it would be very hard for the janitor to explain what he was about to do. It wasn't just that he was once again, for the second day in a row, breaking into the professional premises of Dr. John White Webster, MD, presently of Cambridge, esteemed member of the Geological Society of London and Erving Professor of Chemistry and Mineralogy at Harvard. It was that this time he was breaking into a very specific part of the doctor's premises.

Littlefield was going to smash into the bottom of his toilet.

* * * *

HE'D FAILED.

The janitor opened his eyes, brought the world into focus. He'd failed to wake up early, and according to the hectoring verses that had run in the local newspapers recently, a man's character could be judged by how long he slept.

Nature requires five,
Custom gives us seven—
Laziness takes nine,
And Wickedness eleven.

At first glance, Littlefield wasn't a wicked man: he'd slept only five hours. The problem was, before that he'd been out dancing until four in the morning.

He lumbered into the kitchen for the breakfast his wife had been waiting an hour for him to eat. Waking up late hadn't been his real failure: it was leaving the crawl space work undone. Ephraim had managed to remove only a few bricks. The privy wall was improbably thick; after an hour, his arms aching from the clumsy combination of a hatchet and a chisel, he'd simply given up. Now, with the holiday over, Webster was liable to show up at any time and—

Good morning.

The man himself was at their side door. Just there, like any other visitor, or as if he were still making the rounds from his old physician's practice from decades ago, but uninvited, and inviting himself in regardless.

Professor Webster entered and sat down in the janitor's kitchen. Ephraim and Caroline watched warily as he nonchalantly picked up the day's paper. It was peculiar for the doctor to visit, peculiar for him to make himself at home like this.

"Is there any more news?" Webster paged through headlines.

Why, there was plenty of news that day: a steamboat explosion in New Orleans; Mormon prospectors arrived in California; an Indian attack by the Colorado River. But that was not the news Dr. Webster was interested in.

"Do you hear any further of Dr. Parkman?" he added.

"No," said the janitor cautiously. "I have not."

Well, it seemed that Dr. Webster had. Why, he'd just taken the omnibus into the city with a friend and had stopped by Mr. Henchman's—did Littlefield know Henchman, the apothecary over on Cambridge Street?—and heard that a woman had spotted a large and suspicious bundle stowed into a cab and had taken down the carriage's number.

Worthy police! It had been only a few years ago that Marshal Tukey had decreed the licensing and numbering of hansom cabs—those notorious touts for theater-hall prostitutes—but here the numbering of the cabs had yielded an even greater catch than any embarrassed husband. This woman, the doctor explained, had reported what she'd seen to police, and the cab had been seized. And what did Littlefield think they'd found?

It was covered, Dr. Webster finished his tale triumphantly, *with blood*.

In the silence of the kitchen, the doctor's observation hung like a challenge.

"There are a great many stories flying about," Mr. Littlefield replied. "One does not know what to believe."

The doctor finally left their kitchen, and his footsteps receded up the stairs and away from the stunned husband and wife.

He knows more than he lets on, Ephraim whispered.

Who knew how much time they had? And even if Webster left later for his customary lunch, surely other doctors would be entering and leaving the building before long. They had to act soon. In fact, they had to act that very day.

12

"I SHAL BE KILED"

ONE BY ONE, THE MURDERERS ARRIVED AT THE MEDICAL College.

There was William Corder, the smirking village intellectual who secretly buried his hometown sweetheart, moved to London to get married through the personal ads, and reinvented himself as a schoolmaster. He bore, it was said, an enlarged brain area of Destructiveness. There was the infant-drowning Catharine Welsh, deemed to have "the whole region of animal propensities very large." Not to be outdone, there was also Madeline Albert, the young French girl who killed her mother with a hatchet, and Boutillier, a matricidal child with extreme enlargement of Acquisitiveness. And, most fittingly, there were Burke and Hare, whose impatience to procure cadavers for Edinburgh medical students led to homicidal shortcuts.

The Phrenological Collection was coming to Harvard, and there was little the doctors or staff could do to stop its skullish march.

That Friday morning saw Littlefield hauling plaster busts into Dr. Holmes's anatomy lecture hall and stowing the blank-eyed visages in the storage space under the hall's raked seating. The collection was an awkward present from Professor Emeritus John Warren—who, in the time-honored fashion of retirees, could now rain such gifts as he wished on the department, including and especially those the faculty did not necessarily want. Warren had a fascination with phrenology, even as its brief but powerful pull on academia was beginning to weaken, and he had acquired the immense holdings in plaster heads from the Boston Phrenological Society. For a brief spell a decade earlier, the society had counted scores of Boston doctors among its members and had even published its own journal; now, at the gentle suggestion of this emeritus, Dr. Holmes was to acknowledge the subject of phrenology in this quarter's lectures. The matter was unavoidable, as he'd already accepted Warren's gift of plaster heads—and, more importantly, a $5,000 donation by said emeritus.

But such was the life of a college dean. Holmes had no love for phrenology and admitted that he was "diffident to approach the subject at all," but it would have been irresponsible to turn the gift down. And besides, the busts had a certain macabre charm. Along with what Warren delightedly called his "degenerates and celebrated criminals," they also included the life masks of Samuel Coleridge and mathematician Charles Babbage.

As the murderers and worthies alike took their places, Littlefield turned to Dr. Bigelow, who was overseeing the whole operation. It had been a busy month for the new professor; while finishing his study of his patient with an iron rod through the skull, sorting plaster heads was the least of his concerns.

Sir? He took the doctor aside. *Have you heard any talk concerning Dr. Webster and Dr. Parkman?*

Indeed Bigelow had. And, like everyone in Boston's tight fabric of respectable families, Bigelow had his own connection to the case: his sister was about to become engaged to Dr. Parkman's son.

I am planning to break through the wall of Webster's privy, Littlefield told him. *It is the only place left unsearched.*

To act on the janitor's suspicion was terrible, but not to act could be even worse. And there was another problem: if the body wasn't found, his future in-law's vast estate could be tied up for years.

"Go ahead with it," Bigelow told the janitor, and returned to his plaster heads.

Ephraim wandered the halls of the college, unsure. Bigelow had been in his job for only three weeks, and what did any new professor know? What protection was his word for a mere janitor? He spotted

J.B.S. Jackson toiling away in a side room, and though Dr. Jackson had been on the faculty for only a couple of years, he was already experienced in such matters. When, the previous summer, Littlefield had gotten mixed up in the abortion scandal involving the cadaver of Sarah Furber, it was Dr. Jackson who'd been among the first to spot something very amiss with her body.

The janitor quietly confided his plans to Jackson, and the doctor weighed the prospect of the school being dragged through the mud once again. What, he asked, did Littlefield intend to do if he found anything?

"Go to Dr. Holmes," the janitor said innocently.

"You had better not go to him," the professor advised. This was not a matter for their dean. Holmes was their pillar in the community and in the country; and even more delicately, he had a new book of poetry coming out the very next day. Nor was it a matter for their ambitious new colleague tending to the busts upstairs. No, better to bring in the old man.

"Go to the elder Dr. Bigelow, in Summer Street," Jackson continued. "Then come and tell me. If I am not at home, leave your name on my slate, and—I shall understand it."

If Webster detected even a hint of the excavations, he would most certainly understand what was going on—all too well. One wrong move, and Dr. Parkman might not be the only fresh body found in the medical school.

"Mr. Littlefield, I feel dreadfully about this," Dr. Jackson warned. *"Go through that wall before you sleep tonight."*

* * * *

BY THE early afternoon, Webster had left his lab. Littlefield slipped out of the building and over to the Fuller foundry down the street, aware that trying again to bash through a brick wall with a hatchet and chisel clearly wasn't going to work. He didn't just need the right tools, though; he also needed the right excuse for the tools. How, without letting his real task on, could he explain that he required demolition tools in a building where a man had apparently disappeared?

The steady drip and drain of water in Webster's lab gave one hint: plumbing. It was the perfect excuse. Since Cochituate water had first been piped along this street, Harvard doctors in particular had become great advocates of the salubrious effects of the frigid water. Basins installed in bedrooms and offices were just the thing; better still, one observer at the school drolly observed, were the showers "which poured a feeble stream of cold water upon the shoulders of those whose systems could stand the shock." Running a new service into yet another room of the college was an entirely plausible excuse, and Fuller would be the logical man to ask for tools; he knew all about such matters, for his foundry had produced many of the cast-iron pipes for the city's water mains.

The janitor accosted Leonard Fuller and dutifully explained how he needed a crowbar to knock a hole through a wall—for a water line, you understand. The excuse hung awkwardly in the air; Fuller understood very well indeed. There was still a reward on offer for Parkman's body, after all, and everyone knew that the college was the last place where there'd been a confirmed sighting of the old man. The laconic foundry owner regarded Ephraim with a long look of bemusement.

I need it for a water line, Ephraim insisted.

"I guess you do," Fuller finally said, and slid the tool over to the janitor.

It did not take long for Charles Kingsley, still doggedly making his rounds that afternoon as Parkman's right-hand man, to hear the foundry gossip about Harvard's peculiar new variety of plumbing. It was just another Parkman rumor, of course, and the day had not been lacking in those. One of the better ones had come over lunch, with Cambridge's postmaster hand-delivering a letter addressed to Marshal Tukey. The envelope's extraordinarily crude lettering, seemingly written with a twig, had immediately drawn the postman's attention, so that he'd personally walked it across the river and to city hall. When opened, it had revealed a disturbing scrawled-out message:

> Dr Parkman was took on Bord the ship herculan and this is all I dare say or I shal be kiled. Est Cambridge one of the men gave me his watch but I was feard to keep it and throwd it in water rightside the road to the long brige to Boston

This was a frustrating clue; there was no *"Herculan,"* but there was indeed a schooner named *Herculean*—and it had set sail from Boston Harbor the day before. Its crew would be an unlikely gang of kidnappers: they'd shipped out on unremarkable cotton runs to New Orleans, and earlier that year they'd braved a hurricane to valiantly save a sinking ship's crew on the high seas. Still, Dr. Parkman's watch alone had a $100 reward on it; even the hint of a lead might bring out some rivermen to drag the pilings around the bridge yet again.

Kingsley had been through Webster's rooms twice, but with the latest news of Littlefield's very odd job, they bore visiting again. Joined by a police officer, he crossed North Grove Street and walked up the steps to the Medical College. Kingsley pulled on the door; it didn't budge.

Locked. The janitor was taking no chances.

Kingsley quietly placed his ear up against the cold stone of the school's exterior and listened intently. Faintly, in the subterranean distance, he could make out the steady report of metal striking brickwork. *Clink—clink—clink.*

*　*　*　*

LITTLEFIELD WAS finally making some progress when he heard the hammer pounding over his head: one, two, three, four. The signal. Webster was coming. The janitor scrambled out of the crawl space, his overalls muddy and, once he was back in the heated building, damp with sweat. He'd already shed his usual vest and jacket for the job. Had it not been for his building maintenance duties, his appearance would have been enough to alert anyone; as it was, it was damning enough.

Caroline was waiting for him upstairs, chagrined.

"I've made a fool of you this time," she admitted. "Two gentlemen called here, and I thought one was Dr. Webster; but they are Mr. Kingsley, and Mr. Starkweather. They are at the door now."

Littlefield slid the bolt on the front door, and—still cautious not to let anyone in—stepped outside to meet Kingsley and Officer Starkweather on the front steps.

What private places, Kingsley asked significantly, *have not yet been searched in this building?*

Why, the privy, the janitor replied.

The two were tactful enough not to let on that they'd just been eavesdropping through the wall. Now they were ready to take a more direct route: surely they could simply break through the lock of Webster's privy?

"Let us go into his laboratory," Kingsley urged Littlefield.

Kingsley could hardly be blamed, perhaps, for not understanding that this was not like his employer's squalid tenements. This was Harvard's medical school, and one couldn't simply go about breaking down doors and prying out locks, and certainly not without a warrant. Certain proprieties had to be maintained; these gentlemen were professors.

"Can we not get in, then?" Officer Starkweather pressed.

"No, Dr. Webster has locked it, and has got the key," the janitor said flatly.

The pair left empty-handed. But then George Trenholm walked up—another officer making his rounds. Littlefield had known George for a few years, and trusted him enough to wave him inside and tell him of his plans.

Here—he pointed out the entryway by the dissecting room—*that's where the wall was so hot that I thought the building would catch fire.*

Trenholm instinctively put his hand against the wall, though it had long since gone cold again. There was nothing more to see, and so they strolled out back outside; being called up from beneath the building had simply wasted what precious time Littlefield had to keep digging.

Mrs. Littlefield came bustling over to them.

"You have just saved your bacon," she reported. "Dr. Webster has just passed in."

The doctor was none the wiser. He'd arrived to find the building unlocked and hadn't run into Mr. Littlefield and Officer Trenholm snooping about. Blithely unaware, he collected the long-neglected grapevines from the hallway and dragged them into his laboratory. The door remained slightly ajar for a brief moment—and then he reemerged and locked it again. When the doctor exited the building, Littlefield and Trenholm were still standing outside—just a janitor talking to the passing officer on his beat, idly gossiping about Parkman's disappearance.

Dr. Webster gamely joined in their conversation.

"What about that twenty-dollar bill?" he asked.

Officer Trenholm was puzzled. What twenty-dollar bill?

Why, Webster explained, the one collected on the bridge—the one an Irishman used to a pay a one-cent toll. He'd just been called over to Marshal Tukey's, in fact, to see if he could identify it as one he'd given to Dr. Parkman. But, alas—it was just another twenty-dollar bill. Who knew whether it was one of those he'd handed to Parkman?

"I told him I could not swear to it," Webster admitted.

It was all most regrettable; so many clues, and yet the disappearance seemed bound to remain a mystery.

Well, good day, he bade them, and walked off.

The pair watched him disappear down North Grove Street. *Come back in twenty minutes*, Littlefield told Trenholm—and with that, he ran over to Fuller's for more tools, then slipped back inside the Medical College and down through the trap door again.

It was four in the afternoon by then, and the job was getting harder as he got closer to breaking through. A draft was pulling cold air through the hole in the bricks, nearly blowing out the flame of his lamp; and he knew that once he got inside the privy, there were trenches where river water could collect to the height of a man. But there was no telling when Webster would come back, so the janitor threw himself into smashing away at the bricks, now with hammer and chisel, then with a crowbar, until the hole was just wide enough. He dropped his tools and grabbed his lamp: now was the time.

Littlefield peered inside the opening and thrust his flickering light into the terrible darkness before him.

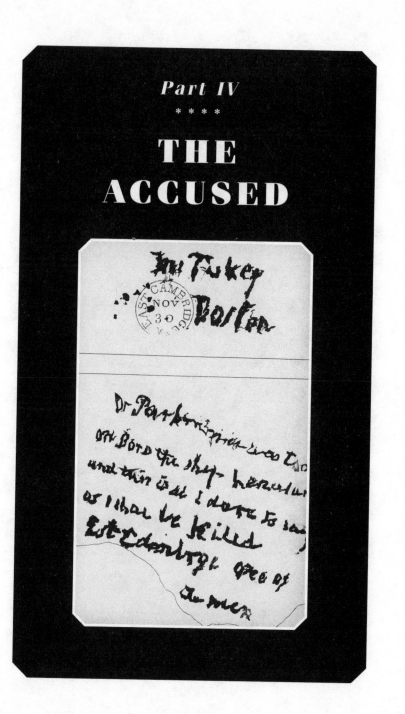

13

PISTOLS DRAWN

DR. BIGELOW WAS JUST SITTING DOWN TO HIS DINNER AS dusk fell over Boston. Soon all the merchants around the city would begin to lock up their businesses for the night, an act of no small fascination to the doctor. He had a fondness for the art of lock picking and owned what one visitor to his home described as "a whole bushel of locks" to practice on. Not for any practical purpose, mind you. Some men whittled; Bigelow picked. With a good set of filed keys, he had found, you could spring even a difficult lock open with a satisfying click. The coming weekend meant a brief respite from doctoring, from the Medical College lectures: time for his locks, time for his painting, time for a good meal.

You have a visitor in your office, he was informed.

Visitors, always visitors. He set aside his napkin and trudged down to his waiting room. There was no patient for him. Instead, there was Ephraim Littlefield—disheveled, and stained with dirt, sweat, and white mortar dust.

Ephraim's hands were trembling.

"Oh," he repeated wildly, almost babbling. "I have found him. *I have found him!*"

His meaning was plain enough; and all the janitor's years of shadowy dealings in cadavers rose up against him. The professor seized Littlefield by the collar and rattled the sobbing man.

"Damn you!" Dr. Bigelow roared. "What did you have to do with it, Littlefield?"

"Nothing!" he protested. "Nothing!"

What must surely come next was clear: the scandal upon the Harvard name, the insult on the grieving donor's family, the board meetings to follow. It was all over; the locals would surely tear the college to pieces now.

Bigelow released his grip on the hysterical janitor and let the man drop.

Go back to the college, he told Littlefield. *I'll get Marshal Tukey.*

The professor marched down the darkened streets to city hall, where he found the marshal, Kingsley, the lawyer James Blake, and assorted officers all mulling over their dwindling search. There were still more leads, every day: leads to other states, leads to other cities, leads that led straight out to sea. Or maybe it was a decidedly local crime. Just the night before, highwaymen had held up a cab on the bridge by the college—jumping out, with one wresting the horse's reins and the other throwing open the carriage door and demanding money. They were deterred only when the driver shot the top off one robber's hat. So there was another new lead: What if these same highwaymen had intercepted Parkman as he'd crossed the bridge to Cambridge?

You can stop looking.

The news from Dr. Bigelow sank in for a moment. Then, Tukey grabbed his revolver, and the men headed out into the night.

* * * *

OFFICER TRENHOLM had already beat them to the scene.

The police arrived at the Medical College and crowded into Littlefield's modest apartment, where they found Trenholm waiting for them. He had, as promised, come back that afternoon, just twenty minutes after talking with the janitor, only to find that the terrified fellow had already run off to fetch Dr. Bigelow. It was Mrs. Littlefield who let him in and led him to the trap door—asking, concernedly, Are you not afraid to go down there?—and when he wasn't, George Trenholm became the second man to venture alone into the breach in Webster's brick vault.

There was, he grimly confirmed to his boss, something to Little-field's report.

The group swelled with more officers, and along with the janitor they filed down the hallway to the hatch in the floor. One by one, they descended through the trap door and into the crawl space. As the slope of the dirt made the roof low to their heads, they crouched down to reach the hole. Tukey had his right-hand enforcer Derastus Clapp by his side, and he asked the detective to pass him the lamp. Then the marshal peered into the vault.

A steady stream was falling inside; the Cochituate water had been left running into the vault, wastefully pouring back into ground already soaked by the river, where it endlessly washed away—what, exactly? Follow the water down in the beam of light, to where it spattered the bottom of the foul brick enclosure: there. In the light glistened what might appear, perhaps, to be heaped cuts of discarded butcher's meat. It was not so easy, at first glance, to discern what variety of creature they had been sliced from.

Dr. Bigelow, the marshal inquired, *is this, was this, a human?*

It is, Dr. Bigelow agreed. It was.

And was Harvard's medical school, the marshal politely asked the janitor, generally in the habit of storing bodies in the toilet?

"No," Littlefield answered.

Somewhere overhead, a board creaked in the darkness, and a real-ization stabbed through the assembled men. The policemen, looking at one another and at Littlefield and Bigelow, registered the fact that every single one of them had descended through the trap door.

They had not left a lookout upstairs.

"That is Webster," one hissed.

Another creak; and then a footfall.

"He is overhead," another whispered.

They could be locked down here for the entire weekend. Worse, Littlefield knew that Webster kept a loaded pistol in the lab; the doctor sometimes experimented with batteries and electrical wires rigged to set off the gun. If desperate enough, the doctor could pick them all off one by one as they emerged through the trap door.

Marshal Tukey pulled out his revolver and indicated to Officers Clapp and Trenholm to follow. Padding to the trap door, they stealthily leapt up into—silence.

No sign of him. But someone *was* in the building.

The men quietly split up, weapons drawn—Tukey toward the lab, the others upstairs to the lecture halls. The marshal slipped into a storeroom, gun drawn, yet somehow outmatched: the arrays of retorts, flasks, and stoppered beakers were, in the darkness, an arsenal of glass and acids. If there should be a crouching figure among them—no, nobody there. But one suspiciously closed-up cabinet, gingerly opened, revealed a most unscientific collection of bottles: the professor's hidden store of wine and liquor.

Of their owner, there was no sign.

Clapp and Trenholm crept up the stairs, past the display cases in the empty school lobby, and up to the doorways that, in the daylight, so many students had blithely passed through with no thoughts of death—save for those of their assigned cadavers. The doors swung into the dark, vacant rooms; inside were benign tools of learning, now phantasmal in the moonlight. The demonstration skeletons grinned unnervingly from the bare lecture stage as the pair checked the sloping auditorium rows, ready to fire; beneath the seats were only the blank stares of the phrenological busts that had been stowed earlier that afternoon.

They were alone—just them, the mute plaster heads, and the skeletons. If Webster had already been here, he'd clearly taken flight. And if he would not come to them—then they would have to go to him.

* * * *

IT WAS about seven that evening when the carriage pulled up just short of Dr. Webster's house in Cambridge. Best to keep it slightly out of sight and not alarm their suspect, Officer Clapp thought; he told

Officers Starkweather and Spurr to hold back. A carriage stopping in front of the professor's house and three officers marching up would arouse suspicion, but one of them on foot would not.

Clapp walked up to the house alone, only to find the doctor himself already outside. Dr. Webster had stepped into the front yard, still in his slippers, to show a visitor to the gate; Clapp caught up to him as he was turning to go back inside. The doctor recognized the old officer immediately.

"How do you do, Mr. Clapp?" he asked amiably.

We're searching the college again, the officer explained apologetically. *Could you come assist us for a moment?*

It was a terrible inconvenience, of course, but it had now been a week to the day since the disappearance; there was some due diligence to show to Parkman's family before winding things down. Webster, of course, was only too glad to help; the family, he remarked, must be in great pain. The pair went briefly into the professor's study, where Webster gamely pulled on his coat, hat, and shoes.

As they passed back out through the front door, the doctor was struck by a realization: he had forgotten something.

"I should like to go back for my keys," he apologized.

That won't be necessary, Clapp explained—they already had plenty of keys to unlock the building.

"Very well," Dr. Webster said, and strode with Clapp to the waiting carriage. A couple of other fellows sat in the front by the driver, and Webster and Clapp took seats in the back. The darkened roads rolled by them as they made their way to Boston, and it idly brought to mind the new railroad. In just weeks, perhaps days, it would arrive in Cambridge. To think, a ride like this might soon become a thing of the past! The two conversed animatedly on the subject; these were indeed extraordinary times they lived in.

Ah, but crime. Carriages had their own problems, of course: one favorite trick at the omnibus stops was for a thief to blow cigar smoke at his mark, distracting him while a confederate picked his pockets clean. But might the coming of the rails not bring the city's filth and wickedness upon Cambridge even faster and more efficiently? The city could be a terrible place for those who knew its darker corners. Officer Clapp had been on the police force for some twenty years, and the things one might see could freeze the blood. A pair of doomed sweethearts who hanged themselves face-to-face, with the same rope over either side of a beam in her father's shop; that had been a bad one. Rat-fighting matches in saloons in the poorer quarters, with men hauling bags of twenty to thirty angry rats down the alleys at night to the contest; they'd collect them from the local stables, trapping them amid the horses' oats. The endless arrests for drunkenness on rum— just terrible. The rails were a fine means of travel, but to what end?

Their carriage rumbled and crackled over the Craigie Bridge. The tide was low, leaving the mud flats exposed in the moonlight. Just a few hours earlier, men had been sounding all around this stretch of river, looking for Dr. Parkman. There was a rumor, come to think of it, that Parkman's hat had been found over at the Navy Yard. But there were also more leads; why, Dr. Webster had just heard another one himself.

"There is a lady over there," Dr. Webster noted helpfully, gesturing toward the port, "a Mrs. Bent, who knows something about it."

She'd apparently also seen Dr. Parkman last Friday, the professor said, and that gave him a splendid idea.

"Suppose we ride over there?" he added brightly.

"We had better postpone it to some other time," Officer Clapp demurred. No need to interrupt her evening, after all. Webster settled back in as they drove onward from the bridge and down Leverett Street, and he watched as they clip-clopped straight past the Brighton Street turnoff. A block later they passed Spring Street, which should have been their next best route.

"You ought to have turned that corner, if you are going to the college," the doctor said.

"The driver is probably green," Clapp remarked apologetically— they'd have to take the long way, maybe down Leverett until

Cambridge Street and then back around again, but they'd get to the college in a few minutes.

Perhaps it was all for the best. Just a few blocks farther down Leverett was a building where the officers needed to needed to stop off for a moment anyway—did Dr. Webster mind? The carriage halted, and Clapp hopped down into the street. "Gentlemen?" he said, summoning his colleagues, and he indicated to Webster that he might as well come along, too. The group strode toward the back of a looming brick building.

"Gentlemen, suppose we walk into the inner office?" Officer Clapp ushered the group forward, as their eyes adjusted to the lights ablaze inside. Dr. Webster followed them through the doorway; once inside, he stopped in astonishment. The door was shut soundly behind him.

They were inside the Leverett Street Jail.

"Mr. Clapp?" The professor spun around to face the officer. "What does this mean?"

In a moment, Derastus Clapp's pleasant demeanor had vanished.

"Dr. Webster, it is no use to disguise our purpose any longer," he said. "You recollect that I called your attention, at the bridge, to sounding above and below the bridge?"

Indeed the doctor did; it had been scarcely a few minutes ago.

"We have been sounding in and about the *college*," Officer Clapp continued, "and have done looking for Dr. Parkman. We shall not look for his body any more."

There was much other work to be done, surely: a writ of mittimus to be drawn up, the coroner to be fetched, a county attorney rousted from his evening's rest, a cell to be prepared in the jail. But the posting of more handbills, sending officers to search the woods and streams for miles around, the long hours spent shining lanterns into attics and basement corners? No, that was not part of their evening's work any longer.

"You are now in custody," Officer Clapp announced, "on a charge of the murder of Dr. Parkman."

14

A RUINED MAN

"WHAT!" DR. WEBSTER BLURTED OUT. "ME?"

"Yes," Clapp replied. "You, sir."

The professor's pockets were promptly emptied by the jail keepers, and an inventory taken: a wallet, $2.40 in cash, a gold watch, an omnibus ticket case, and one rather rusty set of keys. Before committing the doctor to the indignity of the downstairs lockup cell, Clapp needed to check in with the marshal's office. The officers were to watch Webster in the booking office until then—"Don't commit the Doctor until I get back," he told his partner—and so Officer Starkweather kept his charge under observation while the jailers drifted back into their usual duties.

The professor sat in stunned silence for a while, then finally cleared his throat. Could he have a glass of water? Starkweather drew a pitcher for him, and Webster drank several long drafts; it was something to fill the painful silence. Then the prisoner spoke.

"Have they found Dr. Parkman?"

Officer Starkweather wasn't going to answer a question like that.

"You might tell me *something* about it," the doctor protested. "Where did they find him?"

Officer Starkweather wasn't going to answer that, either.

"How came they to suspect me?" the doctor pressed.

This, too, was a subject about which Officer Starkweather was not prepared to speak at this time.

Webster sank back into his chair. For a man who always kept his own home particularly warm, this place had a terrible chill to it. The very walls of these dark chambers went from cold stone to even colder iron: old cannonballs had deliberately been embedded inside them to prevent prisoners from burrowing out. In the distance were the usual grim sounds: the clank of iron, the scrape of days scratched on the walls, the sordid groans of the drunk and the disorderly. Webster began to sob.

"Oh!" he wept. "My children, what will they do! What will they think of me?"

Officer Starkweather, to be fair, really could not answer that question, either. At length the doctor collected himself, reasoning out the impossibility of the whole thing. Clearly they'd found something at the college—something in his offices, if suspicion was on him.

"Nobody has access to my private apartments," Webster puzzled aloud. "None but . . ."

But . . . but . . .

". . . the porter," he finished slowly, "who makes the fire."

The professor sat in dead silence for a full minute.

"That . . . *villain*!" he gasped. "I am a ruined man!"

Webster leapt up and paced the office in wordless anguish. Starkweather watched him warily. Webster's hands fidgeted around his own vest for a moment, and then he brushed a hand over his mouth, as if covering it in horror. In the next moment, his body went into a sudden, ragged spasm.

"Doctor!" Starkweather grabbed him. "Have you been taking anything?"

Oh no, Webster insisted—no medication or anything like that. The professor sank onto a settee, usually kept for the relief of the officers, and lay there without a word for the next hour. When Clapp returned and gave the order—*Take him to the lockup*—Starkweather firmly grabbed the doctor's right arm, ready to lead him away. His prisoner didn't budge. *I can't stand*, Webster explained weakly.

It was true: his body had gone entirely and inexplicably limp. It took two men to lift him up and half-drag him to his cell; they rolled him onto his side on a cot, and Webster slumped over, facedown into his pillow, unmoving. Despite the cold of the jail, the doctor was sweating profusely. Whether he was in withdrawal from an opium habit, in the beginnings of delirium tremens, or undergoing some other nameless terror, it was hard to say. The jailers and officers conferred: Should they call a doctor?

No need, Officer Clapp decided. They should just keep checking on him. The detective wasn't too worried; the jail had taken in something like five thousand prisoners in the last year, and only a couple had died on them—that is, aside from one who was executed.

An hour later, the jailers stood by Webster, waiting to accompany him back upstairs. The county attorney was here to see him, they explained. Webster, still facedown on his pillow, did not move. What few words could be made out seemed to be about his family and his attorney friend, Mr. Prescott. When they raised him up, he was nearly delirious.

"I expected this," Webster muttered, as they lifted his sagging frame heavily and dragged him step by step up the stairs.

Samuel Dunn Parker awaited him in the booking office, exasperated and incredulous at having been called in for DA duties on a Friday night. Parker was nearing seventy, and he'd known John Webster and his father for decades, back to when the old man had run the family pharmacy. They were all Harvard men, both families; Parker's own son was the alumni secretary for the Class of '35. What could one of the most senior professors on campus, of all people, possibly have to do with a murder case? Yet the prisoner half-carried in from the lockup was hardly recognizable as his son's old chemistry professor. Dragged into the booking office, Webster collapsed into an armchair, then nearly slid from it to the floor.

Water, he called out weakly. A glass was held up to his lips; his teeth chattered and bit against it, and the water splashed down the front of his shirt.

"Oh," he mumbled distractedly, "my wife and children!"

Parker, who'd arrived half-expecting a respectable professor indignant over an absurd mistake by the detectives, instead found himself confronted by a man who'd come completely undone. What could one say? There was, he gently reminded Webster, another family whose father had been missing for a week now. Could he not help them?

"We do not come here to distress you," the elderly attorney said soothingly. "It is a sad duty that devolves upon me. I come here to inform you of the dreadful charge against you, and the reason of your confinement in these dreary walls."

Webster's head lolled to the side; he seemed on the verge of fainting..

"It is the hope of all our hearts that you will be enabled to explain away these terrible suspicions," Parker continued. "We will assist you to do this if you will accompany us now to the Medical College. That you may be enabled to remove all doubts of your innocence, is my earnest prayer to God."

Webster would go, though he refused the very premise of the visit. *There isn't anything to explain,* he whispered.

*　*　*　*

THE OFFICERS shivered in the cold at the back entrance of the Medical College, yanking on the bell pull and waiting for someone down in the crowded lab to hear them.

"We've got Dr. Webster here!" one called in. "And he is very faint."

Two of them stood on either side of the doctor, holding his ragged form up; despite the cold, he was still sweating and his face had reddened. The lock rattled, and the door swung open, and at once Littlefield came face-to-face with his bedraggled employer.

"They have arrested me," Webster croaked reproachfully, "and have *taken me from my family,* and did not give me a chance to bid them good-night."

There was nothing for the janitor to say; he wordlessly let the officers and their prisoner pass. It was ten-thirty on a Friday night, and instead of being home asleep or out carousing on theater row, the coroner, the

county attorney, the city marshal, and seemingly every available policeman had crowded into a lab that had rarely seen more than one or two
men at a time. What was a largely solitary workplace in daylight was
now a crime scene, and officers and officials swarmed around the most
ordinary objects, scrutinizing them. Near the entrance to the lecture
hall, one was eyeing a coat hanging on a hook. Evidence!

"That," the doctor said numbly, "is the coat that I lecture in." As
men barged into the small antechamber before the lecture hall, he
added simply, "This is where I make examinations." There was little
else of interest in the area, it seemed. But Officer Starkweather, reaching toward the back of one of the room's shelves, discovered a parcel
wrapped in paper and unwrapped it. A ball of twine rolled out; inside
remained some cod hooks arranged into a grapple, as well as a pound
of lead sinkers.

None of the keys worked on the privy door—"Force the door!" the
yell went up—so a hatchet promptly smashed off the lock, while more
men flooded over into a chemical supply room. Webster, helped over to
watch from the hallway, protested—if they weren't careful while moving about, they would break delicate labware and do great mischief to
the premises. "You will find nothing but some bottles and demijohns,"
he complained. "I don't know what they want there, they won't find
anything improper." That was nearly correct: there was also a set of
filed keys, commonly considered burglar's tools—a curious thing for a
Harvard professor to keep in his office. Still, Webster remained insistent: "There is *nothing* there of importance."

Very well—then they would look where there was indeed something
of importance. Webster was half-carried down to the lower laboratory,
where Littlefield had been telling the officers everything, and with
each step down the stairs, the professor's agitation grew.

"Where is the chimney that was so heated?" one officer called out.

"There is the furnace." Littlefield pointed. A chimney pipe led down
to the lab furnace, and someone, peering in, remarked that there was
something inside. Something in the ashes. Teeth? Then a melted chunk

of gold glinted in the lantern light and, near it, the outline of a lower jaw. Chips of calcined bone were fused with the remnants of coal.

"Don't disturb the bones," the coroner said sharply—better to leave them to him. Webster, who had barely managed to sit up in his chair, began convulsing and losing his balance; the officers steadied him, and he again fumbled a glass of water over himself. As the professor watched, a plank was gently carried up into the laboratory. Arrayed on top of it were glistening chunks of human flesh: a right calf, a right thigh, and a pelvis. They were set down in front of Webster, just out of his reach, and the officers watched him, waiting for the confession. Instead, Webster writhed for some fifteen minutes in silent agony. Tears were now streaming down his face, but not a word passed his lips.

County Attorney Parker, whether in sorrow or disgust, was dumbstruck.

Shall I take him away? a jailer finally asked.

"I have nothing to say," the old attorney answered at length. The officers hoisted Dr. Webster up and dragged him out into the night, and one by one the other officers and officials left. It was nearing midnight. They'd return to investigate further in morning.

Officer Starkweather was left to guard the rooms, and he set about preparing for a long night. He moved the grisly pile of body parts into the privy, where they couldn't be tampered with. Since the lock lay smashed on the floor, he drove a nail halfway into the door frame so that it couldn't be opened. Then he grabbed a pair of pants that were hanging on a nail—J. W. WEBSTER, read a label inside them—evidence, perhaps, but also the softest thing in the room. Starkweather folded the pants into the semblance of a pillow. He'd sleep tonight in a murder scene, his head resting gently upon a murderer's pantaloons. Still, that wasn't what haunted one's mind as the hours ticked past midnight. No, the real mystery was in the cod hooks and twine found on a shelf. True, the Charles River was right here; but why would a Harvard professor come to work to go fishing?

* * * *

IT TOOK a while to get Dr. Webster back to his jail cell.

Not that the professor wasn't cooperating; it was that his body could not. As they called down a carriage at the medical school, the officers found that the doctor's arms and legs had stiffened like boards in the frigid night air, unable to bend. Finally, like householders trying to fit a hat stand into a cab, Officers Cummings and Andrews managed to lift the professor awkwardly into the carriage compartment. Once he was inside, his joints gave way, and he collapsed into the seat, his pants and coat both now soaked with perspiration. Jailer Andrews watched him carefully; the man had seemed on the verge of mania or death for hours now.

As they passed the darkened storefronts and homes, the doctor managed to speak.

"Why don't they ask Littlefield? *He* can explain all this," he murmured. "*He* has the care of the dissecting-room. They wanted me to explain, but they didn't ask me anything." His departure from his study at seven that evening seemed impossibly far away, and his warm home in Cambridge receded farther with each turn of the carriage's wheels. "What will my family think of my absence?" he beseeched Andrews.

The jailer had been on the force for over twenty years now. He'd arrested everyone from dapper counterfeiters to the wild murderer of a night watchman, and he'd never seen anything quite like this.

"I pity you," Andrews said. "And I am sorry for you, dear sir."

Rather than feel comforted, the patrician doctor seemed simply bewildered by this. What pity could some poorly paid turnkey have for a Harvard professor?

"*You* pity me!" Webster blurted out. "You are sorry for me? What for?"

"To see you so excited. I hope you will be calmer."

"Oh!" Webster said distantly. "That's it."

The rest of the ride passed without a word. Back at his jail cell, the men bolstered Webster's head with pillows and placed a lantern nearby so that they could peek in, though there was little to see or hear beside his groans. One o'clock passed, and the doctor lay seemingly inert; an hour later, and he still had not moved an inch.

The contents of his pockets, though, were providing considerably more lively viewing. Inside his wallet were three scraps of paper. The first simply had a single number scrawled on it in pencil: *$483,64*. But unfolding the next scrap revealed two columns dense with notes in the same crabbed hand:

> *Nov. 9 Friday, rec'd*
> *$510,00*
> *234,10 out Dr. Big*
> *Pettee cash —$275, 90*
> *Dr. P came to lecture-room, front left-hand seat,—students stopped— he waited till gone, and came to me and asked for money—Desired for him to wait till Friday 23d, as all the tickets were not paid for, but no doubt wd be then,—he, good deal excited—went away—said I owed him $483,64.*
> *Friday 23d, called at his house about 9 A.M., told him I had the money, and if he wd call soon after one, wd pay him—He called at 1/2 past, and I paid him, $483,64 cts.*

A second column rehearsed the same explanation, but now with a startling difference: a mention of another mortgage, this one for $2,432, a sum larger than Webster's yearly pay at Harvard, and an unusual type of loan and amount for a renter. Dr. Webster, it seemed, had been getting very deeply into debt.

> *9th Due Dr. P, who called at lecture $483,64, by his act.—Desired him to wait until Friday 23d—Angry.*

Friday, 1/2 1, pd him; he to clear mortgage.

Notes, Feb 13, 1847 including smaller one, $2432. $125 due him on loan, which the large note covers, he agreed to give up tow'd's sale of Min'ls.

Bal due, 483,64—paid, and he gave me two notes—had paid the mortgage, but said he wd go and cancel it. Had paid him 325 by Smith

> *125 due*
> *500 the loan*
> *Rest from other persons.*

Who the other persons were the note did not say, but that meant that nearly $1,500 needed by Webster to pay Parkman would have had to come from those vaguely listed "other persons." And what of that unexplained notation of "sale of Min'ls"?

A third scrap revealed a simple list of words:

> *ale*
> *jug mol's*
> *keys*
> *Tin box*
> *Paint*
> *Solder*

It appeared to be a shopping list, the sort written out so carelessly that it would be difficult for anyone else to decipher. And that, indeed, was the problem: the middle letter of "ale" was nearly unreadable. In fact, viewed from another angle, it might spell a different word altogether.

Axe.

15

OLD GRIMES
IS DEAD

When Mrs. Webster opened her front door early on Saturday morning, it was not to find her husband arriving back home.

May we come in? Detective Clapp asked.

It had been scarcely twelve hours since Clapp's last visit, alone, waiting as Dr. Webster pulled on his shoes. This time he had returned in the company of Mrs. Webster's in-law Charles Cunningham, as well as a local policeman. They hadn't brought the doctor with them; what they had brought was a document bearing the freshly inked signature of the Cambridge town judge.

We have a search warrant.

The doctor's bewildered wife ushered them in. Cunningham's purpose there was to reassure Harriet and her daughters—"I thought it would be a disagreeable business to go alone," Detective Clapp would later confide—but, like so many others, Cunningham was both family and a creditor. And it was financial papers, or perhaps something worse, that he and Clapp were looking for. Mrs. Webster and her daughters could be of no help: for all the little economies necessitated by their father's spending, they did not understand the state of his accounts. Just the morning before, they'd sent out invitations around the neighborhood for a grand party.

Clapp and Cunningham quickly focused on Dr. Webster's study, the usual home of his disordered finances. A trunk of papers revealed nothing more than the ordinary accounts of a working Harvard professor. Along with the expected correspondence, and stores of pens, ink, and stationery, a search in a desk drawer produced a checkbook for the Charles River Bank, showing a balance of $136. That couldn't be altogether correct: the scraps in the doctor's own pockets had revealed thousands in debt. Cunningham himself had given money to the Websters, and yet of those transactions there was no sign. The documentation had to be hidden *somewhere*. Surrounded by the doctor's fine library—surely the cause of at least some of that debt—the men puzzled over the absence of his papers.

The books! They rifled through the rows, pulling out the volumes of geology, chemistry, and poetry, flapping open their pages, examining the shelving behind them. Nothing.

By now the Charles River Bank would be open; maybe there they'd find some answers in its ledgers, handled with the usual discretion one would expect of Harvard's local bank. But even as Clapp stepped down from the Websters' porch, word was spreading among the watchful neighbors of Cambridge. Just up the street, Mayor Willard's son walked in with the morning news from Boston and handed a newspaper to his father.

Most papers still didn't have the news, and even the scrappy editors of the eight A.M. *Boston Herald* had barely had time to include a single paragraph on its front page.

STRANGE RUMOR. There is a strange rumor afloat this morning, that the body of Dr. George Parkman had been found at the Massachusetts Medical Hospital, and that Professor Webster has been arrested and committed to Leverett Street Jail, in connection with his death—all of which is too horrible to command belief.

The *Daily Bee* had a better scoop in its morning paper:

DISCOVERY OF THE BODY OF
DR. PARKMAN
**Under the floor of the Massachusetts
Medical College in North Grove St.
Arrest of Prof. John W. Webster**

In scarcely a hundred hurriedly written words, it was all there: the locked laboratory, Littlefield's discovery in the vault, the arrest. Mayor Willard read the morning newspaper in disbelief. How could the Boston papers print something so outlandish, so patently untrue?

"This is atrocious," the mayor scoffed.

"No, sir, this is true," his son shot back. The younger Willard had been speaking just that morning with County Attorney Parker. "And when you have read the evidence, you will think it was deliberate."

Yet the charge was impossible to countenance. Like any respectable citizen in Cambridge, Mayor Willard was tied to both the school and to the Websters himself: his own father had once been the president of Harvard, and before semiretiring to become the mayor, Willard had been a professor of Oriental languages at the school. Webster had been his colleague for decades, and what these papers were claiming was simply inconceivable.

"I always knew Dr. Webster to be a very frivolous man," the old mayor insisted, "but I never thought he was a wicked one."

* * *

FROM DEEP inside Dr. Webster's lab, there came a bloodcurdling cry.

Agghhhh! the policeman shrieked.

Silence.

Agghhhh! he shrieked again.

Eventually one of Officer Fuller's fellow policemen sauntered back down into the lab, not particularly alarmed. Then the two men traded places, with Fuller going upstairs to the second-floor lecture hall, where Dr. Holmes had taught on the day of the murder, amid the skeletons and phrenology busts. Fuller waited dutifully in dead silence; then he went back down to the lab again. His partner had been screaming, too; neither of them had been able to hear the other from two stories away.

So that answered one question. You could stand in Webster's lab screaming bloody murder—and committing it—and Oliver Wendell

Holmes, who'd been lecturing to his students two floors above at the time of Parkman's disappearance, wouldn't hear a thing.

The lab had begun filling with officers and officials at eight-thirty that morning, and more discoveries were surfacing in the cold light of a December day. Almost the moment Coroner Pratt arrived, he lifted out the grate from the lab's furnace, and human teeth spilled out from between the gridirons; among the ashes were hard little bone chips, but shattered and scorched like tiny shells in black sand. In the upper laboratory, they found an earthenware plate with dried black ink, and under a table, a small pine stick with ink-stained cotton wadding on the end: the implement, perhaps, for the crude handwriting of the previous day's letter sending the police to the newly departed schooner *Herculean*.

Back in the lower lab, Fuller eyed a wooden box in a supply closet. It was a plain tea chest, a handy sort of crate sold at the docks down the street, just the thing for storing a professor's spare lab apparatus and samples. Officer Fuller lifted up the lid; this one had chunks of minerals inside, part of Webster's geological collections of chiastolite, spodumene, green feldspar, and the like. The doctor had cushioned his rock samples in a bed of tanning bark, probably from a sack of the stuff he kept nearby. Fuller idly ran his hand down into the bark; there was another layer of mineral samples underneath. Then he thrust his hand farther down into the crate.

There was something else down there. His fingers sank into another object, softer than the rest—it was wet, and cold. He looked about for the officer who had spent the night in the room.

"Starkweather!" he yelled in alarm.

Officers clambered back down the stairs from the upper lab, with Parkman's agent Kingsley accompanying them. They found Fuller pointing at the crate.

"There's something more in there than minerals," he said.

Fuller dragged the box out of the closet and into the middle of the room, its lid removed. Then, as the assembled officers watched, he lifted it up and roughly turned it onto its side. The contents cascaded out onto the floor, and a squarish, sodden shape thudded heavily onto the boards. Bark and minerals trickled out of the chest and onto it, and, from the bottom of the chest, a jackknife came clattering out.

Before them was a headless, limbless clod: a human torso.

The men stared in utter surprise for a long moment. Fuller picked up the knife and pulled it open. The handle was decorated with hunting figures, and the blade looked like it had been newly cleaned and oiled. He snapped it shut, then slid the knife into his pocket for the evidence box. One of the other officers was clumsily using a walking stick to scrape the bark off the back of the torso. *Get away,* Fuller snapped, and then he leaned in for a closer look. There was a length of twine around the back, as if the torso had been trussed for roasting. Gently, he rolled it over to expose its front.

It had been hollowed out. Or, rather, it had been hollowed out and then filled again: the viscera were gone, and in their place another bloody hunk had been forced in, so tightly that the bared ribs were poking into it. It was the missing left thigh, jammed inside like clothing in an overpacked steamer trunk.

The coroner and his attending doctors made their way through the press of officers and peered more closely at the body parts. The marks of cutting on the body didn't quite make sense. The separation of the collarbone from the sternum in cutting off the head actually showed some medical knowledge—heads were surprisingly difficult to cut off with finesse—but the cuts down towards the pelvis were rather poorly executed. They looked, in short, like the half-right job of a chemistry professor who was three decades out of his medical practice. A bit of an embarrassment, atop the scandal of it all. But, regrettable as it was that word was getting out of the arrest, at least the police had thus far managed to keep the very worst specifics away from the penny newspapers and their readers.

Tap. Tap.

A reporter for the *Boston Herald* stood at the laboratory window: Could he come in?

* * * *

THE BLOCK around the Old State House was in an utter tumult. Here, up Washington and along State Street, the former seat of the old colony now lived under the clanking and ceaseless siege of Boston's printers. The building from whose balcony the Declaration of Independence had been read now declaimed the merits of Oak Tooth Wash, Dr. Warren's Sarsaparilla, and Whipple's Daguerreotypes Taken by Steam. Along this block one could find the printing offices for the *Daily Mail*, the *Herald*, the *Daily Atlas*, the *Daily Chronotype*, and a dozen more dailies and weeklies besides, shoulder to shoulder with engravers, express delivery offices, at least five competing news depots, and advertising agencies, whose "drummers" made ceaseless rounds of the sturdy brick buildings along the block. But today, the crowds of readers and deliverymen were gathering to see the latest words emerge from one office: 7 State Street, the home of the *Daily Bee*.

The *Bee* was hardly the most respectable paper—the stodgy mercantile *Daily Advertiser* might have fancied itself in that role—and even among the cheap penny papers, it was not the most popular. That honor, such as it was, went to its scurrilous Democratic neighbor the *Herald*. Somehow, despite being an organ of the ruling local Republican Party, the *Bee* often found itself outsold two to one by the livelier *Herald*. Not today.

"Our office was thronged with people," one reporter recounted, "who stood on tip-toe for the latest revelations." Those seeing the headlines looked searchingly to others next to them, in disbelief. "Can it be true?" they blurted out.

The *Bee*'s connection to local government served it well that day; it was the first with the scoop on Webster's arrest. Other papers, upon asking at the jailhouse and at city hall, had found the story stoutly denied. For the entire morning, the *Bee* had the jump on every other daily in Boston. The elated owners ran their presses at full steam, hurling out thirty-six hundred copies an hour and selling them as fast as they could pass them out the door.

It couldn't last; for one thing, the *Bee* had a sister publication, *Perley's Pic-Nic,* which they had to load in the type for that afternoon. The story then, inevitably, would pass to their rivals at the *Herald.* But by the time the last *Bee* rolled off the printing cylinders, its proprietors had cranked out about twenty thousand copies—quadruple their normal run. And even as the *Pic-Nic* went to press, *Bee* reporters were pumping jailers for more details about Webster's strange breakdown after his arrest, generating copy that threatened to run through all the exclamation marks in the type trays.

"The sight of the water crazed him! He appeared wild, ghastly, filled with fear! He fairly writhed with torment!" the *Bee* reported breathlessly. "It was a sight to curdle the coldest blood, and fill the stoutest man with terror! Tragedies, with scenes like this in them, are often played, but rarely enacted!"

For those across the river who were not connected with the police or the family, the word arrived more slowly, and incredulously. "I nursed the baby as I listened," wrote one Cambridge neighbor, "and felt the milk grow cold in my breast." Harvard's main campus was thrown into utter disbelief as students emerged from their Saturday morning classes. "The excitement, the melancholy, the aghastness of every body are indescribable," wrote a campus librarian. "The Professors *poh!* at the mere supposition that he is guilty. . . . People cannot eat; they feel sick."

Sauntering through it, happily unaware, was Henry Longfellow. He'd made it off-campus and partway into the city, on his way to a friend's lecture to young women on Dante, before beholding the bewildering sight of massed crowds around the school and the newspaper offices. "The whole town," he marveled, "is in the greatest excitement." Soon he found out why. The news was simply baffling. That his old neighbor, the colleague he'd just had dinner with, could be accused of such a thing was unthinkable.

The Dante lecture did not go well. How could it? There was only one topic of discussion that day, and it was not to be the *Purgatorio*— not even for the respectable young ladies of Boston. Turning to Longfellow after the lecture, Mrs. Farrar—an old friend, and a writer on women's etiquette—could keep the matter in no longer, etiquette be damned. Had he heard, she asked, that Mr. Parkman's thigh had been found? Or *presumably* it was Parkman's thigh.

"Of course," she added to Longfellow, scandalously, "nobody could identify that but his wife!"

It truly was quite appalling.

"All minds," the poet lamented, "are soiled by this foul deed."

But even as the young ladies left the lecture, there was a new rumor and a new tragedy, this one nearly as shocking as the first. Webster, it was said, had killed himself in jail.

* * * *

IN THE dimly lit cell Dr. Clark stood up; there was nothing he could do for the prisoner now.

You're fine, he reported.

John White Webster, who was indeed remarkably alive, had recovered enough from the shock of the previous evening that he was not only sitting up on his cot, he was complaining heartily about his case to his jailer, Gustavus Andrews.

"That is no more Dr. Parkman's body than it is mine," he groused. "How in the world it came to be there, I don't know."

Andrews maintained the usual droll reserve his job required around the prisoners. Perhaps he'd land a good souvenir from this one; back when he'd been a constable, his capture of a ring of counterfeiters had netted 660 fake quarters. After the state melted them for assaying— the metal proved worthless—he'd asked for them back as a keepsake.

The massy chunk now sat in his office; he was considering casting it into a dinner bell for the prisoners.

Dr. Webster was still going on about the Medical College; he scarcely even needed prompting anymore.

"I never liked the looks of Littlefield," he confided to his jailer. By his account, he'd warned the school against hiring the janitor in the first place—"I opposed his coming there all I could."

Dr. Webster fell silent around reporters, though. He wasn't willing to talk with them, or with much of anybody from outside the jail. No, he'd talk only with his family and with Franklin Dexter, the lawyer he'd requested. But for the *Herald* reporters showing up at the Leverett Street Jail, ready to seize the story from the *Bee,* Webster's mere survival was story enough. "REPORTED SUICIDE OF WEBSTER UNTRUE!" the next edition promptly proclaimed, joining its fellow headers "DIABOLICAL DEED!" and the always reliable "STARTLING INTELLIGENCE!"

The Medical College was where the story was now, anyway. "A RIOT ANTICIPATED!" the *Herald* announced, perhaps a little too hopefully—and added, nonchalantly, "It is supposed the building will be torn down." There was indeed a crowd gathering around the college, as many as a thousand people, and ready for a fight. The local Irish poor, scapegoated for so much else in the city, had been blamed for Parkman's disappearance, too. They had long suspected—correctly—that the Medical College made off with the cadavers of their paupers. Now, it seemed, Harvard had tampered with the living as well. All those stories of an Irishman with a suspicious twenty-dollar bill to pay the bridge fare by the school—the gall of it, when Parkman's body had been in the college all along. A rich man, killed by another rich man, who pinned it on the poor!

A local urchin, poking around a basement window, briefly tumbled in—presumably into the clutches of the dastardly Harvard professors inside—and the crowd nearly boiled over. He was quickly fished out, and a member of the crowd loudly tried intervening to placate the others.

I saw Dr. Parkman enter this college! the fellow yelled out. It was McGinnis, an Irishman who earned his keep by carting garbage from school. The building getting torn down by an angry mob would not be altogether to his benefit. *I saw it myself,* he yelled, *and then I saw Parkman outside an hour later!*

The mob was unconvinced. The mood blackened, a witness recalled, to one "scarcely less criminal than the dark deed of blood itself." Police reported back to city hall that a riot was surely imminent, and Mayor Bigelow—"whose eyes," a journalist noted, "were a good deal magnified for the occasion"—ordered every available officer to the scene. The local militia was called to arms. The City Guards, New England Guards, and the Artillery altogether had more than one hundred guns at the ready, and the mayor quickly visited their quarters for some rousing words. The sight of a few military uniforms might have been enough: the crowd dispersed, and the rowdies melted away.

In their place, a smaller and more peaceable group emerged that evening, fumbling for some way to recognize the gravity of what had transpired in the building before them. Someone had the idea to sing a hymn; but then they hit upon the latest Stephen Foster song, "Old Uncle Ned" ("Hang up de fiddle and de bow / No more hard work for poor Old Ned / He's gone whar de good N——— go.") At length, though, the voices rose up and over the Medical College and the surrounding homes with a slightly more sedate number:

> *Old Grimes is dead; that good old man*
> *We never shall see more*
> *He used to wear a long, black coat,*
> *All buttoned down before . . .*
> *But good old Grimes is now at rest,*

Nor fears misfortune's frown;
He wore a double-breasted vest,
The stripes ran up and down.

It wasn't quite a church hymn, but it was perhaps the best one could expect from the streets of Boston on a Saturday night.

Still, at least one Bostonian puzzled over the scene before him: Samuel Wentworth, a provisioner with a store on Lynde Street. Like so many in the neighborhood, he too had seen Dr. Parkman out on his rounds on the day of his disappearance. It didn't occur to him to tell the police or anyone else, but he'd spotted Parkman on Court Street, just by Mrs. Kidder's patent medicine store, a thriving business filled with humbugs like Dalley's Magical Pain Extractor and Dr. Morehead's Improved Graduated-Magnetic Machines. It wasn't a place one would expect to find the dour old physician lingering.

And there was another peculiar thing. Wentworth was quite sure he'd seen him there at about three p.m.—a full hour after he was supposed to be dead.

16

A LIFETIME OF
UPRIGHTNESS

PROFESSOR BIGELOW STOOD BEFORE A PACKED LECTURE HALL of students that Monday, their faces expectant. The cold morning light cut across the windows and lecture stage in a building much too new to have suffered its second scandal in as many years.

It was never altogether possible to know, when disaster struck a school, just how the students would react: with scorn and audible scoffing, with visible grief, or with shocked silence and respectful murmurs as they filed in and out of the lecture hall. It depended on that year's cohort, and it depended no less on the professor who faced them. And for this task, the faculty had chosen the young Henry Bigelow. He was their newest professor, and the one closest in age and temperament to the students themselves.

"Gentlemen," Dr. Bigelow began, and the room fell quiet.

"It is with deep regret that I am obliged to announce to the class that in consequence of the solemn and appalling events of the last week, the lectures at the Medical College will be suspended this and the succeeding two days. This measure is rendered necessary by the existing condition of things."

The students gazed at the hall around them, at the existing condition of things. It was a fair question as to whether they'd even be allowed back in after the two succeeding days. They'd had to get police permission to come inside the building; and that day, audible from within the depths of the structure, men could be heard prying up floorboards and planing off samples of wood from the floors and the walls.

"It is due," the young doctor continued, "to the present excited state of public feeling—it is due to the majesty of the law, the investigations of which are not yet completed; above all, it is due to the memory of George Parkman. The melancholy forebodings of the past week, which have ripened into the painful conviction that he no longer survives, have cast a cloud over our whole city. Most of all, gentlemen, it will be felt in this school, which has been the recipient of his bounty, and which is fearfully associated with the last known hours of his existence."

Though one could scarcely tell from the solemnity of Bigelow's speech, the school's alumni and faculty had already swung into action. The forensic evidence had been found, after all, in the very building of those best qualified to examine it; investigating a mutilated body in the Medical College was rather like solving a robbery perpetrated inside a police headquarters. The evidence was quickly parceled out by the coroner: Dr. Nathan Keep ('27) and Professor Jeffries Wyman ('37) would examine the bones and loose teeth found in the furnace. Drs. Winslow Lewis ('22), George Gay ('45), and James Stone ('43) would examine what they dubbed "the fleshy portions of the body" from the tea chest and the privy. The chemical evidence spattered about the offices would be examined by Drs. Martin Gay ('26) and Charles T. Jackson ('29). Handling the carved-up remains of a fellow alumnus and perhaps sending one of their professors to the gallows—all told, it was possibly the worst Harvard reunion on record.

Yet each man brought an extraordinary range of expertise to his forensic task. Dr. Keep was a physician, but he'd also been a personal dentist to both Parkman and Webster. He knew, for instance, that Dr. Parkman inserted his false teeth for socializing and popped them into his back pocket when not in use; the old man often damaged his dentures by then sitting on them. His forensics partner Dr. Wyman was newly prominent for a groundbreaking skeletal analysis announcing the discovery of the African gorilla, a species that had remained remarkably unknown to the Western world until 1847. But now, instead of analyzing a creature that no Bostonian had seen alive,

Wyman faced reconstructing the skeleton of a man who, it seemed, half the city knew by sight.

These teams of Harvard alumni epitomized just how far the field of forensics had come. For years, medical jurisprudence had often occupied itself with questions of abortion, miscarriage, and parentage; it was no accident that Harvard still had a single combined position referred to as "professor of obstetrics and medical jurisprudence." But with the rise of instruction in anatomy and chemistry in the past generation, and the rapid sharing of case studies and experiments through the burgeoning availability of medical journals, forensics was advancing quickly. The primary guide to the field back in Parkman and Webster's medical student days, Farr's *Elements of Medical Jurisprudence,* had filled all of 139 generously margined pages. The standard guide by 1849, Taylor's *Medical Jurisprudence,* ran to more than 800 densely typeset pages and covered everything from death by lightning to gall bladder injuries; nearly half of the chapters were on poisoning alone, be it by antimony, by nightshade, or even by vinegar.

As his colleagues wheeled into action just a few rooms away, Dr. Bigelow maintained the grave and respectful bearing expected of the medical school and its faculty.

"Let us bow," the professor intoned to his students, "before the decrees of Providence, and wait on its wisdom and justice."

* * * *

DR. JOHN White Webster was not waiting on wisdom and justice that morning; he was, however, waiting for his breakfast. He'd largely recovered in the past two days; his hands, steadied now, no longer dashed the water glass or the fork away. Rather than let him suffer the prison fare, one of his wife's Prescott cousins had been footing the bill for orders down the block at Parker's Restaurant—even though, as with the Cunninghams, the Prescotts themselves were owed money by Webster. The previous night, the doctor had enjoyed some oysters;

now, once again spared from the slop served to the others in lockup, he waited for another delivery.

"His numerous friends will be rejoiced to learn that he has not *lost his appetite*," a visitor drily observed that morning.

His meal arrived, and he devoured it. It was peculiar to eat alone, but to be expected; here, on the lowest floor of the jail, where the least light reached the windows, was where prisoners for capital offenses were kept. The higher tiers, lighter and a little closer to heaven, held the thieves, harmless drunks, debtors, and some hapless material witnesses. Neither Webster's wife nor his daughters had visited his cell yet; they wanted to but had been dissuaded for the sake of their own delicate constitutions. It wasn't that his cell was so bad, really. It was a bit dim but whitewashed and clean, and Harriet had sent her husband a few baskets of books and other dainties from the house. He needed a little rug, perhaps, to keep the floor from getting so dreadfully cold.

John?

Outside his cell were Professors Benjamin Peirce and Eben Horsford, the brilliant mathematician and the young star in physics. Fancy seeing them here: Did they know this cell had once held the dread pirate Don Pedro Gilbert? The Terror of the Treasure Coast? Indeed it had. And now it held Harvard's Erving Professor of Chemistry and Mineralogy. Such was the lamentable state of Boston's constabulary and its justice system. Well, it was good they had come, for there was much for them to plan. Eben would have to serve in John's place for the chemistry lectures, once those began again at the school. It had to be Eben; Oliver Wendell Holmes had consulted with him, in his capacity as dean of the school, and he and Webster both agreed. Horsford's work in translating chemical texts from the German was nearly as good as Webster's, and there was no better man to step in while the doctor addressed these charges of, well, the charges of the present matter.

It would take a while, to be sure.

So much damage had been done already. The professor's private financial affairs had been painfully dragged before all of Boston and, even worse, all of Cambridge. A statement in this morning's *Bee* was typical: "The professor has been embarrassed for money for the past few months to an almost extreme degree." Another paper revealed the inheritance he'd received from his late father two decades ago—a tidy $40,000—and noted that he'd squandered most of it on a grand home he'd then sold at a terrible loss. One paper portrayed him as a man of "expensive habits and a love of luxury," while another noted that he'd recently had a nine-dollar check returned due to insufficient funds.

To many across the river in Cambridge, to gentlemen like Peirce and Horsford, the notion of their old colleague embroiled in a crime over money defied any sense at all. "A lifetime of uprightness forbids it," scoffed the *Cambridge Chronicle*. As to who had really committed the crime, well, that was obvious. They scarcely even needed to name him.

"We are at perfect liberty to suppose that *some individual* knowing that Dr. Parkman was to have received money of Dr. Webster, might have accosted him as he came out of Dr. Webster's lecture-room on the main floor of the building, might have asked him down into the basement, and having him in a room with no other person, and not exposed to observation, felled him with a blow," one newspaper theorized. The writer was not very coy about who this unnamed individual would be. "In the hours of midnight, when he was the sole monarch of the College, he would naturally, at any rate, think of disposing the body in the safest way possible." And with the reward offered for the body, of course, this individual would now triple his money or better by subsequently "discovering" the body.

"Of course we cannot believe Dr. Webster guilty, bad as some of the evidence looks," wrote Fanny Longfellow to her sister-in-law. "Many suspect the janitor, who is known to be a bad man, and to have wished for the reward offered for Dr. Parkman's body."

Boston and Cambridge were swiftly separating, observed one reporter, into the "the anti-Webster and the anti-Littlefield parties." The janitor was already known to have handled the college's dark trade in cadavers; who knew what else he was capable of? Three students from the Medical College had recently gone to the district attorney, charging that Littlefield had offered one of them seventy dollars for a gold watch; this, they charged, was surely evidence of his ill-gotten gains. But there was a comically simple explanation: Littlefield had made the comment in jest, *weeks* earlier. And what need had he of a watch from a student, in the middle of a city full of pawnbrokers and jewelers? To the anti-Websterians, this was simply one more attempt, an editorial inveighed, "to throw a deed of blood from a man in high society upon the head of a poor man."

High society did have its uses for Webster. He'd requested a private arraignment, or as close to one as the city could manage, and because he was a respectable citizen, it had been granted. But would he miss lunch through this special arraignment? Ah, well, he might.

Professor Peirce was bewildered by his old colleague. Webster was strangely calm and, during their conversation, kept endlessly circling back to his meals. "His whole mind seems to be running upon his food," Peirce later reported, "and upon the delicacies with which he may pamper his appetite."

It was mystifying. Did the fellow not understand that he was in mortal danger from these charges?

* * * *

JUSTICE IN Boston never slept, but it did take lunch breaks. The jail-house carriage arrived at a courthouse that would normally have been abandoned for the more genial chambers of Parker's and the Union Oyster House. The sergeant at arms was discombobulated, so little did he expect court business at this hour, and no sooner had he opened the large oaken doors to allow Webster and a phalanx of officers inside than he'd shut it to the press. Two lucky reporters made it in—one from the *Courier*, the other from the abolitionist paper the *Daily Chronotype*. They'd never seen the public shut out like this. Just the year before, when a black sailor named Washington Goode had been charged in a sensational murder, there'd been no secrecy at all—quite the opposite. And yet here was a white Harvard man, his case the talk of the town, whisked into the courthouse with scarcely a murmur to the press.

"The color of a man's skin makes a mighty difference with some folks," the *Chronotype* reporter observed acidly.

Webster situated himself at the docket while the arraigning judge pored over the papers. Some interesting cases for the court today: the notorious counterfeiter Madame O'Connor, as well as a miscreant who'd tried extorting $500 from a Bostonian through anonymous letters threatening to burn his house down. But none topped this case. Had he, Professor Webster, read the charges?

No, Webster answered, smiling politely, he had not.

It would take a few minutes to prepare them for the prisoner to read; Webster occupied his wait with a newspaper. It was not altogether comforting reading, as his own case was the biggest story. "ASTOUND-ING DISCLOSURES!" the *Bee* blared, adding, "THE EVIDENCE ACCU-MULATES!" Even with the Medical College cordoned off by police, the rumor was that certain penny papers had been offering bounties of up to fifty dollars for a good scoop. If so, the *Herald* had certainly got its money's worth: that afternoon it was topping all competitors with a shockingly grisly, and disconcertingly accurate, illustration of George Parkman's remains as illicitly viewed inside the Medical College. It was an unheard-of picture to run in a Boston newspaper—a body visibly laid out for public view in the news columns, right alongside the "Receipts of California Gold Dust" and stock quotes for the Connecticut River Railroad. Yet nothing about the case seemed normal anymore. Newspapers had suddenly become so valuable that urchins were stealing them off subscribers' doorsteps to resell in the street. Thanks to the new telegraph lines into the city, soon the story would go national as well; what little reprieve Webster had so far had from that was due to a weekend storm knocking out Boston's lines to New York City.

The *Herald* had also commissioned an artist to draw Webster's portrait; haste was its most notable artistic feature. The result, one commentator scoffed, "looks no more like that gentleman than it looks like Queen Victoria."

At length the complaint was brought over to the docket and handed to the doctor. The first sentence alone was more than two hundred words long, sported four semicolons, and bore that curious mixture of the formal and the visceral that characterized a murder arraignment: "upon search of said Medical College certain portions of a human frame and body, freshly dead, have been found." But it terminated in a sharp point: "John W. Webster, at said Boston, on said 23d, &c., of his malice afterthought, in and upon said George Parkman feloniously did make an assault, and him the said Parkman then and there of his malice afterthought feloniously did kill and murder him in some way and some manner and some weapon to said complainant unknown." The complaint was signed "Charles M. Kingsley"; Parkman's trusty agent had not failed his old employer.

This was not a bailable case, the judge explained to Webster; he'd have to wait in jail for the eventual trial.

And yet, perhaps his situation was not a hopeless one. The prosecution would have to prove the charges beyond a reasonable doubt, and Webster's case promised some very reasonable doubts indeed. How could the prosecutors establish a murder in a building already full of dead bodies? How could they determine that the body was really Parkman's? Even if it was Parkman, how could they show that someone else hadn't put the body there? If Webster had put it there, how could they ascertain that it had been premeditated murder and not manslaughter? And would anyone really believe that a Harvard professor would commit such an act?

How could doubt not seem reasonable in a case like this?

Webster was sent back to his cell, where some turkey and rice arrived from Parker's, and he fell upon it eagerly. Then he sat down to write a letter to his daughter Marianne, whom he had still not seen after three days in jail; as the eldest of his daughters still at home, she would be asked to run errands. "My dearest Marianne," he scratched onto the paper, and he recounted the day's events: the visit by Peirce and Horsford, the arraignment so admirably hidden from the public. But then, inevitably, he thought of all the wonderful food he had been sent:

> They send much more than I can eat and I have directed the steward
> to distribute the surplus to any poor ones here. If you will send me
> a small canister of tea, I can make my own. A little pepper, I may
> want, some day: you can put it up, to come with some bundle. . . .
> Half a dozen Rochelle powders, I should like.

There was another concern on his mind, though, before he set down his pen and sealed the envelope.

"Tell mamma," he added, "*not to open* the little bundle I gave her."

* * * *

AT NINE-THIRTY on Thursday morning, the remains of George Parkman were returned to his home at 8 Walnut Street.

The casket that now lay in the family's house was the closest to a homecoming the Parkman family could hope for. The Reverend Peabody spoke with the immediate family and other relations. A brass plate on the casket bore a few simple words:

GEORGE PARKMAN
Died Nov. 23, 1849
Aged 60 years.

The age was wrong; he hadn't turned sixty just yet. But the casket in their home and the date of death inscribed upon it represented the family's declaration: that this was his body, and that he had indeed died that day in the Medical College.

Those who had known Dr. Parkman best struggled to draw up the kind of amiable remembrances that an occasion like this would demand. There were his kindnesses to the insane, of course. Parkman had donated both an organ and a piano to the Boston Lunatic Hospital—additions much loved by the inmates, but of which few outside its walls would ever learn. The doctor had never quite left medicine, in fact: he had been working on a final paper, it was said, on "the value of electricity in producing active dejection from the bowels."

The favorite story, oft repeated, was about his poor tenants, and the old man's response when a local politician had asked him to donate ten dollars for a showy cannon salute to celebrate an election victory. "Just step with me round the corner," the doctor was said to reply. Then, taking the politician up some rickety stairs, Parkman ushered him into the tenement of a poor consumptive tenant. "Now," Parkman remarked, handing over a bill, "here is ten dollars: you may either fire it away in powder or give it to this poor woman. I won't attempt to bias you." With that, he vanished from the room, leaving his charge to stand there awkwardly, and then sheepishly hand the money to the woman. The story was a telling one: charitable, in its way, but, like Parkman, also rather sharp and unforgiving.

The occasional piano or ten-dollar gift did not quite hide the fact that Parkman's larger operations were not altogether benevolent. George's donation of the land under the Medical College, it seemed, was hardly as munificent as it first appeared—at least, not when one looked at the land under the new nearby jail. The former had been donated to Harvard while Josiah Quincy Sr. was its president; the latter was negotiated shortly afterward with Boston mayor Josiah Quincy Jr.—and at an astronomical twelve-fold markup from what Parkman and Shaw had paid for the land. The deal had profited Parkman and Shaw more than $40,000 apiece. Their plot was not what the city's own commission had recommended; the land was partially underwater at high tide, and so waterlogged that it took nearly $50,000 more in municipal funds for a landfill and a seawall to even make it habitable. The donation looked suspiciously like a quid pro quo, worked out with the Quincys, that enriched Harvard—and George Parkman and Robert Shaw—at the expense of the city of

Boston. The incoming mayor, John Bigelow, was so irked by it that for months he halted construction on the Charles River property, trying to get the jail site moved, before finally concluding that the city's finances were already disastrously committed. For this sleight of hand, George Parkman would now be remembered as a great benefactor.

Not every Parkman was so clever at hiding his tracks. The publicity over George's murder produced the revelation in the papers that years earlier George had helped his brother Samuel—"Naughty Sam," as he was known in the family—flee the law and the country after a murky scandal involving forgeries. Naughty Sam was rumored to be living in Italy, though the family knew better; he was living in debauchery in Paris.

Naughty Sam, alas, could not be present for that day's funeral.

George's casket was loaded onto a bier, and a handful of family members and other relatives followed it across Boston Common in a procession of five carriages. For such decidedly partial remains, Parkman's box was surprisingly heavy. Inside the wooden casket was a sealed leaden coffin; and inside that, the doctor's remains floated, gently suspended in spirits. This was the better to preserve them if they were needed for retrieval during the trial—a clever bit of forensic practicality that Dr. Parkman would have entirely approved of.

If only his reputation could also be preserved under a leaden seal. Instead, the secrets of families on both sides of the Charles River continued their steady drip onto the pages of the press. "Day by day," Longfellow wrote in his journal, "the horrid facts, circumstances, and considerations of the Cambridge Tragedy come oozing like water through an ill-constructed cistern!" To those around Harvard, of course, the plot against Webster was dubbed the *Cambridge* Tragedy; to those in Boston, convinced of Webster's guilt and the persecution of the school's porter, it was now the *Boston* Tragedy.

There was, however, one conviction they all shared: that whatever was to follow, it was indeed going to be a tragedy.

Part V

* * * *

THE
TRIAL

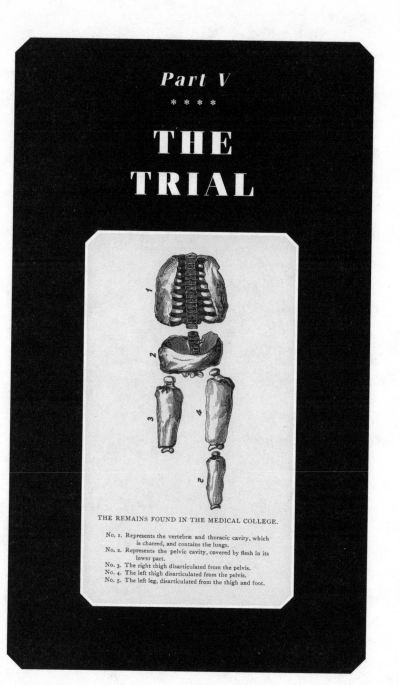

THE REMAINS FOUND IN THE MEDICAL COLLEGE.

No. 1. Represents the vertebræ and thoracic cavity, which is charred, and contains the lungs.
No. 2. Represents the pelvic cavity, covered by flesh in its lower part.
No. 3. The right thigh disarticulated from the pelvis.
No. 4. The left thigh disarticulated from the pelvis.
No. 5. The left leg, disarticulated from the thigh and foot.

17

IN THE
DEAD HOUSE

THE SKELETON KEY SCRAPED INSIDE THE LOCK AND TURNED;
the door swung into darkness.

The men knew they weren't supposed to be there, and they locked
the door behind them. The coroner's inquest was in Ward Room 7
of city hall, but old hands knew that the coroner's storage room—
the "dead house"—was right under Room 7, and that an air vent ran
between the two spaces. The two reporters strained at the grille to
catch any words of the expert testimony: *victim, flesh, caustic, teeth* . . .

Click.

The door swung open under the hand of a court officer.

What are . . .

One trespasser bowled past the lawman, sprinting down the old
planked hallway, but the officer grabbed the other one and hauled him
upstairs before an unamused court—where, it was reported, "he was
taken before the jury, and coroner-mauled."

Desperate measures by reporters were hardly a surprise, though,
with the coroner holding his inquest behind closed doors. This was
nearly unheard of, and widely attacked in Boston and around the country. "SECRET INQUISITION," one Baltimore paper announced. A public
inquest, the DA soothingly explained, would result in "pre-occupying
and misdirecting public opinion" and would make a fair trial impossible. His reasons might have been given credence until he also let it slip
that the Webster and Parkman families wanted the investigation kept
private, and that he'd accommodated them. Boston once again seemed
to have a different justice system for the rich than the poor.

"From the beginning," the *Bee* accused, "there has been shown an evident disposition to conceal and keep back the information in this affair. . . . The public have a right to know."

Perhaps, but more urgently, the newspapers had a *need* to know. Telegraphic coverage of suicides, boiler explosions, and train derailments was growing so rapidly that the *Cambridge Chronicle* drolly reprinted a proposal for constructing a giant awning made of newsprint across the length of America, to contain "17,000,000 columns of reading matter." While there was plenty of national news that December, with the Washington Monument reaching the fifty-foot mark and talk of a proposal to send another Arctic expedition after missing explorer Sir John Franklin, the presses were hungrier still for the sensational and the strange. News of spirit knockings in New York was good; the claim that a Russian inventor had created a steam-powered man was even better.

But nothing sold like murder, and no murder sold like Dr. Parkman's.

Papers across the country had picked up the story now—it was, a Georgia newspaper noted, a ghastly bounty for "lovers of horrors." The New Orleans *Daily Picayune* reported that "The Northern papers teem with the revolting details" and pondered whether "refined education is valueless" if Harvard could be the scene of such depravity: "How can we expect that the illiterate and benighted child of want will remain faithful . . . when he in whose breast the lamp of science brightly burns is found derelict?"

The story traveled on ships across the ocean, steadily sailing west to run in the Honolulu *Polynesian* and the *New Zealand Spectator,* and east to the *Illustrated London News.* That city had itself scarcely recovered from "the Bermondsey Horror," a lurid affair in which a married couple lured the wife's wealthy lover into their Miniver Place home, shot him and beat him with a crowbar, buried his body under the kitchen flagstones, and then double-crossed each other over the money. Such newly proclaimed Tragedies and Horrors seemed to arrive as regularly as the latest monthly installment of *David Copperfield.*

With business thriving, the real scandal of the reporter found in the dead house was, perhaps, that he'd been foolish enough to get caught.

"He was exceedingly sorry—that the officer had discovered his cool contrivance for getting the materials for an Extra," a *Post* reporter dryly commented, and the *Journal* promptly picked up the story as well. The two other papers typically suspected of such high jinks were the *Herald* and perhaps the *Bee;* but the *Herald* hinted in owl puns that an evening penny paper—the ostensibly more respectable *Transcript*—had done the deed: "WHO was caught in the dead house? Who?" it needled. The *Bee* worked up a sly fable of an owl haunting the rafters of city hall: "The owl is killed and is in the dead-house—where an inquest will be held today, and which—on account of the feelings of the coroner—no reporters will be allowed. We hear that a locksmith has been at work all night on another *skeleton key*."

The *Transcript* still clung to an air of respectability, even while it printed the bloody details of the case. As readers settled in for the Christmas season, the paper ran a poem titled "Murder-Worship," scolding them for reading the very thing its own columns provided:

> . . . *We chronicle the foul minutiae*
> *Of the dark deeds of crime;—nay! stop not here,*
> *But sift their very prison–life, and draw*
> *The veil from off their hidden histories:*
> *We crowd to see their waxen effigies;*
> *We make their portraits household gods, and rear*
> *Them shrines, where Murder–worship is allowed by Law.*

The poem, like so much else in American papers, was pirated from Britain; it had run in *Punch* as a comment on the Bermondsey Horror. Not a word was changed, nor needed to be, for what had been true of Miniver Place in London was just as true of North Grove Street in Boston.

* * * *

THE NEW Year of 1850 arrived in Boston with both sleigh rides in the moonlight and the inaugural journey of the rail line between Cambridge and Boston. Modern life had come to Harvard, and the smoke-belching locomotive was the fitting end to the first half of the century. "What stupendous discoveries, what great events it has produced!" rhapsodized the *Evening Transcript*. "The steamboat, the railroad, the daguerreotype, the magnetic telegraph, etherization. . . . It has been a grand, a magnificent era, whatever the grumblers may say."

Longfellow was delighted by this wondrous conveyance; he rode the rails into town and did not find himself missing hour-long waits in the old omnibus office. The railway terminus in Boston, admittedly, lacked grandeur. The trip, he judged, was "very pleasant, though it leaves down by North End, by no means the most desirable end of a journey." But then, if one's final destination was to be the Leverett Street Jail, as Longfellow's was to be today, perhaps no journey could end well anyway.

The jail guards showed the poet in and walked him down to Webster's cell. "There," Longfellow noted in his journal, "sat the doctor reading."

John was voluble, nervous with the bottled-up energy of a sociable man now in his second month of confinement. It was not as cold inside the jail as Longfellow imagined—but it was just as dark. Yet Webster was reading incessantly, more like a cloistered scholar than a prisoner, fortified in the morning by copies of the *Advertiser* and the *Courier*, and then writing back to his family and colleagues for the latest books he'd seen mentioned. During his jail time, Charlotte Brontë's *Shirley* and Washington Irving's biography of Mohammed were published, and he was particularly keen to lay hands on the latter volume.

The details of his own case did not make for such pleasant reading. Just that morning the papers had run a claim that he'd been complaining of other prisoners taunting him with "Murderer!" when he tried to sleep. But, one account noted, after a guard was posted overnight and heard nothing, Webster had still complained of voices the next morning. "The doctor's imagination is so wrought upon," concluded a reporter, "as to produce in some degree mental aberration."

Such fanciful reports by the press, Webster grumbled, left the "public mind inflamed—blind to truth."

It was a relief to have Longfellow visit; he was a link to the world Webster had lost, of the pleasant dilemmas of a Harvard family man—what Longfellow dubbed the "Hesperian Gardens of college life." President Sparks was pleading with the poet to teach more literature lectures in the coming year, which wasn't really in his contract, but how could he say no? A few days ago, he'd spent some hours building snow forts outside the house with his children; what a world away that seemed from this grim place, where the fortifications were real. Meals with future senator Charles Sumner, tea with Emerson; over a dinner with literary friends, they'd passed the hat around for Hawthorne, who, it was whispered, "was really in want." The poor fellow had a novel coming out, about a respectable Puritan minister hiding an adultery scandal. What market was there for that quaint stuff, when you could read in any newspaper about a Harvard professor facing a murder charge?

Webster had his own sheaf of writing in the works. The prison had furnished his cell with a rudely fitted table, where he penned sheet after sheet of notes on his defense. He sketched pages of maps and drawings—some showing the positions of potentially removable panels and latches on his laboratory doors, the better to demonstrate how vulnerable they were to intruders.

So someone might have gained entry to his lab—but who?

The janitor, Webster claimed. Littlefield was capable of anything for a few dollars' profit. Why, when they'd moved into the new medical school building, a few years ago, Littlefield had, for some extra pay, taken on the very worst jobs involving in clearing out the old premises. "Dr. Lawrence hired Littlefield to clean out the bodies etc. accumulated in the vault of the old college, and he did it for 200 dollars I think he told me," Webster sniffed. "Shows he was ready to do any thing for money." That his own lab made this work that now he looked down upon was hardly the point to Webster; how could it be, when the first question was, What sort of man would *take* that work?

It was simple, really. Parkman had been murdered elsewhere—perhaps by an angry tenant—and his body was bundled into a sack as a black-market cadaver. "The body was probably brought to the college to sell as a subject," Webster theorized. "On discovering whose body it was, it would have been the first impulse to get rid of it." As to the parts winding up in his own privy, Dr. Webster suspected that Little-field secretly had an extra key. Maybe, he helpfully added, they should search the janitor's privy, too. "Would it not be well," he suggested, "to employ a man to look below[?]"

"He talked freely about his case," Longfellow marveled, "but showed no particular emotion, save when I told him that the Musical Asso-ciation Concerts had been given up in Cambridge out of a feeling of sympathy for him."

It was shocking for the doctor to hear that Harvard's alumni con-certs had fallen silent. Music was a pure joy of Webster's home life in Cambridge, and that life, it seemed, was slipping inexorably away.

* * * *

THE BITTER cold continued for days, and the Bostonian vogue for using the newly installed plumbing to wash down the sidewalks quickly turned the streets into treacherous sheets of ice. Soon even the Charles River itself had hardened into glass. Locals ventured out onto the ice with their skates, and the river by the Medical College echoed with the cries of delighted children. When a lad named Jerome trudged into the senior Dr. Bigelow's office, it might just as easily have been to ask for someone to administer to a clumsy skater.

I've got something for Dr. Ware, the boy explained.

That wasn't unusual; Jerome sometimes ran errands for Ware. But this time it was something he'd found in the river—under the ice, in fact, while he'd been skating. Bigelow knew that Ware was in the middle of a lecture with the medical students. Leave it with me, he told the boy. When Ware emerged from his lecture hall, his colleague was waiting for him.

"Found the hands of Dr. Parkman," the old professor laconically informed him.

They were indeed hands: the fingers swollen, the flesh stripped off and still stuck to the ice, but unmistakably two human hands. The boy had found them well out from shore; Dr. Ware mused that perhaps they'd been disarticulated from the body and flung as far out into the river as possible. The school would have to inform the family, of course.

The mystery, however, was quickly solved by a third professor: *I* put those out there, he explained. He'd buried them in the sandy bank a week ago, before the freeze—just curiosity, really, to study the rate of decomposition—and clearly he hadn't buried them deeply enough. The hands were those of an ordinary college cadaver. But then, such discoveries were to be expected: the school both being a medical college and occupying a riverfront building in a large city, there'd always be *some* dead bodies about. In the first days of searching for Parkman, the police had even found a dead newborn, abandoned out on the nearby empty lot where the jail was to be built. Then, as the *Herald* noted, "a rather good-looking young girl" also proved to be missing from her house-servant job nearby. She later turned up alive in a South Boston workhouse, and the story was quietly forgotten.

With Bostonians attuned to any hint of mystery around North Grove Street, though, every such find was reported in the newspapers. Impresarios and merchants took note, and one of the most shameless used a false headline to sucker readers into a notice for a mesmerist:

THE PARKMAN TRAGEDY in the glow of its excitement, scarcely produced more interest in the minds of our citizens, than the wonderful and almost superhuman experiments in the science of "electro biology" nightly made at the Melodeon by the able and educated Mr. Fiske.

One bookseller, Redding & Co., took advantage of the scandal to unload its stock of one hundred copies of Webster's 1821 book *A Description of the Island of St. Michael,* a pleasantly dull tome. It hardly mattered that even the merchant admitted that it was "Dry, physical fact. . . . There is hardly such a thing as a sentiment in the whole volume."

If moldering books by Webster had a market, there was an even greater one for books *about* Webster. That week, even as newspapers ran ads for the latest "Despairing, Raving, Mad, Heart-Killing, High Flown, Lampooning, Romantic" valentine cards from London, there appeared notices for *The Boston Tragedy!,* a twelve-and-a-half-cent rush job that tidily summarized the case and whose pages promised "evidence of the blackest character." Its publisher soon claimed that twenty thousand copies sold in the first week alone.

The relentless publicity was so disheartening that Harvard's recently retired president, Edward Everett, briefly mulled the idea of teaming up with two fellow Harvard alumni to start their own edifying newspaper, "for gratuitous circulation, or nearly so, to counteract the detestable penny papers which are filled with ribaldry and exercise the worst possible influence." But Everett was not always a man of the most practical ideas: as president, he'd changed the university's name to "The University at Cambridge," reissuing the school stationery and retitling the school's bulletins accordingly. Perhaps he imagined an eventual merger with the institution's British cousin; in any case, the new name did not outlast his three years in the office.

Actual penny-paper proprietors were, alas, considerably more tenacious than Everett. On February 28, *Herald* readers were greeted with a headline that roared, "HIGHLY IMPORTANT! DISCOVERY OF A DEAD BODY *supposed to be that of* DR G PARKMAN!" A body found in the river near Roxbury, the article claimed, had been judged by an inquest to probably be Parkman's, what with its "long, attenuated limbs—the apparent age—the peculiar bend of the body." News of the discovery was halfway across the country even as Bostonians subsequently learned that the inquest had actually said nothing of the sort. The body was that of a missing thirty-eight-year-old carriage-smith, despondent after his employer went bust—not a fifty-nine-year-old doctor who'd been out collecting rents. The other newspapers leapt upon what they dubbed "the Parkman Hoax." The *Herald,* unrepentant as ever, retreated into a time-honored sanctuary for humbug: moralizing.

"We never wantonly trifle with the feelings of the public, especially on a subject so awful and momentous as the one in question," the paper piously announced. "That revolting atrocities—moral abominations, and other descriptions of iniquities, appear in the *Herald,* is not our fault, but that of the wicked world in which we live."

* * * *

SOMEHOW, BACK in Cambridge, life continued in the Webster household.

The few times Harriet and the girls had seen John had scarcely lasted over an hour; they'd spent more time with him in a single evening at home over Milton and violin practice than they'd had together in three months of his imprisonment at Leverett Street.

The family, in turn, was imprisoned in their house, besieged by letters from attorneys— *Dear Mrs. Webster, Please accept my deepest sympathies in this trying time. If I might offer my services*—none of whom would have bothered writing if they'd known that Harriet and her daughters had resorted to needlework just to get by. Their combined sewing brought in barely fifty dollars a month, less than a third of Dr. Webster's salary. And then, too, Mrs. Webster had once quietly earned much-needed extra money by having her relatives in the Azores send fashionable straw hats and stockings hidden in their parcels. It was not *exactly* legal; but she had quietly resold the items at a fine price, having avoided the steep duties on such goods. Now, however, she could hardly leave the house: visiting the docks for shipping would bring an intolerable gauntlet of stares. Even visitors to the house were not to be trusted. One peddler, let into the kitchen to talk with their helper Anne, had inquired so pointedly about their affairs that they became convinced he was a spy—whether sent by the Parkmans, the police, or the newspapers, it hardly mattered.

The daguerreotypes on the bureau were their best company now, though even they were reminders of what had been lost. There was one of Sarah and her baby, taken in the Azores; she alone of the daughters had been married and shipped off before this disaster struck. And in other frames, views of Porta Delgada, from Mrs. Webster's childhood home—an ocean and a lifetime away from this imprisonment in a frigid New England winter.

They'd have to sell some books from the professor's library. Perhaps, he helpfully suggested, they could sell more than that from his office. "There are also some good pictures, some pieces of statuary," he added. These, he thought, might be "of interest to persons of taste."

But they were still desperately short of money.

A carriage came by each morning to pick the women up for a brief respite in the outside world. The carriage wasn't theirs—they didn't dare hire such an extravagance—but, rather, the thoughtful favor of a Harvard friend. Anything outside the carriage was less calming, especially the newspapers. There terrible, cruel things were said about the girls' father: the mocking revelation that he'd been dubbed "Skyrocket Jack" by his students, for his milquetoast manner and his sometimes inept proclivity for chemical explosions; the oddly contrary claims of his cruelty and his "devilish" temper; and humiliating revelations about the family's shaky finances, coming just as his daughters were becoming marriageable. But the news was harder, perhaps, for the false hope it offered. As February slipped into March, and the body found in Roxbury was forgotten, attention turned instead to an extraordinary letter received months earlier by the *New Orleans Delta*:

Dear Sir: It is with difficulty that I can get paper to rite you; but I am induced to do so for the safety of Dr. Webster. He is not guilty of the deed. I myself perpetrated the Deed that he is charged with.

And I am off for Californiar.
Yours, ORONOKA
the 23rd of November was a Bad Day for me

Newspapers, not to mention both the Parkman and the Webster families, received all kinds of wild letters. One from Philadelphia claimed that Parkman had been murdered by a tenant in a Charles Street apartment—just as Webster himself had theorized—and then his body dumped off at the college.

Yet the Oronoka letter looked more convincing than most. It had been postmarked in Washington, Texas—some eighty miles outside Houston—and witnesses stated that a mysterious man from Boston's suburbs *had* been in the region. Follow-up reports noted that a "John Weeks" signed himself into a nearby hotel at the time and died of cholera a few weeks later on a steamboat—perhaps bound for California. His effects revealed his identity as Benjamin F. Cannon, who'd disappeared from his Wendell, Massachusetts, home in November, on the run from creditors. Some maintained that the news couldn't have reached Texas in time for a hoaxer to write it based on the newspaper accounts; the letter writer, they said, must have been someone with personal knowledge of the crime who had left Boston before the body was discovered.

This might have been a convincing argument, were it not for some simple arithmetic: the letter was mailed twenty-seven days after the public revelation of the crime; yet the first word of the letter appeared in Boston twenty-one days after *that*. So news could indeed travel between those locations in just three weeks. Its author might have had a week to read of the affair in the papers and then amuse himself with a hoax. Moreover, there was no hint that Cannon had been seen in Boston or around Parkman, or that there was anything incriminating in his trunk of personal effects that was sent home to his daughters, or, indeed, that there was anything remarkable about a man fleeing creditors to reinvent himself out west.

This story, like all the others, dissipated and left Mrs. Webster with nothing. Nothing, that is, but the sure knowledge that on March 19, her husband would stand trial on a capital charge of murder.

THE COMMONWEALTH OF MASSACHUSETTS V. JOHN WHITE WEBSTER

SUPREME JUDICIAL COURT OF MASSACHUSETTS,
NEW COURT HOUSE, CITY OF BOSTON

March 19th — April 1st, 1850

Hon. Lemuel Shaw, Esq.

Chief Justice of the Massachusetts Supreme Judicial Court

Hon. Samuel S. Wilde, *Associate Justice*
Hon. Charles A. Dewey, *Associate Justice*
Hon. Theron Metcalf, *Associate Justice*

George C. Wilde, Esq., *Clerk of the Supreme Judicial Court*

Dr. John White Webster
Defendant

COUNSEL FOR THE PRISONER   PROSECUTORS

Hon. Pliny Merrick   John Clifford, Esq., Attorney General

Edward D. Sohier, Esq.   George Bemis, Esq.

MEMBERS OF THE JURY

Thomas Barrett
John Borrowscale
Robert J. Byram (Foreman)
James Crosby
John E. Davenport
Albert Day
Joseph Eustis
Daniel T. Fuller
Benjamin H. Greene
Arnold Hayward
Frederick A. Henderson
Stephen A. Stackpole

18

GOOD MEN AND TRUE

THE BOSTON *HERALD*?

Draw.

The *Boston Courier*?

Draw.

The Boston *Mail*?

Draw.

About a dozen reporters gathered in the empty courtroom, drawing straws from the hand of Sheriff Eveleth, vying for the press chairs closest to the witness stand. The courthouse still smelled of sawdust; all weekend Sheriff Eveleth had had carpenters in here, barricading all but two entrances and strategically rerouting the remaining entryways. Hastily erected hallways and extra railings would smoothly sluice the massed public through only the upper galleries of the courtroom, and then back downstairs, out through the cellar, and into the street. A separate new hallway, guarded by police officers, would admit the trial judges, lawyers, and witnesses into the main floor of the courtroom.

The New York *Globe*?

Draw.

The New York papers had reporters there for the trial, too. For days, Boston newspapers had been priming their readers, with the *Bee* going into a reverie at the prospects: "This, without question, will be the most exciting trial that ever took place in this country. — THE PEOPLE demand all the facts concerning this MOST MYSTERIOUS TRAGEDY, and as one of the people's agents, we mean to do our part towards answering that demand." The *Herald*, boasting of "one of the fastest presses, an extra set of hands, and a steam engine," promised its readers hourly editions so that the "mazy web of this unprecedented transaction will be unveiled before the public."

But a newer medium was also seizing the moment. Local inventor John Adams Whipple was one of the first Americans to manufacture photography chemicals, and his ads for "Daguerreotypes by Steam" were a staple of Boston newspapers. He also dabbled in work as a showman, at night turning his studio into a twenty-five-cent magic lantern show of "dissolving views" projected onto the wall "as large as life." He had a scholarly side, too, working with Harvard's observatory to create some of the very first astronomical images. Whipple, however, knew where the money was at the moment with Harvard photographs, and it wasn't up on the moon. Redding & Co., the same bookstore that had used the scandal to unload old copies of Professor Webster's rather sleepy monograph, now offered twenty-five-cent engravings of Webster "from a daguerreotype by Mr. Whipple."

All the attention on Dr. Webster had almost worked *too* well. There had been talk of moving the trial to a performance space like the Melodeon theater, or to Tremont Hall—the latter seating some twenty-six hundred—before settling on the more sober environs of a customary courtroom. But the city's largest room could fit only about five hundred. The applicants could have filled the room twelve times over; still more, neither knowing nor caring about tickets, would show up wanting to get in. Observing the usual courtesies meant that medical and law students, as well as their professional elders, were given special priority in applying for trial passes, which they eagerly took; in the end, only a fraction of the upper gallery seating was left for the public.

This also left the newspapers jockeying for prime spots on the courtroom floor. The sheriff had done his best; his carpenters had even built some press tables specially for the trial, situated between the jury box and the sheriff's desk.

The *Boston Traveller?*

Draw.

Really, the crowding couldn't be helped. Why, the witnesses alone would number up to 120 people. Sheriff Eveleth could only shrug at the madness of it all.

"I don't know what else can be done," he told the reporters.

* * * *

THE CROWDS began forming at seven that morning, gathering in the snow and on the southern steps of the courthouse, electrified by the approach of any important-looking carriage.

"That's him!" one of the onlookers yelled.

"That be damned," another scoffed, "that's not Webster."

Policemen stood outside the thick, bronze-sheathed doors, opening and closing them to one ticket holder at a time, "to keep at bay the unfavored multitude," as an observer drily put it. Slowly the gallery and the floor filled, and the air swelled with the spectators' animated discussions until, at eight forty-five a.m., a sudden hush fell upon the room: Dr. Webster had arrived.

"All stretched forward to scan his looks," one reporter observed, "for instinctively all men are physiognomists."

Webster's manner betrayed little. The doctor was no stranger to the courtroom, having served as an expert witness upon occasion. Led up to his seat in the dock—a cushioned armchair—he bowed slightly and smiled at several friends in the crowd before sitting down. He looked exactly like what, in fact, he was: a bespectacled grandfather who taught chemistry at Harvard. Still, with phrenology's hold on the public imagination, some saw in his features all the marks of criminality that a professional demeanor could not hide.

"The countenance of the prisoner indicated to the physiognomist strong animal passion and irascible temperament," opined the New York *Globe*. "His general appearance makes no favorable impression."

The four judges arrived to another hush. Capital cases required a majority of the state supreme court's justices, and four of the five judges were here today, with Chief Justice Lemuel Shaw presiding. At sixty-nine, Shaw was now in his twentieth year as chief justice, and already the longest serving in the state's history; his past three predecessors had all died in office, and the dour and dogged Shaw would likely be no different. He was inextricable from the business and culture of Boston; his opinions had shaped New England's burgeoning railroads and industries, and his new son-in-law Herman Melville had ambitions to shape its literature as well.

A skeptic might have pointed out that Shaw, as a member of Harvard's Board of Overseers, had a conflict of interest in this case. But that was not how the law worked in Boston, and particularly not how the law worked at Harvard. Shaw was also presiding over an endlessly disputed will by one Edward Phillips, whose heirs contested provisos that included a $100,000 bequest to Harvard's observatory. That Lemuel Shaw was judging that case elicited little comment; how could a connection to Harvard be a conflict of interest, when Harvard was every Boston gentleman's common interest? And in this day's case, not only were the accused and the victim from Harvard, but so were Webster's defense team of Pliny Merrick and Edward Sohier; and so, for that matter, was the associate prosecutor, George Bemis, and many of the witnesses.

The general public, however, was a different matter altogether—for in selecting a jury, an attorney needed to exercise care in assessing each man's associations and opinions.

"John Borrowscale!" the court clerk called out, taking roll as each man answered. "Hiram Bosworth! . . . George Frothingham!"

Of the sixty men in the jury pool, fifteen were quickly excused: ten for medical reasons, three under an exemption for militia members, one for no longer living in the county, and the last out of sheer old age. Forty-five men were left to choose from.

"I now move, Your Honors," the court clerk announced to the four justices, "that a jury be empanelled to try the issue."

Dr. Webster was called to the bar, and the jury selection—a process he'd seen many times as a medical expert, but not as the accused—was explained to him.

"John W. Webster: you are now set to the bar to be tried, and these good men whom I shall call, are to pass between the Commonwealth and you, upon your trial. If you would object to any of them, you will do so as they are called, and before they are sworn." Twenty jurors could be removed peremptorily, without reason; more could be challenged with reason. And those reasons, to both the judge and the legal teams, were not difficult to ascertain.

"Prisoner, look upon the juror," the clerk intoned. "Juror, look upon the prisoner."

The first juror scarcely made it past locking eyes with Webster; the second, Charles Appleton, lasted long enough to meet a pointed question from Chief Justice Shaw.

"Mr. Appleton," he began, "it is necessary that we know whether you are completely unprejudiced. It is immaterial which way the opinion is. Have you formed any opinion upon the subject of the prisoner's guilt or innocence, and have you expressed such opinion?"

"I *have* both formed and expressed an opinion," Appleton admitted, drawing his short career as a Webster juror to an immediate close.

The third juror claimed no such bias, but then found a second question waiting for him from the chief justice.

"There are many persons in the community who believe that it is wrong to inflict capital punishment on any criminal," Shaw explained. The old judge peered at his subject: Was he, Mr. William Barly, one of *those persons*? Ah! Indeed he was.

With each succeeding juror struck down, a buzz passed through the assembled crowd. Would *any* Bostonian qualify? Who had not expressed an opinion on Dr. Webster? When the fourth man in the jury pool—a printer named Thomas Barrett—prevailed and was sworn in, there was visible relief. From there a jury slowly emerged; when the forty-eighth of the sixty members of the jury pool was called at ten-thirty, they had their dozen jurors. With only white male voters allowed to serve, it read like a downtown office directory: two clerks, two merchants, a wheelwright, a slater, a painter, a carpenter, a furnisher, a printer, a bookseller, and a locksmith.

The twelve men seated themselves in the jury box, and the court clerk turned back to the prisoner.

"John W. Webster," the clerk announced, "hold up your right hand."

The doctor stood at the iron railing of the bar, his hand held aloft, and his face twitched subtly as the murder charges were read aloud: murder by knife, by hammer, by "mortal strokes" of hands and feet. His hand trembled slightly as the clerk finished.

"To this indictment, Gentlemen of the Jury, the prisoner at the bar has pleaded Not Guilty," the clerk continued. "You are now sworn to try the issue. If he is guilty, you will say so; if he is not guilty, you will say so, and no more."

And now, with the state's age-old invocation, the trial could truly begin.

"Good men and true!" the court clerk called out. "Stand together and hearken to your evidence!"

*   *   *   *

ATTORNEY GENERAL John Clifford hadn't really wanted to stand before this jury.

His plan was simple enough: his duties as the state's attorney general and a Whig politician already occupied him so thoroughly that he'd handed this case to a young star lawyer, George Bemis. At thirty-three, Bemis was a brilliant but unwilling legal mind: he mingled in the same circles as Longfellow and complained that his law work was a distraction from the higher life of the mind that he found when dining or praying with Emerson, Alcott, and Channing. And like all Harvard graduates his age, he'd known Dr. Webster as part of the deeply familiar campus pantheon of professors. Bemis, however, was proving difficult for Clifford to retain for a harder and more unexpected reason:

he was distracted by his father, who'd been bedridden for weeks with chest pains. For that matter, Bemis himself was only just getting over a long and miserable cold. In the end, Bemis had stayed only by extracting a promise from the attorney general: he'd handle the witnesses, but Clifford would orate the opening and closing arguments.

And so, rather to his own surprise, Attorney General Clifford now found himself standing up to open the most sensational case of his altogether sober career.

"Here, Gentlemen," he began, "in the clear, calm light of justice, we are called to investigate an issue, and endeavor to ascertain the simple truth of the accusation brought by the Grand Jury against the prisoner at the bar. That presentment involves two general propositions. The first is, that Dr. George Parkman, the person named in the indictment, has been murdered. The second is, that he was murdered by John W. Webster, the prisoner at the bar."

The packed courthouse listened intently as the attorney general addressed the jury, watching Webster's face for any sign of guilt. The professor, though occasionally fiddling with his spectacles, showed scarcely a hint of concern.

"We shall offer, then, Gentlemen, evidence to show you that Dr. George Parkman, a well-known and highly respectable citizen of Boston, was living, in good health and cheerful spirits, on Friday, the twenty-third day of November last; that he was engaged in his usual occupations on that day, up until fifteen minutes before two o'clock, which time he was last seen alive, entering the Medical Building in Grove Street. Dr. Parkman left some lettuce in a shop near the Medical College, with the intention of returning to take it, and thence to carry it home. He did not return. His friends and family became alarmed. Notices were published in the evening papers of Saturday, calling the attention of the entire public to the fact of his disappearance."

Chief Justice Shaw was already worried about keeping track of all these details.

"Was Friday the day?" he asked, interrupting the attorney general.

"Friday was the day of his disappearance, Saturday the day of the publication," Clifford said solicitously, and turned back to the jury. "Gentlemen, the entire police of this city were brought into requisition. Handbills were issued, offering the most liberal rewards . . . $3000, one of them. Hope gave way, and the conjecture and apprehension which had possessed the minds of his friends, the police and the public, deepened into certainty, that he was not in the land of the living."

Clifford moved on to the physical evidence: "On the 30th of November, the Friday after his disappearance, in the vault of a privy connected with the defendant's laboratory at the Medical College, were found parts answering to the description of Dr. Parkman. On that day, Friday, and the next day, Saturday, were found in the furnace of Dr. Webster's laboratory, a great number of bones. On Saturday there was found a tea-chest containing, imbedded in a quantity of tan, and covered with minerals, the thorax or entire trunk of a human body. Of the bones found in the furnace, not a fragment was found which duplicates any found in the vault or the tea-chest. Unless by a miracle they agreed, the parts all constituted portions of *one human body.*"

The spectator's gallery broke out in shocked whispers and murmurs, and from the floor of the courthouse Sheriff Eveleth immediately berated the townspeople in the upper seats.

"Silence in the gallery!" he yelled. "Silence!"

"Gentlemen," Clifford continued, "you will have placed for your inspection a block of mineral teeth found in that furnace, which will be testified to by two gentlemen, accomplished dentists, to be the teeth of Dr. Parkman. Dr. Keep distinctly recollects, recognizing his own work, that if he had seen them in Africa, or beyond the sea, he should have known them to be the teeth he made for Dr. George Parkman. Dr. Keep has in his possession the peculiar mold of Dr. Parkman's jaw—a peculiarity so great, that you could not find, through any caprice of nature, another precisely like it."

The crowd swelled up again, for this was astonishing, nearly unheard of—teeth as evidence?

"Quiet in the gallery!" the sheriff bellowed again.

George Bemis, sitting in the other chair of the prosecution table, quietly watched Attorney General Clifford at work. The jury selection had gone better than he'd expected, and Clifford was no slouch at oration—even if Bemis had needed to write most of the opening argument for him. Now, however, would come the real revelations to the jury and the public: not just means but the motive.

"Well, Gentlemen," his partner continued, "if Dr. Parkman was murdered, then comes the other great question. Was it by the prisoner at the bar? We shall offer evidence to show the connection between the deceased and the prisoner since the year 1842, when there was a loan of money made by Dr. Parkman to Dr. Webster. Dr. Webster had been embarrassed, even reduced to great straits, for money. At the time when this death of Dr. Parkman occurred, *all* the personal property which Dr. Webster had in the world was under mortgage to Dr. George Parkman."

It was this revelation that Webster, almost more than any accusation of murder, had tried so hard to avoid fully revealing, even to his own family: that though he was both the inheritor of a small fortune and an established faculty member of Harvard, the very basis of his gentility had been a sham for years.

"*This* was the relation of those parties on that fatal 23rd of November," Clifford announced decisively to the crowd. "The improvident debtor evading payment of his debt! The creditor resolutely pursuing!"

* * * *

AMONG THE first witnesses to be called was one who understood Parkman's financial dealings well: his brother-in-law and business partner, Robert Shaw.

"The last time I saw Dr. Parkman was on the day of his disappearance," he stated. "He called at my house between nine and ten o'clock in the morning of that day, and we walked down State Street together. We parted about ten o'clock, at the Merchant's Bank."

When the doctor went missing, it was Shaw who had gone to the city marshal, dictated the missing notices in the newspapers, and guaranteed the $3,000 reward. And it was Shaw, too, who then took custody of the doctor's body and arranged his funeral.

Do you believe those remains were Parkman? Bemis asked.

Sohier hastily objected. Without a positive identification, surely the question was a leading one? Bemis, unimpressed with Sohier, turned back to the witness and duly rephrased his question.

"What appearances," he asked Shaw drily, "if any, did you observe, showing a resemblance to *any* person?"

"I saw appearances about these remains, which induced me to believe them to belong to the body of Dr. George Parkman," Shaw explained. "The hair on the breast and leg, the color of which exactly corresponded with what I had seen. The hair on his leg I had seen in an early part of November . . ." The patrician Shaw paused delicately; he was speaking before hundreds of people, after all—and, as one observer noted, a number of "well dressed females" were among the crowds trying to get in.

"Shall I relate the circumstance?" he finally asked.

"Yes."

"He came to my house early one morning," Shaw continued. "A cold morning—and to my remark that he wasn't dressed warm enough, he replied that he had not on even drawers, and pulled up his pantaloons to show it."

It was a fine bit of entertainment for the gallery: *Silence!* But what Shaw had to reveal next would strike much deeper into real scandal. What, he was asked, was his financial relation to the prisoner in the dock?

"On the 18th of April, 1848, I received a note from Dr. Webster, asking to have a private interview with me," Shaw recalled. "He came the next day, and expressed to me his great embarrassment, and great want of money. He said that he expected the sheriff would be at his house to take away his furniture if he could not raise a certain sum of money."

Webster offered to sell his last possession of real value—his mineral cabinet—for a mere $1,200. Shaw didn't really want the cabinet, but he loaned the doctor $600 toward a possible eventual purchase, with the condition that Webster could keep the cabinet if he paid the interest. The professor never did pay the interest, and Shaw, with larger and less awkward business interests to tend to, quietly let the debt remain unspoken.

"Subsequently to this," Shaw revealed, "I was walking with Dr. Parkman one day in Mount Vernon Street, when we met Dr. Webster. I asked Dr. Parkman, after we passed, what salary Dr. Webster was receiving at Cambridge—"

Objection! Sohier countered. Surely this was both hearsay and immaterial.

But it was not, and not least to the chief justice, who sat on Harvard's board. Webster's salary, and everyone else's on the faculty, was public knowledge from Harvard's annual report, and money mattered a great deal in Webster's relations to those around him.

Go ahead, the judge said.

"He replied $1,200," the witness continued. "I then said, 'That is not half enough to support his family,' and went on to speak of his sale to me of his minerals. Dr. Parkman said, 'They are not his to sell. I have a mortgage on them, and if you will come to my house, I will show it to you.'"

The mortgage was a terrifyingly thorough document. Nearly every item in Webster's possession—every mineral, every book, every stick of furniture, everything down to his house linens—had already been pledged to Parkman as security on a $2,400 loan. For Dr. Parkman, it was just business; for Dr. Webster, it was ruin. The man had become so desperate that he'd pledged the same mineral cabinet to two business partners scarcely a block apart from each other. It was also rumored that at least two *other* creditors, the brothers Abbot and Amos Lawrence, had also made a $1,500 loan on the very same cabinet. They'd been either too discreet or too chagrined to collect on it; and to that delicacy, perhaps, they now owed their lives.

But George Parkman, a relentless creditor at the best of times, was furious when he learned of the professor's deception.

"He said that he would see Dr. Webster, and give him a piece of his mind," Shaw testified, each word building a fatal motive. "That it was a downright fraud, and that he ought to be *punished*."

19

THE CATALOG
OF BONES

AS DR. WEBSTER WAS MANACLED AND LED OUT TO THE
waiting prison carriage at eight o'clock the next morning, hundreds
watched from the sidewalks and windows of Leverett Street, hoping
to catch a glimpse of him. Some had to work harder for their view: in
the barred windows of the jail, the hands of prisoners could be seen
holding out small mirrors and slivers of silvered glass, tilting them just
right to provide a view of the jail's most famous resident, while the men
blindly called out questions and mocking replies to each other.

"So much for one nob murdering another," yelled one inmate.

"D'you believe he settled that feller?" another called back.

"Yes—just as much as though I'd been there."

Among sporting types in the city, betting pools were already forming over the verdict. What wasn't in dispute, though, was the likely
sentence for someone in the upper crust. "Public opinion is divided as
to the conviction of Webster," the *Boston Daily Mail* noted, "but none
seem to think for a moment that he will ever be publicly doomed to an
ignominious death of your common murderers."

Even as Webster's carriage was readying to go to the courthouse, a
few streets away another was taking on jurors. They'd spent the night
sequestered in an inn with a constable watching over them; and though
he missed home, juror James Crosby admitted that his comrades "seem
like a pleasant set of men." Even the food and drink being provided
were surprisingly passable. That morning they were taken to the Medical College to view Webster's lecture hall, his laboratory, and, finally,
his privy.

The murder scene was the most peaceful place they'd see that day. When the jury arrived at the courthouse at nine-thirty, they were let in past a mob scene of men trying to barge in. *I'm a lawyer, a member of the bar,* one would-be spectator claimed to a policeman standing guard at the entrance, though it was apparent that the only bar he belonged to sold ale for a nickel a pint. Another, shoving his ticket at a constable as he breezed past, was promptly grabbed; his ticket was a forgery. "If tickets were ever at a premium," a reporter marveled, "they were on this occasion."

Down on the courtroom floor, the judges seated themselves and the clerk called roll for the jury—"Frederick Henderson!" *Here.* "Stephen Stackpole!"—and then launched into the second day by calling to the stand the famed Francis Tukey.

"I am the City Marshal," Tukey explained, "and as such, have partially the superintendence and direction of the police." Though Mrs. Parkman hadn't subjected her nerves to the trial, the victim's brother Francis and son George Jr. sat nearby and heard the marshal assure Boston—and not least them—that no effort had been spared to find Dr. Parkman.

"It would have been impossible to make a more extensive search," the marshal explained. "Messengers were sent in all direction, for fifty or sixty miles. We searched over land and water. We published and circulated, among other things, 28,000 handbills of four difference notices. They were published as advertisements in all the Boston papers. The search for the deceased was prosecuted till the remains were found."

With the morning visit to the crime scene fresh in the jurors' minds, they now had an extraordinary exhibit placed before them: a wooden model of the college, commissioned from local carver James Hobbs. Usually hired for fine woodwork in ship salons and state houses, Hobbs had rendered a beautifully detailed miniature of the North Grove Street building. Each floor lifted out, so that the marshal could point to the locations and how they stood in relation to one another.

"When we arrived, from Mr. Littlefield's apartments, we went into the cellar, and thence down through the trap-door into the basement." Tukey pointed out each location, and then lifted the laboratory floor up, to reveal the basement and the vault. "After descending through the trap-door, we crawled along the ground underneath the floor, some sixty feet," the marshal explained, leading the jurors' gaze to where the privy was located in the model, and showing them where Littlefield had smashed out the brickwork. "I looked in, and saw several pieces of human flesh. The water from the sink was running down spattering over them. I asked Dr. Bigelow, if they were from a dissecting room. He said it was not the place for them."

Tukey produced another exhibit: an evidence box that contained bone chips from the laboratory furnace—and, he noted, "various other things, which I now produce and identify."

From the box the marshal drew out a knife he'd found in Webster's laboratory—not a scalpel but a Turkish *yatagan*, with a silver handle and long and slightly curved blade, the sort of combat knife used by soldiers in the Balkans. A jolt of electricity passed through the crowd, setting the gallery abuzz: *Was this what killed George Parkman?* One juror glanced for a moment from the wickedly sharp blade to the face of its alleged owner and was startled to catch the doctor's reaction. For whether it was from incredulity at Tukey's implication or simple bravado—Professor Webster was laughing.

*   *   *   *

As a matter of fact, Dr. Woodbridge Strong was rather amused by the case, too.

A string of witnesses from grocers and blacksmiths to schoolboys were questioned in quick succession to establish that Dr. Parkman had been seen walking up North Grove Street and into the college at two-fifteen p.m. on November 23. The victim's older brother, the Reverend Francis Parkman, gave a moving account of Webster telling him of the missing man's visit to the college—and how the professor had, the reverend puzzled aloud, "no expression of surprise at the disappearance, and none of sympathy." But these witnesses were a formality: nobody, not even Webster, contested the fact that Parkman had visited the college that day. Whether he had ever reemerged—whether he'd been murdered, and whether the body found there was his—were the real questions. And for those, the court needed Webster's own professional peers. Dr. Jeffries Wyman, for instance, took the stand with a painstaking catalog of bones and a chart that showed just where all the recovered bone fragments could be found in a single body.

Then there was Dr. Woodbridge Strong.

"I am a practicing physician in this city, and have been since 1820," he announced to the court, and he cast his mind happily back to his youth. He was the same age as George Parkman but as jolly in his sangfroid as his old friend George had been dour. "When I was a student with the late Dr. Nathan Smith," Strong recalled, "I took *every* opportunity to practice dissection. One winter, in particular, I occupied most of my time in dissecting, sometimes from eight in the morning till twelve at night! I have had a subject at my table for three months together. In the pursuit of my anatomical studies, I have had considerable experience in burning up, or getting rid of human remains by fire."

As it happened, Dr. Strong had seen Parkman on the day of his disappearance. Even if he hadn't known him, how could he not notice a hatchet-chinned and bony fellow like that? Dr. Strong was a connoisseur of what he termed "out of shape" bodies—not in bad health, necessarily, just literally the wrong shape. "If I see a man with one shoulder higher than the other, I always notice it," he explained to the jury. "If I see a woman in the street with a crook in her back, I always notice it."

He also noticed the beauties of the body, he added drolly.

But that wasn't why the prosecution had called him. He stood before the jury as an expert on just how to get rid of a human body; in fact, on how to do it with only an ordinary fireplace. He'd had plenty of experience in his very own offices as a physician.

"Once, in particular," he explained enthusiastically, "I had a pirate given to me by the United States Marshal, for dissection. It being warm weather, I wanted to get rid of the flesh, and preserve only the bones. He was a muscular, stout man, and I began upon it one night with a wood fire, in a large, old-fashioned fire-place. I built a rousing fire! And sat by it all night, piling on the wood and the flesh, and had not got it consumed by morning."

The crowd was mesmerized by the doctor's weird enthusiasm; Dr. Strong was unfazed by the most grisly subject matter. "Sickening," one juror wrote in his notes. But Woodbridge Strong was just getting started—warming to his subject, so to speak.

"I was afraid of a visit by the police," he blithely continued. "By eleven o'clock, they gave me a call, to know what made such a smell in the street." What made such a smell was the damnably hard task he been given. "I look upon it as no small operation to burn up a body," he lectured. "It needs the right sort of fuel. Wood is better than coal, and the lighter the wood, the better. Pine kindlings would be good for the purpose." The little furnace in Webster's laboratory? Amateur stuff, and perfectly dreadful for burning up bodies. "That appeared to me the most inconvenient place for such a purpose."

As one of the doctors who had gathered in Webster's laboratory after the discovery of the body, Dr. Strong had taken particular interest in the hole poked into the limbless thorax. It was a clean cut straight through, under the sixth rib, through the membrane. That meant it had been made when the flesh was tense—when, the doctor deduced, the victim was alive.

"After death, the elasticity of a body is gone, and it would be very difficult to make a good clean cut like this," he explained. "I have *tried* it."

The courtroom had become so packed that the air was suffocating, so the windows were thrown open to let the cold March wind inside. Delivery trucks and other loud passersby could be heard outside, their clatter interrupting the terrible silence of the courtroom, as Woodbridge Strong thought out loud about just what, he reckoned, would hint at a cause of death.

"These remains were *unusually bloodless*," he mused. They were like cuts from a butcher—"as much so as meat that is sold. My inference from this would be that the person bled to death from violence."

* * * *

THE PAPERS could scarcely keep up. The *Daily Mail*'s editor watched a mountain of extra newsprint he'd ordered in the morning—"a monstrous size, a perfect barricade to the press"—diminish by noon, so that "like the unsubstantial fabric of a vision, there was not a wreck of it left behind." Over at the *Herald*, the steam presses boiled with a triple-sized run of 37,880 copies—in a city of about 130,000, the equivalent of a *Herald* for every Boston household.

But there was one courtroom writer Bostonians couldn't read: Dr. Webster himself. With a neat little correspondence book and a pencil, he was earnestly taking notes, his expression largely inscrutable as a third day of prosecution witnesses were brought to the stand. One of the first was a Medical College protégé, Charles T. Jackson. Twelve years younger than Webster, Dr. Jackson was his professional doppelgänger, a man who'd made a name for himself more through his work in chemistry and geology than his expertise in medicine. He was connected through marriage to the prominent families of Boston; in his case, as Ralph Waldo Emerson's brother-in-law. And like Webster, Jackson was also a frustrated inventor, but had seen much larger prizes slip from his grasp: after pursuing a claim against Samuel Morse for the invention of the telegraph, he'd also unsuccessfully claimed invention of anesthetic ether.

Court testimony was second nature to Jackson. But against his old Harvard professor? Yet even he had to admit that he immediately recognized the *yatagan* knife as one from Webster's lab, and, what was more, he was familiar with its presumed victim.

"I knew the late Dr. George Parkman, very well," Dr. Jackson testified. "He was frequently at my office. He was a tall, slender man, of somewhat peculiar figure; rather flat in the chest, and broad across the pelvis. I saw nothing in the remains dissimilar from what I should suppose was Dr. Parkman's formation."

Joining the police in the search of Webster's laboratory, Jackson had observed strange green spots on the floors and in the stairwell. Chemist that he was, he'd grabbed some filter paper and absorbed the fluid into the quarter-sized pieces. His analysis: nitrate of copper. Whether it had been used to cover up or destroy bloodstains, Jackson wasn't sure. But he could answer another question—one about a seemingly exonerating circumstance the newspapers had puzzled over in the aftermath of Webster's arrest. Why, with a laboratory at his disposal, didn't the chemistry professor simply dissolve all the evidence?

"If the bones were taken out, and the flesh cut into fine pieces," Dr. Jackson hypothesized, "I think that with the proper quantity of acid, it might be entirely dissolved in half a day, so as to become a dense, yellow liquid. The quantity of acid, I should fix at the weight of the body." But Webster didn't have 140 pints of acid sitting in his laboratory; that was an amount fit for a rendering factory. Nor did he have a large vat to place 140 pounds of human matter into. "The largest kettle which I saw," Jackson noted, "was a tin-boiler with a copper bottom, such as is used for washing clothes—some twelve or fifteen inches square. That would not admit a thorax—or even a thigh."

Even as slender as he was, the sheer bulk of George Parkman—or any adult, really—would quickly overwhelm all the caustic bottles on Webster's shelves, just as his little assay stove had been outmatched. Dr. Jackson had taken special note of the cinders in that stove, too; he'd recovered and weighed the gold teeth found in there, and placed the metal at nearly 174 grains, or $6.94 worth. But as to why gold teeth were in there in the first place, that question best went to another witness: the victim's dentist.

* * * *

LIKE NEARLY everyone taking the stand this day, Nathan Cooley Keep was himself a Harvard-trained physician—just two classes before Dr. Jackson in the medical school, in fact—and his general practitioner work included a pioneering use of ether during Fanny Longfellow's most recent pregnancy. Dr. Keep had also turned a youthful apprenticeship with a Newark jeweler to use in his medical practice. Thanks to his skill with metalwork and porcelain, he'd developed a specialty in the emerging field of modern dentistry, hawking "artificial teeth of the most approved materials, arranged with the least possible inconvenience."

Testifying in a trial was another matter, though. Dental evidence had never before been used in an American capital case. In fact, when dental records had been used by prosecutors in a Scottish grave-robbing case in 1814, it had backfired and resulted in an acquittal. The closest precedent in America was almost entirely out of living memory: after the Battle of Bunker Hill, Paul Revere had used his metalworking sideline in crafting false teeth to identify a patient of his from among the dead. But Revere's judgment had risked, at worse, placing the wrong marker on a grave. Were Clifford and Bemis seriously contemplating determining a living man's guilt, in a capital murder case, on such a wildly untested form of evidence?

I call Dr. Nathan Keep, the attorney general calmly announced.

Taking the stand, Dr. Keep was handed the jaw fragments and blocks of dentures recovered from the assay furnace. He'd seen them before, back in December. Professor Webster watched as his old student turned them over in his hands again, carefully examining them one more time.

"These blocks, now shown before me, are the same which I made for Dr. Parkman," Dr. Keep confirmed. The old tycoon's famously jutting chin had particular meaning for his dentist. "Parkman's mouth," he testified, "was a very peculiar one: so marked, in respect to its shape, and the relation of the upper and lower jaws, that the impression of it on my mind was very distinct."

Dr. Keep had been Parkman's dentist for twenty-four years, but he best remembered crafting the doctor's last set of dentures, because the old man had asked on short notice for a new set in time for the opening of the Medical College building. "He wished," Keep recalled, "to have the set finished by that time, or he did not wish to have them at all." It was no small challenge. All of Parkman's upper teeth were gone, though he had a few lower ones; and rather than having them pulled to more easily allow a full set of dentures, the old man had insisted on keeping them, which demanded a triptych of plates for his lower mouth alone. That meant taking beeswax molds of the interior of Parkman's mouth, creating plaster molds, then tin test plates, and then permanent gold plates. Into that, porcelain teeth were fitted, and the roof and gums painted a natural-looking pink—an unusual artistic touch that Keep prided himself on.

"The two sets were connected together by spiral springs, which enabled the wearer to open and shut his mouth. The teeth were fastened in with platinum pins," the dentist explained, passing some molds to the jury. "I have another model, showing the length of the lower teeth."

It was just about then, as noon approached, that somebody outside the courthouse yelled, *Fire!*

* * * *

CITY HALL wildly rang its bell in alarm, and those rushing to the open windows in the courtroom and around the neighborhood soon saw why: the upper stories of the Tremont House hotel were in flames. Attorney General Clifford stood up—*he* was staying at the Tremont. Chief Justice Shaw quickly granted a recess, and Clifford departed to save his papers and his baggage with as much haste as the dignity of his office allowed.

As the stunned crowd milled around the courtroom during the impromptu recess, whispered speculations could be heard: Was it arson? Had someone set it deliberately to derail the trial? Dr. Webster, with the attention on him momentarily loosened, leaned across the bar to chat amicably with his colleagues in the ranks of the medical witnesses. He was improbably impressed with the wooden model of their college the prosecutors had brought in.

"Wyman," he said, "we ought to have that model for the college! It would be a capital thing."

Sometimes the gravity of the situation sank back in, though.

I fear some could misinterpret your testimony, he gently chided his colleague Dr. Jackson. The doctor was surprised at this, and he worried that he'd hurt his old teacher.

I can testify again, if you like—for the defense, Dr. Jackson hastily assured him.

Well, they'd have to see what the coming days would bring. Today's testimony had been so peculiar that it was hard to say what would need clarifying next—not least because of the current witness. Even before the trial, news that dental remains were being examined by Dr. Keep had occasioned some skepticism. "It would be very difficult to make a man's life turn on such a recognition," the *Chronotype* had opined after Webster's arrest. "If there is a considerable chance of a witness being mistaken with an entire corpse before him, how much more with a few teeth of one!"

Webster wasn't so sure about Dr. Keep's vaunted reputation as a dentist, either.

"*I* employed Keep in my family, and his work all failed," he scoffed to his defense team. "When I paid Keep I told him my mind. The children can testify the teeth he filled for them gave out."

Attorney General Clifford returned a half hour later, his papers and bags moved to a new hotel. He'd been lucky to escape both fire and water; the city's new water supply had such terrific pressure that, as the fireman ran their fire hose through the Tremont's entrance and down hallways, it burst inside the building with as much damage as the fire itself. But there'd been nothing more nefarious behind the fire, it seemed, than a sooty chimney; the only people arrested were half a dozen pickpockets who'd taken the opportunity to work the crowd of gawkers outside the hotel.

Those idlers, it seemed, now shifted their attention back to the courthouse. Afraid to lose their places, spectators refused to move along during the recess, and a crowd was building outside the courtroom doors. A long line snaked up the stairs and into the gallery, with men and boys pushing and shoving anyone who didn't let them forward or who didn't, at least, have news to bring back from the gallery. "They hung along the stairs and lobbies like bees," a *Mail* reporter wrote, "and as one after another left the gallery and was endeavoring to extricate himself from the jam, he furnished the 'latest news' to the excited mass, and by this means saved himself from many a severe punch in the ribs or the 'bread basket.'"

The crowd surged forward, and a door splintered; the shouting outside the courtroom became unhinged, even dangerous. *Get the police over here,* the chief justice demanded. After a final surge that knocked two officers off their feet, the roiling tide began to recede under the yells and billy clubs of Tukey's men.

And then, for the first time that day, the courthouse was almost quiet. Dr. Keep resumed his testimony.

"He called on me the day before his disappearance, and stayed some fifteen minutes, inquiring about a servant that had lived with me," Keep continued. Dr. Parkman had also visited some two weeks earlier, late at night, and had woken him to get the springs on his dentures fixed. "This was my last professional intercourse with him," Keep stated.

It was not, however, the last time he'd seen Dr. Parkman's teeth. Upon returning from a Thanksgiving in the country, he'd heard the terrible news.

"On my return, Dr. Winslow Lewis Jr. presented to me these three portions of mineral-teeth. On looking at them, I recognized them to be the same teeth I had made for Dr. Parkman." Keep began handling the various pieces before the jury, and fitting them into the molds of

Parkman's jaw, which he had stored at his office. The match was exact. "The most perfect piece that remained, was *that* block, that belonged to the lower left jaw. I recognized the shape and outline, as being identical with the impressions on my mind, of those that I labored so long." He held up the matched block, his voice choked, and tears began to well up. "The resemblance was so striking, that I could no longer have any doubt that they were his."

Keep stopped to dab his eyes and compose himself. Webster, one reporter noted, "sat as unmoved as a rock."

The dentist tried his best to continue. The mineral teeth, he ventured, had been put into the furnace while still inside their head. On their own, they'd have heated rapidly and exploded from the moisture contained within, he remarked: "I have known such explosions to take place in new teeth, when heated suddenly." With that, Dr. Keep couldn't maintain his professional distance anymore. As he recalled his first words upon seeing the dental evidence, he broke down at the stand, crying into his handkerchief.

"When Dr. Lewis showed the teeth to me," the dentist sobbed, "I said, '*Dr. Parkman is gone: we shall see him no more!*'"

20

MESMERIC
REVELATION

EPHRAIM HATED MORNINGS, BUT THIS ONE WAS DIFFER-
ent. In the groggy half-light of dawn that Friday, he picked as handsome an outfit as a man on a college janitor's salary might own: a blue
frock coat, a blue silk scarf, which he wore around his neck as a cravat,
and a carefully pressed standing collar. He wasn't, however, going out
dancing; he had a very different sort of engagement that day.

State your name, he was asked in the courthouse that morning.

Ephraim Littlefield, he said, adding, "I have no middle name."

The packed room stretched before him, an impossible distance from
where he should have been this time of the morning—at the Medical
College, sweeping classrooms, stoking furnaces, and drawing water
for the laboratory. Instead, just a few feet away sat Dr. Webster, busily
taking notes again. Littlefield kept his gaze steadily on Webster, even
when the doctor did not look up at him.

"I am janitor of the Medical College," he began. "I have known Dr.
Webster seven years, last October, since my first connection with the
College. I had known Dr. Parkman twenty years.

"I was present at the interview between Dr. Parkman and Dr. Webster on Monday of the week of the disappearance," he continued. "The
19th of the month, I think. I was helping Dr. Webster, who had three
or four candles burning in the room. The Doctor stood at a table, looking at a chemical book; I stood by the stove, stirring some water, in
which a solution was to be made. Dr. Parkman came into the back
room from the door leading from the lecture room. Dr. Webster looked
round and appeared surprised to see him enter so suddenly. He said,

'Dr. Webster, are you ready for me tonight?' Dr. Parkman spoke quick and loud. Dr. Webster made the answer, 'No.' Dr. Parkman accused Dr. Webster of selling something that had been mortgaged a second time, or something like that. He took some papers out of his pocket. Dr. Webster said, 'I was not aware of it.' Dr. Parkman said, 'It is so, and you know it. . . . Doctor, something must be accomplished tomorrow.'"

Littlefield calmly recited the now-famous tale of what he'd witnessed in the days that followed: Dr. Parkman entering the building but not leaving; how a sledgehammer went missing that same day from the basement; the locked lab doors and water then running night and day inside; the scorching-hot walls by the doctor's furnace; the nerve-racking small talk with Webster before creeping downstairs to hammer through the privy wall in the basement.

Listening from the defense table, however, what Dr. Webster really objected to was—Littlefield's turkey story. The strange incident involving the turkey had happened before Thanksgiving in the back room behind the lecture hall, the janitor explained.

"He stood at the side of a table, and appeared to be reading a paper, which he held in his hands—a newspaper, I mean. He asked me if I had bought my Thanksgiving turkey. I told him that I had not. He then handed me an order, saying, 'Take that, and get a nice turkey, as I am in the habit of giving two or three away.'" Littlefield earnestly looked at the jury and the judge, then again at the prisoner. But that was just it, he explained—Dr. Webster was not in the habit of giving turkeys or anything else away. "It was," he remarked, "the first time that Dr. Webster ever gave me anything.'"

Nonsense, the doctor bristled to his defense team. Why, he'd given Littlefield something just last year—*a used gown*. This ungrateful janitor's character, he explained, was wide open to attack. The prosecutors had been wise to not rely on, say, Francis Tukey for much of their witness testimony; the city marshal's own distinctly criminal past—and, if the *Herald* was to be believed, present—would have left him open to character attacks. But was Littlefield much more reliable?

"Dr. George Hayman can say something about Littlefield's habits and intemperance," the doctor insisted to his lawyers. "Captain Stacy of the Custom House can tell about Littlefield's being turned out of his temperance lodge."

His wife's got a reputation too, he added significantly.

When it came time to cross-exam Littlefield, Webster's attorneys saw their chance.

"Where were you," Sohier asked the janitor, "on the Thursday night previous to Dr. Parkman's disappearance? What time were you home?"

"I was home at one o'clock," Littlefield ventured.

But where inside the college was he that night? Had he been in Webster's lab?

"Where were you that night?" the lawyer pressed.

"I can't say," the janitor admitted.

"Until you left home, that last night, were you there?"

"I don't know."

And then Sohier sprung his trap.

"Had you not made use of the Doctor's room, on that night, to play cards?"

The genial, honest-looking janitor suddenly became curiously reticent.

"I decline answering that question."

The spectators in the room burst out in laughter—and Sohier, emboldened, pressed harder upon the man trapped at the witness stand.

"Had you not been there gambling?"

"I decline answering that question," the janitor insisted, to another burst of laughter from the crowd.

"Do you know," Sohier asked triumphantly, "that the Doctor found out you were gambling?"

"I don't know," the janitor shot back. "He never said anything to me about it."

Cast your mind to the day the building nearly caught fire, Sohier asked him. "Did you try to get into the privy that afternoon?"

"I did not."

"Did you go home that night?"

The questions were becoming uncomfortable, and finding a theme.

"I did not," Littlefield finally answered.

"Where did you go?"

"I went to a cotillion party."

The courtroom burst into laughter again, and Sohier relished the moment.

"You stated that you had suspicions about the privy, and that you did not go into it," the lawyer asked incredulously, "but that you went to a *cotillion party?*"

"Yes," Littlefield answered stubbornly.

Sohier picked up a handbill and brandished it before the witness: the word REWARD was emblazoned boldly upon it.

"Did you ever see that paper?"

"I did."

"What did you do when you first saw it?"

"I went down to the college and showed it. I saw some of them stuck up round the college in all directions."

That reward was *three thousand dollars.* Wasn't that motive enough for an immoral dancer and gambler like Littlefield to besmirch his employer and frame the man for murder?

There was just one problem: the jury wasn't buying it. Ephraim Littlefield seemed like a man who liked a drink and a dance, true; and yet all along, when looking at the jury and the prisoner, he'd held his gaze steady. Boston still had a puritanical streak, but among the merchants and craftsmen in the jury box, Littlefield was someone they themselves might have hired in their businesses: a plainspoken hard worker whose free time was decidedly his own.

"Every appearance has been in his favor," juror James Crosby wrote in his journal. "His testimony has been straightforward and consistent throughout and his manner has impressed me frequently." The attempt to cast suspicion on Littlefield himself was unconvincing: "I cannot believe that he is a guilty man."

As to who the guilty man might really be, Crosby had some dreadful premonitions.

*   *   *   *

SUNDAY BROUGHT blessed relief. The jury was exhausted and homesick; the case weighed so heavily upon them that when the sheriff offered two church services to go to—Reverend Huntington's in the morning, and Reverend Beecher's in the afternoon—many jurors went to both. Their families were allowed to attend, though kept safely apart by pews and a security detail of four men. The sequestered husbands and their wives gave wordless waves and smiles to each other, and the officers softened enough to bring the very smallest prattling children over to kiss their fathers. The other parishioners out that Sunday could hardly help stealing a glance at their famous visitors.

"Been stared at to my heart's content," Crosby mused.

After strolling back to their hotel—following days of snow and ice, the weather had turned improbably beautiful—they heard what news their sequestration allowed them. There had been another sighting of a sea serpent. Senator Calhoun was ailing, and thought to be in his final hours. Hawthorne's new novel had landed a fine review in the *Journal*, while over in the *Transcript*, the trial coverage was abutted by a review of Judge Shaw's son-in-law, Herman Melville, and his new novel *White-Jacket*—which was deemed a return to form "in the best vein of the author of *Typee* and *Omoo*." A new installment of *David Copperfield* had arrived at the jurors' quarters and was read avidly. But for sheer fiction, nothing topped the overheated stories of the trial itself. The jury was drolly informed that reporters were claiming that their fellow juror Ben Greene was violently ill. That, Crosby noted, produced "a hearty laugh," for "he had suffered from a headache."

Monday and most of Tuesday passed with a new parade of witnesses—the police on Webster's spasms after his arrest, an expert in twine to identify the string around the torso in the tea chest, a tinsmith from whom the professor had commissioned a sealable box. The latter wisely purchased an ad for his Waterman's Patent Refrigerators that ran in a column next to the trial coverage. But when jailer Gustavus Andrews stepped up to the stand, the crowd took notice, for not only did he have a story of the doctor sweating and shivering through his arrest, he also held a document in his hand.

"I have in my possession," the jailer explained, "a letter of the prisoner's, brought to my office. The turnkey called my attention to a certain clause in it, and asked me if I should let it go out. My answer was that I should keep it."

He handed the letter to the prosecutor, Mr. Bemis, who prepared to read it aloud to the crowd before him.

"'My dearest Marianne . . .'" he began.

Dr. Webster, listening intently to the testimony, now had to hear his own private letter to his daughter declaimed to a packed courtroom. It was all there: the offhand admission that his arraignment had been timed to avoid publicity, his having bitten his tongue so badly during his arrest spasms that it had swollen. But one sentence had made Andrews save the letter: "Tell mamma, *not to open* the little bundle I gave her the other day, but to keep it just as she received it."

Nor was this note the only one the police had puzzled over. Before Webster's arrest, they'd received at least three anonymous letters that seemed to actively misdirect their search, including the one placing Parkman on the recently departed cargo ship *Herculean*. On Wednesday morning, spectators arrived to find a curiously familiar elderly man being led to the stand.

I am Nathaniel Gould, he informed the clerk, continuing: "I am a resident of this city; have been so for many years."

A trained violinist, Gould had tutored music and singing at Harvard for years. In his hours off-campus, he was a deacon in his church, and devoted to church music. Gould's name was familiar to other Bostonians from his handwriting guides and patent writing paper. For many in the room, it was as if one of their old schoolbooks had begun talking to them.

"I know the prisoner by sight, but I have had no personal acquaintance with him," the handwriting instructor continued. His son certainly knew Webster; he was an alumnus of the medical school. And, Gould added, "I *am* familiar with his signature. I have seen it appended to the diplomas given by the Medical College, for twenty years, from having been employed as a penman to fill out those diplomas."

The prosecutor passed the anonymous notes to Gould.

"Please look at these three letters before you," Bemis said. "State, if you can, in whose handwriting they are."

Webster's team was flabbergasted; the professor could barely conceal his incredulity. Testimony by his fellow doctors, yes—but this? "We object to this proof," Sohier called out. "The witness has never seen the prisoner write, nor heard him admit any writing to be his."

Justice Shaw, having handled both Webster's memos and Gould's beautifully inked diplomas for years as a Harvard trustee, was unmoved.

"He has had occasion, officially, to know his writing, for many years," the chief justice gently reminded the defense lawyer.

"This kind of evidence, if admissible at all, belongs to a class exceedingly liable to error," Sohier persisted.

"I may be permitted, perhaps, to refer to two other trials," the attorney general interposed. "That of George Miller, where both of my learned friends were engaged, and that of Eastman, Fondey & Company. In both these cases, experts were admitted to testify to handwriting." Clifford was perhaps too polite to point out to the defense that Gould himself had been one of the handwriting experts to testify at Miller's 1848 forgery trial—and that Miller had been convicted.

Shaw conferred with his fellow justices, then turned back to the attorneys.

"We do not see that the precise point presented gives rise to the objection. There are other cases; one is in the prosecution of threatening letters, or arson." Just a few months earlier, even as Webster was being arraigned, the city had witnessed the arrest of the "Charlestown Incendiaries," extortionists whose notes threatened their victims with arson.

"The evidence," Chief Justice Shaw added, "has always been considered admissible in those instances."

Bemis returned to his witness.

"Please state, then, whether you recognize the handwriting of *this* letter," he asked, handing over a note sent to the police and signed "Civis."

"I think it is Dr. Webster's handwriting," Gould said plainly. "When one undertakes to forge a hand, there are only two ways in which he can do it. Either by carelessly letting his hand play entirely loose, or by carefully guarding every stroke. In this latter mode, it is next to impossible for any person to continue any great length of time without making some of those letters which are peculiar to himself. Now, in this letter, I find three letters which are entirely different from Professor Webster's common mode of writing—the small letter *a*, the small letter *r*, and the character *&*. In all other letters, there is nothing dissimilar from his usual style of writing. Of those the most similar, the capital *I* can hardly be mistaken. The capital *P*'s are similar. So are the capital *D*'s. More than one-half of the capitals are made on the same mark. That is, the pen is carried up again on the same stroke. The figures 1, 3, 4, and 9 are all exactly alike. The *f*'s are all exactly similar—never made with a loop at the top, but at the bottom."

As for the other two notes—though bearing different signatures, different ink, and different paper—Gould also deemed them to be Webster's.

Nor was he to be the only handwriting expert. George Smith, an established local engraver and calligrapher who published a popular map of Boston, was also called up to the stand. "I am acquainted with the defendant's signature," he explained. "I have also received notes from him in former years." Though unsure of two of the letters, he stopped cold at one of them.

"In regard to the 'Civis' letter, I am compelled to say that it is in Professor Webster's handwriting," he testified. The sadness in Smith's testimony weighed heavily in the air. "I am very sorry to say," the engraver added, "that I feel quite confident of this."

* * * *

THE DEFENSE lawyers had their opening arguments ready; now all they needed was for Webster to not get killed first.

Heavily manacled, the professor trudged into the prison carriage the next morning for the brief journey over to the courthouse. They had scarcely got under way when a sudden *crack* sent jailer, prisoner, and driver lurching and falling forward. The carriage's front axle had snapped, forcing it to hurtle into the ground. A crowd massed, jostling the shaken prisoner as he was extricated, and it was only by good fortune that the jailer was able to load his clanking, bewildered ward into another carriage before the crowd's curiosity turned ugly.

What awaited Webster in the courtroom was scarcely more reassuring. He had been fortunate to retain Ned Sohier and Pliny Merrick, but they hadn't been his first choice of counsel. Franklin Dexter had turned him down, and his second choice, the renowned Rufus Choate, had also declined. Choate had the gall to attend the trial anyway—as a spectator. But then, so had prominent lawyers for miles around. Sohier and Merrick, both Harvard graduates who'd passed under Webster's eye as students, were an odd team to watch in action. The gregarious Merrick was a former DA and a judge of the court of common pleas. The reserved and drably dressed Sohier, in contrast, was one of the city's top finance lawyers, and hardly the obvious choice for a criminal trial. Sohier's quiet manner hid a droll sense of humor; he amused himself with Latin puns, and after buying a horse that refused to cross any bridge, he advertised it for sale because "the owner wished to leave town."

Today, though, he would have to speak in all earnestness.

"May it please Your Honor, and gentlemen of the jury," Sohier began, "I am aware that it is usual for counsel to call the attention of the jury to the situation of their client. I might see nothing but the man—who, for more than a quarter of a century, has been a respected professor in that university, which is the pride of our state, and a respected lecturer in that college, which is one of the boasts of our city. The man, under whose instructions, numbers now present—myself, among the rest—were educated. I might think of these things, gentlemen, and I might forget the case."

Sohier walked quickly and with a habitual stoop, hands thrust into his pockets. In his preoccupied way, he asked the jury to think deeply upon just what the case meant.

"A serious duty has devolved upon all of us, in this more than mortal struggle. Whether Professor Webster shall go hence to his family, and there remain what he has ever been to them—the very center of their purest and holiest affections, the very object of their idolatry—or, whether he shall go hence to the scaffold. Whether the fire upon his hearth-stone shall henceforth beam brightly, and its light be shed on happy faces, beaming kindly upon his; or whether your breath, Mr. Foreman, when you pronounce the verdict, shall extinguish that fire."

The gaze of the crowd produced an unwelcome moment of attention for Mr. Byram, the foreman; normally he'd be working in the comfortable anonymity of his locksmith job at this hour. He hadn't even *wanted* to be jury foreman.

"Now," Sohier continued, "speaking in all frankness, am I to forget the excitement in this city, when it was first bruited about that George Parkman was missing? How men quitted their avocations? How they clustered together on the exchange, in the workshops, at the corners of the streets, in the porches of the church? Can you, or I, forget that burst of indignation when it was announced that George Parkman's body had been found in the laboratory of the Medical College? They are burned into our memories, we cannot forget them."

Sohier then turned the tables on the men in the jury box, asking, What if the object of that outrage and attention had been one of them? There were technical objections to the case, of course: the difference between the government's charge of premeditated murder, as opposed to an inadvertent manslaughter. But there was also the simpler question of whether Webster had done nothing wrong at all.

"*Any one of you* may be charged with an offence," the lawyer warned, "committed by another, at a time when you were alone, or in company only with your wife. Witnesses may be mistaken, and honestly so, as to your identity. You cannot prove the negative, that you did not commit the offence. And what is your protection? You prove your previous *character*—a character perfectly inconsistent with the possibility of your having committed the crime in question. And you rely upon this rule of law, touching reasonable doubt. This, then, is your only protection. This reasonable doubt is intended by the law as a shield for the innocent."

And for that, he reminded them of one of the oldest concepts in the law, one that stretched back to Abraham's plea to save the city of Sodom and was now enshrined in what every lawyer knew as Blackstone's ratio. "Although guilty men sometimes take shelter behind it," Sohier urged the jury, "the humane maxim of the law is that *it is better that a hundred guilty men should escape, rather than one innocent man be convicted.*"

The question now was this: Could the defense establish that reasonable doubt?

*   *   *

JARED SPARKS wasn't just the president of Harvard; he was also a public figure in his own right. Along with editing and publishing the *North American Review,* the country's highest perch for public intellectuals, he'd written major works on the Founding Fathers that drew on his correspondence with such eminences as Madison and Jefferson themselves. Sparks was one of the country's great historians—but, until today, not a man in the habit of participating in history.

"I reside in Cambridge," he testified, and "am the President of Harvard University. I have been intimately acquainted as a neighbor there with Professor Webster for seventeen years."

He may have been a neighbor for seventeen years, but he'd followed Webster a good deal longer than that. As early as 1824, he'd sat in on Webster's lectures and admired his work—impressed, he wrote privately, with "his lucid manner of communicating the more difficult topics of the Science, and the happy & successful manner of performing the experiments."

"From my own observation of him," Sparks now assured the court, "I have never known anything of him but as a kind and amiable man." This was the best sort of character reference Webster might hope for from his employer, if a carefully phrased one. The professor, on the other hand, in a fight for his life, felt little compunction about hurting his old school. "No delicacy as to the college ought to interfere if any thing can be done for my benefit," he'd quietly instructed his lawyers.

The defense called dozens of character witnesses—the mayor of Cambridge, the town's marshal, Webster's neighbors and fellow Harvard men—at one point running through ten of them in a single hour. A second day of witnesses attested to Webster's calm demeanor in the week after the murder, though it was with the appearance of the professor's three daughters at the stand that spectators fell into a fascinated hush.

"On Friday the 23rd, Father was home at tea a little before six o'clock," Marianne explained. "He remained at home till eight o'clock and then went to a neighbor's house with us." The Webster women, though desperately pressed for money, had mustered their most charming clothing for their court appearance, and Marianne's purple dress and dark green scarf made a striking contrast to the usual drab woolen coat favored by her father's lawyer. "He accompanied Mother, my two sisters, and myself to a friend's house to a small party, and left us at the gate," she testified. "When we returned at half-past twelve, he opened the door for us."

In the interim, Webster had spent an utterly unremarkable evening visiting his old medical coeditor Daniel Treadwell, at whose home he chatted with his colleague Dr. Morrill Wyman and other Cambridge worthies—though about what, scarcely anyone could recall. "I think one subject broached with Dr. Wyman was in regard to recent improvements or discoveries in ventilation," a local judge remembered.

If Webster's character and his conduct were not that of a guilty man, the defense team argued, then what of the claim that the body was Parkman's? The prominent dentist William Morton—a onetime collaborator of Nathan Keep's, and now his rival in claiming the discovery of anesthetic ether—was brought out to scoff at Keep's claim of being able to recognize any one tooth, jaw, or denture as Parkman's. Pressed by the prosecution, though, Morton admitted that all of them fitting together would be an extraordinarily unlikely coincidence.

More promising were the witnesses who'd seen George Parkman on the streets of Boston after he was alleged to have been murdered in Webster's quarters. A neighbor recalled spotting the old doctor, with his inimitable quick stride, his chin high and haughty in the air, on Cambridge Street at one-fifty that afternoon—about five or ten minutes after he'd last been seen entering the Medical College.

"I mentioned it to my sister, to cheer her up and make her smile, as she was rather gloomy. I told my sister that I had met *Chin* in the street," she explained, to the guffaws in the courtroom.

Other locals placed Parkman in front of Mrs. Kidder's drugstore at two-thirty; on Washington Street at three-fifteen; and by yet another apothecary shop, this one on Green Street, at four forty-five. There was just one problem: each witness had only *seen* Parkman—or thought they had—and none had spoken with him. For the identification to really stick, the defense needed someone who knew Parkman's face well. And for that, they had their perfect witness: William Thompson.

"I am a clerk in the Registry of Deeds," he explained. As someone who worked with real estate transactions, he certainly knew Parkman—and, crucially, had seen him a half hour after he was supposed to have died at Webster's hands.

"I had seen him very frequently during the past five years. I saw him last on Friday the 23rd of November, in Causeway Street. I should think it was ten or fifteen minutes past two that afternoon," the clerk explained. They'd met in the middle of a block, just in front of a carpenter's shop, and though they hadn't spoken, the doctor's appearance was unmistakable: "When I saw him, he had his hands behind him, and appeared excited, as if angry about some matter."

Yes, the clerk had surely *seen* Parkman, plain as day.

Use spectacles, do you? the prosecutor asked.

"I never use spectacles. I don't think that I am near-sighted," Thompson assured him. Then the clerk immediately contradicted himself: "Some parts of the day, my eyes are weak, and I use glasses which are slightly colored."

A murmur of laughter began to run through the crowd. And did the witness also have to carry a magnifying glass?

"I do not carry a magnifying glass for my own use," Thompson announced. Wait—he did not, except for the one that was currently in his pocket.

As the laughter built, Bemis pounced.

"Have you never told anyone," he asked grandly, "that you could write in the mesmeric state?"

"No sir!" the clerk snapped as the courtroom burst out in merriment.

"You never said *anything*?" Bemis pressed on delightedly.

"I never used the term *mesmeric*," Thompson struggled to explain. "I may have said something about the biological state. I sometimes lecture on biology."

Now even the attending doctors were hooting with derisive laughter. Boston had been swept that year by a fad for "electro-biology," chiefly through the concept's promotion by competing and immensely popular quack shows run by former phrenologist "Reverend" Theophilus Fiske and the mesmerist "Professor" J. S. Grimes. These were really just mesmerism shows, but trendily renamed and using zinc-plated copper coins that mysteriously conducted spiritual electricity across crowds of hundreds or even thousands. Both men had been hauled into court and fined "for exhibiting for the public amusement, without license," but not before leaving local acolytes who set up shop and claimed that electro-biology could cure "Rheumatism, Neuralgia, Deafness, Dimness of Sight, Stammering, and all such diseases as have their origin in derangement of the nervous system."

That had nothing to do with his spectacles, Thompson insisted, or with the magnifying glass he carried with him. "I simply carried the glass for others to use," he explained. "I do not pretend to say that I can see better in the biological state than in the natural."

As far as the crowd was concerned, Thompson couldn't say he saw much of anything at all; the hapless clerk "appeared to be regularly purblind," one *Herald* reporter snorted. The defense team frantically tried to call out the manner of the cross-examination itself.

Objection! Sohier called out as their witness's credibility hopelessly dissolved in a wave of laughter. But it was too late: one of the Webster camp's best hopes for the defense had just been destroyed before their very eyes.

Part VI

* * * *

THE
VERDICT

21

TWELVE MEN IN
MASSACHUSETTS

EVEN AS WILLIAM THOMPSON WAS PREPARING TO TESTIFY
on his "biological" eyesight, a slim envelope arrived at a warren of law
offices on Court Street, bearing a Boston postmark and addressed to
"E. D. Sohier, Esq., Member of the Bar, Boston, Mass." When opened
it revealed a remarkable message—and in a curiously familiar hand:

> MR. E. D. SOHIER:
> *I am very desirous to inform you, that there has been a great mistake made in
> the testimony of some of the witnesses with regard to that "Civis" letter. Now, I
> must inform you that I wrote that letter, myself. I first saw that letter published
> in the "Herald" of this evening. . . . You can compare this writing with that of
> the "Civis" letter, and see if it does not exactly resemble it.*

The correspondent obligingly wrote out all the upper- and lowercase
letters of the alphabet, the numbers 0 through 9, and a few phrases
they recalled using, including "Dr. Parkman" and "cut in small pieces."
"When I wrote that letter, I did not think so much notice would be
taken of it," the writer apologized.

It looked remarkably like the first Civis letter—so much that Sohier,
now knowing which newspaper his correspondent read, placed a notice
in the *Herald,* to run atop its coverage on Friday, March 29:

Important Notice.

If the writer of the letter signed "Civis," received by the counsel of
Dr. Webster from the Boston Post Office on Thursday at half past

12 o'clock, wishes to be of any service in the case on trial,
let him call in person on the counsel immediately.

*   *   *   *

IN THE courtroom that morning, Webster looked revived, even hopeful.

"Did you hear what they said about that letter?" he asked a court officer.

"No," the guard responded. "What letter do you mean?"

"Why, the Civis letter," Dr. Webster responded triumphantly. "They say they have received a letter, in the same handwriting, from the man who wrote it."

Alas, no more mail was forthcoming—none, at least, save for a not particularly helpful letter to Merrick from one of Dr. Webster's old students, who recalled the professor as a milquetoast who might snap under bullying. "It was the regular practice to throw things about Dr. W's lecture room, drop his minerals on the floor, &c. &c.," sometimes bringing the professor to tears, the writer confided. "We actually almost despised his want of spirit."

Prosecutors had their own new torments waiting for the hapless Webster. While calling on four dentists to attest that Nathan Keep could indeed recognize his own handiwork—a strategy only slightly disrupted when one fumbled the evidence box and broke one of Parkman's teeth—Bemis lobbed out a question that landed in the courtroom like a grenade.

"Suppose," he asked the chief justice between dentists, "that there was an individual who had certain great peculiarities." Such peculiarities, say, that might cause him to be mistaken for Dr. Parkman, and for several people to have approached him and discovered their mistake. And what if the prosecutors had five witnesses who had seen and spoken to him? "Would not these last persons be introduced in a case like this?"

Objection! The defense rose. The notion of a George Parkman look-alike walking the streets of Boston was altogether speculative; why was an error by these five would-be prosecution witnesses necessarily pertinent to the defense's own witnesses?

The chief justice agreed—*maybe if you brought in the look-alike him-self,* he conceded—but the damage was already done. A rumor went out that Parkman's uncanny double was "a gentleman distinguished in railroad enterprises." Even if the fellow was never introduced into the courtroom, his possible existence now cast a shadow over the defense team's best chance to save their client: the closing argument.

* * * *

THE VISITORS pouring through the gallery had mounted with each passing day. Even though the gallery accommodated only a fraction of the room's capacity of five hundred, by moving the crowds in quickly, in brief shifts, the police had marched more than seven thousand spectators through on the first day alone. Court officers now worked the entrances as smoothly as the ushers for a Jenny Lind concert, though the crowds themselves hadn't become any more polite—one man was spotted walking down the exit stairs with a bloody nose for his attempts to better see the trial. But when Merrick took to the floor to deliver his closing argument, even the rowdies fell silent.

Not one witness, Merrick charged, could provide an absolute proof of the body's identity, of Webster committing murder, or a confessed motive. It was all supposition. Yet the defense had five people who'd seen Parkman alive after his meeting with Webster.

"They may indeed be mistaken," the attorney admitted, "but is it *certain* that they are? Contrast this direct and decisive evidence with the mangled remains of the human, whoever he was, which were found in the Medical College. The Attorney General is asking you to believe that these remains are but the mutilated parts of the body of Dr. Parkman. He is also asking you to believe that responsible and intelligent men and women were mistaken, not in the naked leg, but respecting the open face, the erect form, the attitude, the movements, and the peculiarities of the living man."

Nor, he argued, could the remains adequately show a cause of death; aside from the notions put forth by Drs. Wyman and Strong, nobody had offered any theory of injury to the body parts prior to death. The mutilations *after* death hardly offered any guide: "To take off a man's head with a saw, undoubtedly kills him—to tear out his breast-bone, and remove all the inwards parts of his body, kills him—cut off his arms, his leg, and his thighs, and he will die—hold his head in the fire till it is burnt to cinders, and he will perish. All these things manifestly occurred to the several parts of this body. But *when* did they occur? Was the head or were the limbs of the living man thrust into that narrow and contracted assay-furnace, of ten inches in circumference, and forcibly held there, until life was extinct?" Were the jurors to believe that in a building whose entire history spoke to the likelihood of a body being a graveyard cadaver, Parkman had met a violent end?

"The proposition is too absurd," the defense attorney scoffed.

And, Merrick added, what if Webster *had* killed Parkman? After all, he admitted, "the parties did meet under most untoward circumstances." But were they to believe that a professor deliberately planned in cold blood to kill his school's biggest donor, in the building he'd helped create, even as a lecture was being given in the floor above them? A charge of manslaughter was at least conceivable, as was the panicked hiding of a body. But the prosecution's claim of premeditated murder was absurd. "Men of such character," Merrick averred, "and in such a position as his, do not, at a single effort, leap away from all the influences of education, social life, and religious instruction, and commit at once the highest and worst crime which can be perpetrated against their fellow-beings."

The handwriting evidence was fanciful—"Mr. Gould is too much of a visionary to be relied upon by a jury"—and as for Ephraim Littlefield's testimony, its hypocrisy was obvious. How could Littlefield accept a Thanksgiving turkey from Dr. Webster if he suspected him of murder? "I can hardly conceive how he touched that order if he believed he was taking it from the red right hand of a bloody murderer," Merrick marveled. Come to think of it, how did Littlefield just *happen* to break through the right spot in the privy wall to find the body parts? "Is this accuracy of the work upon the wall consistent with an ignorance of their position within the vault?" Merrick asked pointedly.

Littlefield, sitting among the trial spectators, now heard made plain what the attorneys usually only hinted at. Perhaps his low place in society was, next to Webster's high standing, all the more reason to suspect him.

"He lays before you the testimonials of a whole community, from the President of the University to the mechanic at his bench," Merrick declared of his client. "When evidence is conflicted with complicating possibilities, that integrity comes as a protecting shield. It is then that the law declares that *he in whom virtue has been embalmed in an upright life shall at last be saved by its power*."

This was Webster's strongest defense of all: that a fellow like him simply *couldn't* have done it. He was, after all, a Harvard man.

* * * *

EVEN BOSTON'S criminals seemed to have given up on doing anything but following the trial. Either that, or the police were too absorbed in the trial to chase local malefactors. The criminal court's lockup at one point dwindled down to a single prisoner—a hapless fellow collared for robbing a junk shop of "a quantity of old brass, an old hat, and six pigeons." For everyone else that Saturday, Chief Justice Shaw's courtroom was the place to be.

Attorney General Clifford stood before the jury on the eleventh day of the trial, knowing that his closing argument might indeed make it the final day.

"Gentlemen of the jury," he asked pointedly, "how many murderers, think you, would ever be punished if a jury were required to wait for direct evidence of an eyewitness to remove all reasonable doubt from their minds? When crimes like these are committed, men take no witnesses; they avoid the sights of all eyes except that of the all-seeing one, to whom the darkness is as the light, but whose presence is then forgotten."

The jurors had been presented with everything from body parts examined by doctors and dentists to bank statements that showed that Webster could not have paid Parkman. Yet, Clifford noted, the defense's closing statement had barely addressed any of this, instead fixating on technicalities in the indictment. "We had the extraordinary spectacle of the counsel devoting two hours and five minutes to the discussion of the law, and ten minutes to the presentation of the facts," he pointed out. They'd quibbled over the means of death, be it by knife, fist, or hammer, when the real question was of murder, "no matter how he did it."

And those who thought they later saw Dr. Parkman alive—what of them?

"What was Dr. George Parkman doing on that day when witnesses think they saw him?" the prosecutor scoffed. "Now in Cambridge Street, then in Causeway Street; now in Washington Street, going towards Roxbury, then in Court Street, examining the roofs of houses; again in Cambridge Street, and afterwards in Green Street. Was there ever anything so preposterous?"

How many times had they, the men of the jury, been mistaken for someone else—or made the same mistake themselves?

Curiously, though Webster himself had claimed to have dined at Brigham's restaurant that afternoon, and then gone out to buy cologne, nobody seemed to have seen *him*, not even by mistake, for most of that fateful Friday afternoon. "Where did he dine that day?" the attorney general demanded. "Did his counsel explain that?"

Then there was the evidence procured by Ephraim Littlefield, and the suspicions heaped upon him in return. The janitor, still sitting in the courtroom, had been scrutinized by the police and the public for months now, suffering patiently through the foulest rumors.

"To him," Clifford insisted, "and to his wife and children, his reputation is as dear as that of a college professor. Those children of his must hear Dr. Webster and Dr. Webster's friends impute to their father, if not a murder, a most foul and unrighteous conspiracy. . . . Gentlemen, are we in a Christian court-room? I do not put Mr. Littlefield upon this stand as a man of culture. I put him here as an honest man, who fills reputably his position in life—an honest, though a humble one."

This struck at the heart of the case. If Littlefield had been the debtor in whose rooms Parkman had vanished—if Dr. Webster had suspected him, and found a body in his quarters—wouldn't that janitor have been convicted already? So why was evidence that convicted a humble servant any less true when found against a man of higher class?

"*He* held a Professorship in Harvard College. And it is honorable that we hold education in such high respect that, when an educated man holding such high social position is charged with a crime, our people—not the educated alone, but the humble, the illiterate—repel at once the probability of its truth," Clifford admitted. Yet many a man had been driven to murder by less than what Webster faced. "What can he do? To what is he exposed? The disclosure to the world of his false reputation? The exposure of his fraud? The loss of caste! The loss of reputation! No poor, illiterate outcast, from the dregs of social life, who prowls out from his hiding-place to steal bread for his starving wife and children, ever had a motive with more force."

But most damning was Dr. Webster's seeming lack of concern. The letter sent to his wife after his arrest had a mysterious request not to open a package—but what else did it have? "A paltry enumeration of his physical wants!" Clifford charged. "A little pepper! And a little tea! And so on! This is not a letter from an innocent father." And to the families affected, who had seen their father's reputation attacked in public, or remains buried in pieces, Webster had evinced even less care.

"Gentlemen," Clifford added, "appeals have been made in behalf of the prisoner's family. God forbid that we should forget them, though the prisoner did! We will remember them better than he remembered the family of Littlefield. We will think of them more than he thought of the family of Dr. Parkman, when he was endeavoring to impress by a great audacious falsehood that Dr. Parkman was insane."

The line was a nasty shock for Webster, not least because it was true. He *had* quietly put about the possibility that Dr. Parkman was insane, including to his own lawyers. "Dr. Bell's Lunatic Asylum perhaps knows something," he'd suggested. But the prosecutors hadn't let on until now that *they* knew of his rumors.

What of Parkman's wife? Clifford demanded. Or his ailing daughter, or his son returned from Europe to a family overtaken by horror? Didn't they deserve justice?

"Gentlemen," the prosecutor concluded, "there is resting upon you a higher responsibility than ever before rested upon twelve men in Massachusetts."

* * * *

OF THE many murders, frauds, and acts of infamy perpetrated in the state of Massachusetts, there was indeed something different about this one.

"John W. Webster," Chief Justice Shaw began, and his voice broke. He was an overseer of Webster's school; the victim was an old acquaintance. The strain of taking on a case perhaps better left to another justice had now become audible. Yet the chief justice pressed onward: "Before committing this cause to the jury, if you have anything to add to the arguments that have been urged on your behalf by your counsel, anything which you deem material, you are at liberty now to address it to the jury."

The defendant had been constrained to silence for the entire trial; this was the one time available to him to speak on his own behalf—"a privilege," the judge added, "of which you may avail yourself or not, at your own discretion."

Dr. Webster stood up, trembling; he most certainly did intend to avail himself.

"I am much obliged to Your Honors," the professor began, nervously addressing the chief justice and the associate justices. "I will not enter into any explanation—though I have desired to do so—of the complicated network of circumstances which the Government has thrown around me, and which for many months has been crushing me. Testimony had been placed in the hands of my counsel; and my innocence would have been fully established had they produced it. They were highly recommended to me . . ." His voice turned scornful. "But in their *superior wisdom*, they have not seen fit to bring forward the evidence prepared by me and which would have exonerated me."

The courtroom fell dead silent, half aghast as Sohier and Merrick bore a fifteen-minute-long attack by their client, dismissing points large and small by the prosecution. The letter to his daughter was about a common household package of citric acid, Webster scoffed. The inability to reconcile his accounts with having paid Parkman was because he hid cash in a trunk; it wasn't visible in bank statements. The spots of nitrate of copper found on his lab floor, imagined to hide bloodstains—nonsense! They were just splashes from ordinary lab accidents. The contention that he hadn't habitually locked his lab door before that Friday disappearance? All wrong—"perversions," he snapped.

"I placed some evidence in the hands of my counsel about where I was at different times on Friday, which they have not used," he continued. His trembling stopped; his voice hardened with anger. "I left the College about three o'clock that afternoon. As I walked towards the omnibus-office, I came to the place at the corner of Hanover Street, called Concert Hall, or Brigham's, and got a mutton-chop. I waited there some time, then went to Mr. Kidder's, and afterwards took the omnibus." His counsel had left this out, he said, adding, "I might mention a great many other matters. But I will not detain the court by detailing them."

The doctor sat back down, brimming with indignation, then leapt back up.

"Will the court allow me to say one thing more?" Webster demanded. "I have felt more distressed by the production of these various anonymous letters than, I had almost said, by anything else that has occurred during the trial. And I call God to my witness—and if it should be the last word that I should ever be allowed to speak—I positively declare that I *never* wrote those letters. My counsel has received a letter from this very 'Civis.' A notice has been inserted in the newspapers, I believe, calling upon him to come forth; but he has not yet shown himself."

Professor Webster looked about the courtroom—searchingly, almost wildly, into the eyes of his spectators, his accusers, his judges.

"If he is present here in this court-room," the doctor cried, "and has a spark of humanity in his breast, *I call upon him to come forward and declare himself!*"

For an electric moment, his words hung in the air of the courtroom. There was no response. Webster sank back down into his chair.

Chief Justice Shaw turned to his two fellow supreme court justices, and there was some nodding and thoughtful murmuring. It was just past five o'clock on a Saturday; everyone surely wanted to go home, but they couldn't allow it. Shaw stood and turned wearily to the jury.

"Gentlemen of the jury, we feel unwilling, notwithstanding the lateness of the hour, to postpone this duty to another day, which must necessarily extend the trial into another week," he explained. "And therefore, painful, responsible, and laborious as this duty is, we think, upon some deliberation, that it is best now to proceed."

Shaw laid out the task before them: they were to decide on a charge of murder. Massachusetts did not yet recognize degrees of this crime. Murder, he reminded them, simply meant with malice aforethought, which didn't mean deliberation—just *intent*. A person who kills another by slowly poisoning them to death is certainly a murderer; but so is a suddenly enraged man who levels his gun at another's head. A fatal punch might indeed have not been meant to kill; that was man-slaughter. And the suspected crime scene made the means particularly mysterious: What if, for instance, such new inventions as chloroform had been used in committing the crime?

The jurors had seen much evidence of the most complex sort; they had heard alibis, testimony about conflicting time lines, reports on medical and financial evidence. They'd grappled with the legal concept of corpus delicti—whether a body found in a medical college, of all places, meant that any crime had occurred at all—and pondered circumstantial evidence to infer the guilt of an act that nobody had seen. But not all the circumstantial evidence was equally pertinent. Littlefield was not on trial, Shaw reminded them; nor, for that matter, were anonymous letters necessarily material to the case, even if the jurors believed that Webster wrote them. After all, even an innocent person, afraid of being charged, could try to throw off an investigation.

So how sure did the men on the jury need to be that Professor Webster had murdered Dr. Parkman? Their determination needed to be beyond a reasonable doubt, which was a relatively modern standard in courtrooms, having largely gained credence in Shaw's own lifetime. But reasonable doubt drew in part on the Enlightenment philosophy epitomized by John Locke's 1689 *Essay Concerning Human Understanding*. There were absolute and objective physical and mathematical certainties: that ice is cold and fire is hot, and that two plus two equals four. But then there was indirect knowledge from the testimony of others—what some called *moral* certainties of the existence of particular facts. As Locke's contemporary John Wilkins had put it, only "a fantastical incredulous fool" would doubt these. "I am sufficiently assured," Wilkins noted, "that there was such a person as Queen *Elizabeth*; that there is such a place as *Spain*."

This meant, one legal guide of the time explained, that while wild arguments might be made to persuade a juror to doubt testimony and its obvious interpretation, the jury's job was to indulge in only reasonable doubts: "To acquit upon light, trivial and fanciful suppositions and remote conjectures, is a virtual violation of the juror's oath." But if there was a reasonable doubt, then a presumption of innocence meant that a verdict of not guilty was the just result.

Yet neither the state of Massachusetts nor the federal courts had a standard definition or instruction of "reasonable doubt" for judges to give to jurors. Chief Justice Shaw's remarkably clear explanation of the concept would instantly become one of the most influential innovations of the trial.

"This is to be proved beyond reasonable doubt," Shaw explained. "Then, what is reasonable doubt? It is a term often used, probably pretty well understood, but not easily defined. It is not mere possible doubt; because everything relating to human affairs and depending upon moral evidence is open to some possible or imaginary doubts. It is that state of the case, which, after the entire comparison and consideration of all the evidence, leaves the minds of jurors in that condition that they cannot say they feel an abiding conviction, to a moral certainty, of the truth of the charge. The burden of proof is upon the prosecutor. All the presumptions of law independent of evidence are in favor of innocence; and every person is presumed to be innocent until he is proved guilty. If upon such proof there is reasonable doubt remaining, the accused is entitled to the benefit of it by an acquittal. For it is not sufficient to establish a probability, though a strong one . . . the evidence must establish the truth of the fact to a reasonable and moral certainty. . . . This we take to be reasonable doubt; because if the law should go further than this, and require absolute certainty, it would exclude circumstantial evidence altogether."

As the hour approached eight in the evening, Shaw gave the jurors one last reassurance before setting them off to their lonely task.

"Gentlemen," he concluded, "when it is said we may err, it is true. But it is nothing more than to say that we are human. Take sufficient time; weigh the evidence; and give such a verdict as will satisfy your own judgments and your own enlightened consciences, and we can have no doubt that it will be a true one."

Writing in his journal, juror Crosby already felt the awful gravity of what lay before them.

"All I can say," he concluded, "is God help us to judge aright."

* * * *

OFFICER JONES led Dr. Webster to an anteroom, and there the two considered the extraordinary events that had just transpired before their eyes.

So? Jones asked. *What do you think of the case?*

"Don't know." Dr. Webster breathed out, then added drily, "Trust in God."

Actually, Dr. Webster had been thinking that his odds were rather good. It was whispered that his family had already bought tickets to the island of Fayal, on a ship sailing in three weeks—just enough time to pack up and leave. He had a daughter, a son-in-law, and a grandson waiting there for him; they could go back to the island home Mrs. Webster had left so many years ago, far from the stain that even a verdict of not guilty would leave. The revelations of the family's debt had been humiliating, and a quiet dismissal lurked in his future; Dr. Webster knew that his old friend Bachi had been dismissed from Harvard for far less. In Fayal the Websters could begin again, far from Boston, far from Cambridge—and far from their creditors.

Officer Jones had more practical concerns in mind.

Do you want some tea? he asked. *Something to eat?*

Dr. Webster was not a man to turn down the offer of a good meal.

Might as well have a proper supper, the professor replied.

As Webster ate, the crowd in the courtroom waited. The spectators nearest the defense and prosecution tables were a veritable reunion of Harvard Law School, and knots of attorneys now formed on the floor of the courtroom, earnestly discussing points of the case with their old classmates. Had the defense dithered too much on technicalities in the indictment and failed to protest their client's innocence enough? What about the scarcely established alibi or the contradictory sightings of Parkman? And what of—as one observer on the floor delicately put it—the "definite character of the judge's charge" to the jury? Had he been sufficiently impartial?

Any reporter attempting to sneak toward the jury room would have found no answer there; from outside its door, there was only dead silence within.

The hours passed with little to fill them but the rumors happily fanned by papers like the *Herald*. Was it true that some of the later witnesses claiming to have seen Parkman had retracted their testimony? Was it true that Webster and three jury members were Freemasons? The newspaper advertisers also merrily went joyriding upon the trial's final dash to the finish; one dentist's ad began with the words "MURDER! MURDER!" and other businesses placed newspaper items that at first glance appeared to be trial coverage:

PROFESSOR WEBSTER'S FATE. He will unquestionably be convicted of murder in the first degree, but will probably go to the penitentiary for life. Professor Webster is one of the best chemists of his day, but we doubt whether anybody else ever produced so much real good, as Mrs. Tilley, whose Vegetable Cough Syrup is now conceded to be the best article in Boston for the cure of Colds, Coughs, Hoarseness, Sore-throat, Cramp, Hosping Cough, &c., 25 cents a bottle. Sold by Reading & Co., 8 State Street.

Reporters ferried the news out of the courtroom trial for transcripts that were already being hurriedly typeset into books; all that remained now was adding the type and slathering on the ink for the final page that would reveal the verdict.

Bemis and Clifford waited patiently at their prosecution table; Merrick and Sohier, at theirs for the defense. There was nothing to do but rub their eyes, drum their fingers on the hard wooden chairs, and look up to the high ceilings. The prosecutors occupied themselves with getting the windows open, to let the cold night air into the stuffy courtroom.

It was ten-forty p.m. when the court officer approached the clerk.

"The jury have agreed," he whispered.

A murmur promptly ran through the room; the county coroner, slipping back into the courtroom, whispered, *Not guilty.* The younger Professor Bigelow darted among his Medical College colleagues, spreading the word—*Acquittal! Acquittal!* But even as the news raced like fire around the courtroom, another ran through the crowd: "He's convicted," men whispered to one another.

Back in the anteroom, Dr. Webster had finished his meal when the word came in.

You're wanted in the courtroom, Officer Jones told him—the jury have a verdict.

"Ah! Do they?" Webster stood up. "*Do* they?"

A hush fell as Webster was led back into the courtroom; then the judges entered through one side door, and the jury through another. The jurymen took their chairs slowly, solemnly, as if carrying the weight of duty on their shoulders. After a tense silence, the clerk turned to them.

"Gentlemen of the jury, have you agreed upon your verdict?"

"We have," the foreman answered, bowing a little.

The clerk turned back to the prisoner.

"John W. Webster," he announced. "Hold up your right hand!"

The professor, shaking ever so slightly, held up his arm. Within mere feet of him were all the men determining his fate: Bemis, watching him intently; Littlefield, sitting close by among the spectators; and the justices and the jury.

"Foreman," the clerk continued. "Look upon the prisoner!"

Byram locked eyes with Webster; the professor stared back at him fixedly.

"What say you, Mr. Foreman?" the clerk called out. "Is John W. Webster, the prisoner at the bar, guilty, or not guilty?"

The locksmith's voice rang out to break the awful silence.

"Guilty."

22

LAW MANUFACTURED FOR THE OCCASION

GUILTY.

With that single word, Webster, an old student of his wrote, "started as if shot." The doctor's uplifted hand fell to the bar with a dull thud, his chin dropped upon his chest; he wavered, and slumped backward into his chair. Webster crumpled, nearly senseless, into silence broken only by the sound of weeping—in the galleries, on the floor, and even on the bench itself. Merrick grasped Webster's hand earnestly, reassuringly, and whispered a few words to his client; the doctor finally nodded and rubbed his eyes, wiping away tears and leaving his spectacles slightly askew upon his face.

"Gentlemen of the jury, hearken to your verdict, as the Court have recorded it," the clerk intoned. "You, upon your oaths, do say, that John W. Webster, the prisoner at the bar, is guilty; so you say, Mr. Foreman; so, Gentlemen, you all say."

Remand the prisoner to his cell, Judge Shaw said quietly.

For a long moment, nobody moved; nobody knew quite what to say.

"What do you want to keep me here for?" Webster said heavily. "I don't want to stay here to be gazed at."

As the doctor was led off in manacles, a *Daily Atlas* reporter turned to see Ephraim Littlefield; tears were running down the janitor's cheeks. He had told the truth, Littlefield explained, even though that truth had condemned another man. "If I was conscious of having uttered one single word that I had any doubt about," he said, fumbling for words, "I would never forgive myself."

Webster sat through the short ride down the darkened Boston streets and back to the Leverett Street Jail. He hadn't planned on still being in jail tomorrow morning, and hadn't put in an order at Parker's Restaurant; as they passed through the jail office, he turned to jail keeper Gustavus Andrews. "I suppose I shall have meals from Parker's, as usual?" he asked. But as they wended their way back to his cell, he saw the guards making a different series of preparations for the night; they were, without a word, quietly removing the cutlery and a razor from among his possessions.

"There's no need of that," Webster protested gloomily. "I'm too much of a Christian to think of committing suicide."

Dr. Webster was locked into his cell, and he lit a small alcohol lamp, warmed a cup of tea over its flame, and sat alone with his thoughts. His family hadn't been waiting for him here; they'd been home, visiting with their old friend Judge Fay, who'd been reassuring them that the trial was going fine. Now, as Saturday night crawled over into Sunday, Webster sat with the lonely knowledge that his slumbering family would wake in the morning unaware of what all their neighbors would already surely know.

His wife's sister was chosen to deliver the verdict. Her carriage approached Webster's Cambridge home slowly that Sunday morning; the news was carried up the stairs to his wife. Mrs. Webster had largely stayed in bed for weeks, ailing and anxious; and when she received the word—*guilty*—her response was mute, stricken silence. But in this, Marianne, Catherine, and Hattie were not like their mother.

"The daughters uttered the most heartrending screams, which were heard by passersby going to church," wrote a Harvard librarian in his journal that day.

Sentencing the following day proved no better. The professor was rousted early from his cell, and he was bustled over to the courthouse in the hope of arriving before the crowds gathered. But it was altogether too late for such modesty. The courthouse had seen some sixty thousand visitors during the trial, and that day's concourse of onlookers seemed the greatest of all. Men and boys jockeyed for position, frustrated by a wall of gentlemen's stovepipes.

"Hats off in the front!" the crowd yelled.

Inside it was as drowsy as the outside was boisterous. As the galleries filled, and the lawyers for the defense and the prosecution took their accustomed seats, Dr. Webster sat in his armchair, waiting for the clock to inch toward nine. His eyelids grew heavy, and his head nodded.

"There's the court," came the whisper, and the professor opened his eyes and straightened himself in chair. It was the court indeed. The formalities took scarcely five minutes, with Chief Justice Shaw pausing to note the law of the state.

"*Every person who shall commit the crime of murder shall suffer the punishment of death for the same.* The manifest object of this law is the protection and security of human life, the most important object of a just and paternal government," he explained gravely. "God grant that your example may afford a solemn warning to all, especially the young."

The example Dr. Webster would provide would be a chillingly stark one—simpler than any first fall lecture, and more final than any spring examination.

Professor John W. Webster was to "be hung by the neck," the judge told him, "until you are *dead.*"

* * * *

COME IN, *come in,* Officer Spurr showed the stream of visitors down the stairs in the laboratory. *Down these steps, this way.*

It was all still there: the acid splashes on the wooden steps, the assay furnace where Parkman's teeth had been found, even the tea chest with bloodstains still visible inside it. The Medical College faculty, rather than make a hopeless attempt to hush up the case, had succumbed to inevitability and voted to invite the public in to view the building. Crowds came gushing in, as if Webster's basement were a hole below the city's moral waterline. Even as Officer Spurr lectured visitors, women could be spotted quietly slipping splinters and scraps from the laboratory into their purses as souvenirs.

Webster had become, his friend Longfellow mused dejectedly, "another Eugene Aram"—the English schoolmaster hanged for murder a century before, betrayed at the height of his scholarly powers by the discovery of buried bones from a disappearance fourteen years earlier. He'd eventually confessed, and the Boston newspapers were just as sure that Webster's death would prove equally warranted.

The trial, wrote the *Courier,* presented "an unbroken chain of indubitable proof." The guilty verdict was, the *Mail* agreed, the inevitable conclusion of anyone who had actually followed the trial in person. In the view of the *Evening Transcript,* Webster had hurt himself even more through a statement to the court that expressed no sympathy to the Parkman family and that quibbled over minutiae instead of passionately denying the charge. Nevertheless, all the papers expressed a curious sense of loss and tragedy in Webster's guilt; all, that is, except for the *Boston Daily Bee.* "EXTRA," it announced in large type the following Saturday, touting an issue whose entire front page covered nothing but the foulness of "the murderer and mangler" John White Webster.

The case presented, the paper charged, "a new problem in human nature—a cool, deliberate, cruel, atrocious murder, perpetrated by one of the oldest professors in a University devoted to 'Christ and the Church.' . . . A man in one of the most distinguished and honorable positions in all of Christendom—a scientific sage, a philosopher and Christian, to be brought out in a vulgar fraud!"

The *Bee* spewed forth accusations: Webster was a mediocre chemist; he was a hack whose books simply restated the work of others. Worse still, the paper repeated a rumor that Webster had killed his mother through "a prank" that knocked her down a flight of stairs. The charges of mediocrity were familiar ones for any scholar, but subjective enough; the latter was wild speculation. More uncomfortably, the *Bee* had searched through the public records of Redford Webster's will, and reminded readers that Dr. Webster had squandered an inheritance of some $40,000 or $50,000, depending on how it was calculated—more than some readers could hope to earn in their entire lives—and that trusts made out the Webster children hinted that even Webster's own father didn't believe that he could be relied upon to safeguard that money. The doctor, the paper charged, had likely squandered those funds as well. Webster's reputation for gluttony did not help matters. Perhaps, the *Bee* scoffed, he had spent his estate "in studying conchology and chemistry at Brigham's"—in buying oysters and alcohol.

Rising to Webster's defense against the *Bee* was, improbably, the *Boston Herald,* which rather resembled being defended from one angry drunk by another even angrier drunk. "We have never seen an example of such baseness and malignity," the *Herald* piously declared. "The writer of that article deserves hanging more than Dr. Webster." The *Herald,* though, still merrily joined in with other newspapers in repeating a cacophony of rumors. Webster had confessed to taking strychnine in a suicide attempt after his arrest; a medical student saw Webster's crime and fled to Vermont; a witness had recanted her testimony about seeing Parkman in the street; Webster had abandoned a woman in Edinburgh when he was a medical student; Webster had tried triple-selling his mineral cabinet by proposing a sale to a Medical College student from Baltimore.

It was the last rumor that really nettled Dr. Webster.

Passing along a letter in secret—the trial had taught him that guards were liable to intercept and keep mail—Webster had a sealed letter smuggled out to his old physician colleague Winslow Lewis. "This is an utter falsehood," he wrote. "By reference to the catalogue you will see there *was no student from Baltimore.*" Webster wrote a suggested "Letter to the Editor"—to come from Lewis, not Webster—that would run in the *Boston Courier* to debunk the story. The letter duly ran soon afterward. But if Webster was able to quietly influence the public, he was still hobbled by the simplest of barriers: the guard outside his cell.

"You must not let it be known that you have rec'd a letter from me, as I am not allowed to send sealed letters," Webster pleaded in his note to Lewis. "If it should be discovered that I did, all means of communicating with friends *would be cut off.*"

Though if Dr. Webster hoped to control the story or save his reputation, it was already far too late. Six competing editions of trial transcripts had been rushed to press in Boston, New York, and even London—with the *Herald* crowing that its twelve-and-a-half-cent edition featured "superior Engravings" of crime scenes and body parts, and the *Boston Daily Mail* boasting within days of the trial that it already had thirty thousand copies printed. Towering over these slender and hastily produced copies, though, was the prospect of a complete transcription by Dr. James Stone, stenographer extraordinaire. Stone was a physician himself—he'd even served as a minor witness in the trial—and also one of the city's leading proselytizers of shorthand, teaching it to roomfuls of children and corresponding with educational reformers like Horace Mann. His knowledge of both medicine and shorthand promised an ideal edition; but when Sohier visited the State Street publisher Phillips, Sampson & Company to see the manuscript, he found that "most of our unhappy arguments had already been cast in stereotype," the pages riddled with "errors so numerous that I should decline trying to do anything about it." The prosecution's arguments did not look much better. Worried letters flew back and forth between the defense counsel and the prosecutor; Sohier considered the edition to contain "the vilest caricatures which can be possibly imagined," and Attorney General Clifford pleaded with Phillips & Sampson. Let both legal teams correct the text, he suggested, and it could be sold as a definitive edition—the company, he pointed out, "will have a monopoly of the market!" But there was too much money to be made, and too fast; the publisher offered only a paltry errata page to be crammed into the back of the book.

When the bound volumes of *Report of the Trial of Prof. John W. Webster* arrived in bookstores just two weeks after the verdict, it was to angry newspaper notices by the lawyers disowning the edition. It flew off the shelves anyway.

* * * *

VISITORS WANDERING under the grand front steps of the medical school—the tours ran through a service entryway, not the front lobby—now found themselves confronted by a new sign on the door:

NO ADMITTENCE

"They probably do not give lessons in spelling at the Medical College," one visitor ventured.

Multitudes had already filed through the crime scene—fifty thousand, by one estimate, almost as many as had visited the trial—and souvenir hunters had begun turning on Littlefield himself and snipping off locks of his hair. Now the put-upon janitor was getting his reward; he'd pulled the door to the lab shut and had gone to collect the $3,000 promised to him by Parkman's family.

For others around the country, though, the show had only just begun. New Yorkers strolling along Broadway found handbills promising two lifelike wax statues of the fatal enemies, as well as thrilling financial action: *"Dr. Parkman stands in the attitude of a creditor! Importuning a debtor, in his hand, and on the table, are seen the papers!"* Those who climbed the stairs up to the exhibition found two statues, "clothed by actual measurements from their wardrobes," and a man said to be Dr. Parkman's old barber on hand to attest to their veracity. The waxen tycoon, one reporter drolly noted, "bore his head down, as if calculating an indefinite amount of rent: while the professor—with the jet black hair always, we believe, assigned to desperate villains on the stage and in wax exhibitions—carried his head aloft, and seemed to be calculating when to strike."

But many Americans weren't so sure that Webster was guilty. Editorials in other cities tore into Boston's most famous trial, claiming that it had had a timid defense, a biased judge, and suspect testimony. New Yorkers immediately began circulating a petition to Governor George Briggs of Massachusetts requesting that in Webster's case, "the mercy of the Executive may be extended." Within days, more petitions were circulating in Philadelphia, Dayton, Richmond, Louisville, and Augusta. Southern editors were especially vociferous in their criticism, with one Richmond paper appalled that any man could hang on the testimony "of that most disgusting of all bipeds, Ephraim Littlefield." Taunted by years of criticism by Boston abolitionists, southern writers now saw their chance to pounce on Yankee injustice.

It didn't help that one of the jurors, Albert Day, now revealed that the jury had entered deliberations with an already crushing sense of Webster's guilt—that "so fully had the evidence pointed to the prisoner as the guilty man—and to NO ONE ELSE" that they had spent a half hour in silence and despair, with the incriminating evidence spread out on the table before them. At length, Day recalled, the foreman had suggested "that we seek for Divine wisdom and guidance"—and after a prayer, they methodically set about looking at the evidence. None doubted that Webster had killed Parkman, but a sole juror voted against the crime being premeditated. After another long silence, which the jurymen spent praying, reading, or simply staring into space, the holdout changed his vote.

Day's account of a briefly split vote excited little controversy; more unexpectedly, the *prayer* did. Bostonians were not ones to boast or to make an overly public show of faith, and Day's revelation played upon the worst memories and caricatures of the old colony. One critic compared it to "the prayers of devout Puritans, while burning witches and hanging Quakers to the greater glory of God." Day found himself stoutly denying any puritanical fervor.

"I am no fanatic—no bigot," he vowed.

Professor Webster, by contrast, was becoming markedly more pious. Local minister George Putnam started visiting Webster, despite scarcely knowing him; the doctor chose him, it was said, precisely because he wanted to talk to someone unassociated with his own past. Webster began promising to say grace over family meals once he was released. His daughters especially encouraged the newfound religion of their innocent father, with Marianne carefully praying over every jar of preserves and other gifts of food they sent to him.

Not everyone around Dr. Webster was convinced. His sister-in-law quietly believed him guilty, and his new faith a sham—and even his Harvard colleague Benjamin Peirce had come to the same conclusion. Writing to a friend in Philadelphia, he deflated the fashion for circulating petitions. "We are quite astonished in Boston that there should be any hesitation as to the justice of the verdict in Webster's case," he remarked. "His staunchest friend here admits it, and believes the murder to have been premeditated."

Almost as unsettling, Professor Peirce wrote, was how he'd found Webster becoming utterly fixated on eating: "In the course of the trial, Prof Treadwell told him that he should see his family in Cambridge, and asked if he had any messages to send. 'Yes,' said he, 'ask them to send me some custards.' On the morning of the sentence, he asked the jailer for a piece of paper on which he wrote in his most eager and excited manner an order for Parker to send him some cream cakes for dinner." Indeed, it wasn't just "some" cream cakes; Webster had ordered a *dozen* for his dinner.

"There is a very faint hope," Peirce added in his letter, "that he might prove to be insane."

* * * *

IT WAS just about then that the Websters' son-in-law arrived.

Harriet and her daughters had no notion that John Dabney would be coming out from Fayal to visit; when he reached shore on April 30th, the solid ground of Boston still rolling under his feet "after a stormy and most tedious passage," he found a household in shock. Word of the verdict hadn't reached across the Atlantic when he'd departed, and as he settled into a guest room in the gloomy Webster house, he gingerly set a daguerreotype of his wife and their toddler, Carl, by the head of his bed and penned a letter back to Fayal. As much as his wife, he fretted over their child.

"You will have heard dearest Sally ere this reaches you of the result of the trial," he wrote. "Recollect that the life of another depends upon your calmness." There were still petitions afoot, he reassured her. "All yet may go well," he promised, and added, "I found your dear mother much better than I expect[ed]."

In the Webster home, Dabney was nearly as confined as he had been on the high seas; Mrs. Webster and her daughters never went out anymore, he observed, except to take a carriage for their Tuesday and Friday visits to their father in jail. There was not much for them to see there, either. Dabney found Webster physically barred from visitors; he could speak to his unseen father-in-law only through the outer grates of a cell window. Smuggling letters out of the jail had come back to haunt Webster; it was even rumored that the guards had run a needle through the paper and envelopes they gave him, and that the second "Civis" letter bore the telltale pinprick. But if little could get out, food was still allowed in. The bohemian writer George Thompson, imprisoned in the next cell for shooting a pistol during a theater brawl, was the fortunate recipient of the professor's excess windfall of books, newspapers, sardines, jam, and wine. He particularly appreciated the wine—and, like most Bostonians, quietly thought his generous neighbor was guilty of murder anyway.

The Webster women absolutely refused to entertain such notions.

"He is the victim of circumstances, a deeply injured man," his daughter Hattie insisted. "That he is innocent, we his family *know*, and nothing on earth will ever take from us this conviction."

The family didn't just want a guilty man's commutation—they wanted an innocent man's full pardon. On April 24, Dr. Webster had filed a pardon request with the governor; and this time, he'd been careful to acknowledge Parkman as well, claiming that "I never entertained any other than the kindest feelings towards him; and that I never had any inducement to injure, in any way, him whom I have long numbered among my best friends." He again put forward the idea of a conspiracy, or perhaps the nefarious work of "an individual."

After a month of stony silence from the governor's office, Webster quietly withdrew the letter.

Instead, Sohier and Merrick crafted a writ of error—an attack on the trial on technical grounds for "certain errors in the proceeding and judgment of the court." In this claim of a faulty trial, Webster's defense team found inadvertent allies, though some were error-prone themselves. An entire pamphlet—*A Review of the Webster Case, by a Member of the New York Bar*—had excoriated the defense team for its "silence and timidity of cross-examination." Written anonymously by future New York mayor A. Oakey Hall, the pamphlet was effective in its rhetoric but careless in its reading of the case; working from Dr. Stone's inexact transcript, he'd skimmed through an entire day of cross-examination of Littlefield and apparently hadn't bothered to read the defense's more aggressive closing arguments. There were also more convincing grounds to argue for a faulty trial; an article in the local *Monthly Law Reporter* had already given a drubbing to Judge Shaw's jury instructions, and another pamphlet had attacked his novel explanation of "beyond a reasonable doubt" as "law manufactured for the occasion."

But before the principals could meet in court again to argue the writ, they first had to gather to view a dead body—and it was not Dr. Parkman's.

23

A MAN
IN ERROR

Bodies were now turning up all over Boston.

No sooner had Webster been sentenced than the *Boston Daily Mail* ran a headline shouting, "DR. PARKMAN FOUND!" Children playing near a storage shed had looked inside and found the mangled remains of an old man; it proved to be an ordinary cadaver in an undeclared workshop kept by medical students. Days later, merely a block or two from the courthouse, construction revealed more remains. Three skeletons, all thrown down an old privy, and all complete except for the unnerving absence from each of a spinal column. The building eventually proved to be the old residence of a Harvard professor, where he and his medical students had been in the habit of practicing their dissections.

But most mysterious of all was a woman identified only as Asch-ph*****. The asterisks were part of the mystery—for Asch-ph***** was an Egyptian mummy, brought to delighted Bostonians by former Cairo diplomat George Gliddon. Part of the mummy's name was obliterated on her sarcophagus; but it was indeed known, Gliddon announced, that she was the daughter of a high priest of Thebes. The newspapers were abuzz over Gliddon's promise to saw into "the intact coffin, unopened for 30 centuries," and to strip away her wrappings that June at the city's Tremont Temple—and to reveal, for perhaps the first time in America, a wondrously preserved three-thousand-year-old woman.

"She may have witnessed the ten plagues of Egypt," the *Evening Transcript* rhapsodized, "or mourned the loss of brothers, sons, or cousins, drowned in the Red Sea."

Boston's elite snapped up five-dollar subscriptions for the unveiling. Chief Justice Shaw subscribed; so did President Sparks of Harvard, Governor Briggs, soon-to-be senator Charles Sumner, Professors Longfellow and Peirce, and indeed most of the Harvard medical school faculty. An array of doctors, including Holmes and Bigelow—the dean and the new hire, the latter fresh from completing an article on Phineas Gage and the infamous bar through his head—would be onstage to carefully observe Gliddon's actions. So would the university's famed naturalist Louis Agassiz. After the miseries of the Webster trial, here was a forensic examination that promised history instead of scandal, enlightened knowledge of the past instead of uneasy revelations about the present.

At long last, on the night of Friday, June 7, the unveiling arrived. After carefully sawing through a bitumen-sealed sycamore inner coffin, Gliddon lifted the lid; the crowd burst into applause when the light of the nineteenth century dawned inside to reveal a mummy "in beautiful condition, as if it had been deposited in its case but yesterday instead of 1500 years before the birth of Christ." She lacked the jewels and treasures they might have hoped for, but who knew what surprises lay beneath the bandages themselves? Professor Agassiz warmed up the crowd by unwrapping a mummified ibis; and then George Gliddon began the final unveiling to the world of this noble daughter of Egypt. The wrappings had been soaked in tree resin by their makers; and now with each stiffened strip pulled away, ancient dust kicked up into the crowd and set Boston's gentry sneezing. As Gliddon drew the final strips away from about the hips, he revealed her ancient—what?

A roar of laughter burst out from the crowd.

"The daughter of the high priest of Thebes," Longfellow noted in his journal, "turns out to be a man!" His fellow author Donald Mitchell, known to the public as "Ik Marvel," recorded the more science-minded reaction of the medical faculty: "Dr. Bigelow blushed, and Professor Agassiz put his hands into his pockets."

Gliddon stammered out an explanation—he'd read the hieroglyphics correctly, but ancient Egyptian mortuaries had handled a great many dead, and surely someone had placed the wrong body in the coffin. The crowd clapped politely at his theory, but for newspapers the story produced weeks of fun, from poems that dutifully rhymed "mummy" with "dummy" to a faux account that concluded with the wrappings unscrolling to reveal these words:

SUPPOSE

YOUR AUNT

SHOULD BE

YOUR UNCLE!

* * * *

A FEW days later, when the principals of Webster's trial reconvened in court on June 12, it was for a considerably more melancholy variety of human fallibility. This time all five state supreme court justices were present, and the defense table was also more crowded than before; another attorney, Charles Bishop Goodrich, sat with Pliny Merrick and Edward Sohier. As the prosecution team of George Bemis and Attorney General Clifford looked on, Merrick stood up and addressed the court.

"May it please Your Honors, it is the wish of the petitioner that Charles B. Goodrich, Esquire, should participate in the argument upon the present application for a writ of error, in connection with his previous counsel. Mr. Goodrich is now present, and prepared, with the leave of the court, to render that service in his behalf."

Proceed.

Webster had complained loudly in his trial speech and in his initial pardon request about his lawyers, and the new attorney seemed an implicit criticism. But Goodrich was well known in Boston—he'd unsuccessfully run for mayor in 1847—and he was a talented lawyer in his own right. Though not fond of jury trials, he excelled in "chamber practice" behind the scenes; arguing on fine technical grounds was his forte.

Proper jurisdiction hadn't been established, he argued; the case hadn't been properly transferred from municipal court to the supreme court. Furthermore, the law said that a place of execution was to be stated, and it hadn't been. The list continued, but Webster's writ was really something of a scarecrow made of lots of little straws bound together to appear frightful; on closer inspection, it was still merely . . . straw.

After hours of learned argument, the attorney general rose to address the court.

"My experience in the courts has failed to teach me a most important lesson, if I could be surprised by this application, or by the ingenuity and subtlety with which it has been urged in the argument," Clifford said drily.

The court was not surprised, either: the writ was denied.

Webster's only hope now was to plead to the state's governor and his Executive Counsel for a commutation. But when the State House hearing for Webster's appeal arrived, on July 2, it was not Sohier, or Merrick, or even Goodrich who rose to address the governor's committee. Instead, at noon, the councilors responded to a request that they first meet with Webster's jailhouse minister, the Reverend George Putnam.

He had a document to read to them, the minister explained.

"The human remains found in the Medical College in November last *were* those of the late Dr. George Parkman," Putnam announced. "I am enabled to present, from Dr. Webster's own lips, a statement of facts connected with the homicide."

*   *   *   *

PUTNAM HAD done the impossible and, to Webster's own family, the inconceivable: he'd landed a confession.

That hadn't been his goal, the reverend quickly explained, as he'd hardly been a confidant of Webster's before. "My acquaintance with Dr. Webster before his trial had been of the slightest and most casual kind," he told the council. But nor had they been unknown to each other. The minister had delivered the election sermon to the state legislature—a profound mark of honor in the commonwealth—and he'd very narrowly missed being appointed to Harvard's Board of Overseers. It had been only a few years since the university had offered him its Hollis Chair in Divinity—though, in the end, he'd turned it down to focus on his ministry.

Now that same ministry had brought him back to Harvard in its darkest hour. After weeks of praying with Webster, and nearly two months after the jury had delivered its verdict, he'd finally broached the topic that weighed on them both.

"On the 23rd of May, I had made up my mind to address him in a wholly new strain, and to demand of him a full statement of the facts," the minister explained. "He said immediately, 'I am ready to tell you all. It will be a relief to me.' He then proceeded to relate the facts which I have since embodied in the statement now to be presented."

Dr. Parkman's death, Putnam explained, had been a hideous mistake. He began to read carefully from Webster's statement to the court. It had all started, just as the prosecution claimed, with Webster's terrible debts and Parkman's visit to the college on the afternoon of November 23, 1849—in the very classroom where Webster taught.

"He came in at the lecture-room door," the minister read out. "I was engaged in removing some glasses from my lecture-room table into the room in the rear, called the upper laboratory. He came very rapidly down the steps and followed me into the laboratory. He immediately addressed me with great energy: 'Are you ready for me, sir? Have you got the money?' I replied, 'No, Dr. Parkman;' and was beginning to state my condition, and make my appeal to him.

"He would not listen to me, but interrupted me with much vehemence. He called me 'scoundrel' and 'liar,' and went on heaping upon me the most bitter taunts and opprobrious epithets. While he was talking, he drew a handful of papers from his pocket, and took from among them my two notes, and also an old letter from Dr. Hosack, written many years ago, and congratulating him (Dr. P.) on his success in getting me appointed professor of chemistry. 'You see,' he said, 'I got you into your office, and now I will get you out of it.'

"I cannot tell how long the torrent of threats and invectives continued. At first I kept interposing, trying to pacify him. But I could not stop him, and soon my own temper was up. I forgot everything. While he was thrusting the letter and his fist into my face, in my fury I seized whatever thing was handiest—it was a stick of wood—and dealt him an instantaneous blow with all the force that passion could give it. I did not know, nor think, nor care where I should hit him, nor how hard, nor what the effect would be."

The effect, Putnam read on, was the worst possible: struck at full force on the side of the head, with nothing to break the blow, Dr. Parkman fell instantly to the floor, a trickle of blood flowing out of his open mouth. Professor Webster dropped his weapon—a thick, tough length of grapevine wood—and grabbed some ammonia and applied it under Dr. Parkman's nose, trying to revive him. "Perhaps I spent some ten minutes in attempts to resuscitate him," Webster explained, "but I found he was absolutely dead. In my horror and consternation I ran instinctively to the doors and bolted them—the doors of the lecture room, and the laboratory below. And then, what was I to do?"

In that moment, Webster revealed, he made three fateful decisions. He decided not to go to the police, he decided to grab the promissory notes from Parkman's dead fingers, and then . . . he decided to dispose of the body. Even as he dragged Dr. Parkman's cooling body down the stairs and into his lower laboratory, just above him Dr. Holmes's afternoon lecture was proceeding; he had to work quickly.

"My next move," the confession continued, "was to get the body into the sink which stands in the small private room—setting up the body partially erect against the corner, and getting up into the sink myself. There it was entirely dismembered. It was quickly done, as a work of terrible and desperate necessity. The only instrument used was the knife found by the officers in the tea-chest, and which I had kept for cutting corks."

The showy Turkish knife, he explained, was just that—something he kept for show; he'd brought it into town merely to have its hilt repaired. The sledgehammer that Littlefield hadn't been able to find, and which some had suspected of being the weapon, also played no role in the crime; Webster didn't know where it was either. The acid spots in the stairwell were simply that—ordinary lab spatters. The filed keys discovered in a drawer really were just a curiosity he'd found in the street one day. And the sealable tin box and fish hooks hadn't been bought to dispose of the body—the former was for mailing plants to Fayal, and the latter for lowering experiments in and out of a vault— but he *had* indeed decided to then use them, after the search died down, to fetch and permanently dispose of Parkman's remains.

The rest was largely as the prosecution had described it: the burning of the head and some limbs in the furnace, the disposal or temporary hiding of other parts in the privy and the tea chest. Parkman's watch was at the bottom of the Charles River. The stab wound in the thorax was simply a slip of the knife during the carving up of the dead body; and as for the package Webster had told his wife not to open, that was merely some household acid that needed to be kept closed.

"I wrote but one of the anonymous letters produced at the trial," he added. The "Civis" letters were his, as was the letter suggesting a search of neighboring basements; but the one allegedly sent from aboard the *Herculean* was someone else's idea of a joke.

And he had one more mystery to dispel: his convulsions on the night of his arrest.

"When I found that we went over Craigie's Bridge," the minister read out, "I thought the arrest was probable. When I found that the carriage was stopping at the jail, I was sure of my fate; and before leaving the carriage, I took a dose of strychnine from my pocket and swallowed it."

But the dose was wrong: instead of dying, he'd gone into wild convulsions and sweating and foaming, feeling that he was dying even as he was carried by policemen to confront the body parts in his laboratory. After a delirious night racked with pain, he'd come to his senses the next morning to find himself—miserably—still alive.

"I never had a thought of injuring Dr. Parkman," Webster had insisted to the minister after finishing his confession.

I believe him, Putnam added, addressing the council. After the confession, he'd advised Webster to withdraw his initial pardon request, since he knew in his heart that he was not an innocent man. And that, Putnam revealed, was why Webster had then withdrawn it. Instead, the professor now came to them to plead for his life as a guilty man—but guilty of a terrible crime of a moment, not of premeditated murder.

It would now be up to the governor and his Executive Council to decide whether the Commonwealth of Massachusetts would, with a noose and scaffold, finish the job that Professor John Webster had already failed at on the night of his arrest.

* * * *

In a State House antechamber, Governor Briggs faced a row of weeping women: Mrs. Harriet Webster, dressed in black mourning clothes—"the very picture of distress and sorrow," one observer wrote—and her daughters, each wearing a modest pink dress, their faces hidden beneath veils. Their father was still back in his jail cell, waiting for the governor's decision.

The Webster women hadn't known of his confession until shortly before the Executive Council did. Up until that point, they'd refused visitors who even spoke of the possibility of his guilt. "How could I believe my husband to be guilty," Mrs. Webster had explained to one friend, "when he frequently said, in coming in from the garden with the knife in his hand, 'They are searching the Medical College'?" He'd been perfectly calm handling knives, in talking with policemen and neighbors, in reading out the "MISSING" posters to them on their outings. Now they faced the realization that his apparent calmness had hidden a crime from even his closest family members.

Our petition for a pardon was a sincere one, her daughters explained. *We truly believed him to be innocent.*

"We feel assured of that," Governor Briggs sympathized. "No one doubts your sincerity."

"I feel that he must have committed the deed in a moment of *great* provocation," Mrs. Webster pleaded. "He doted upon his children—he was a good, kind, husband—and oh, sir, we earnestly hope and pray that you may find it consistent with justice and humanity, to save him and our whole family."

The lieutenant governor, sitting closest to Mrs. Webster, spoke blandly about their duties and the limits of the office, and Mrs. Webster burst out crying.

"Did you say, Sir, it is impossible to commute his sentence?"

"Oh!" the official fumbled. "I can't tell you that, Madam—the subject is before the committee. All I can say is we will try most conscientiously to serve you and save your husband. It is a most painful duty."

It was also becoming a most prolonged duty. Though the councilors had initially hoped to reach their decision by July 6, they called additional meetings and moved that date to July 16, as now they would have to consider the claims Webster made in his confession. At the next hearing, three doctors testified that people could indeed die of a single blow to the head, and sometimes in as little as ten minutes. Jeffries Wyman, the Harvard colleague who'd carefully cataloged Parkman's bones for the trial, now helped come to Webster's defense. Just like other bones, Wyman explained, the skulls of the elderly could become thin and brittle—some were "not thicker than cartridge paper, and would yield to the pressure of the thumb." In handling the fragments of Parkman's skull from the furnace, he'd found the old doctor's "slightly below average" in thickness.

Other signs hinted that Webster was perhaps not guilty of the most cold-blooded sort of murder. A local physician testified that Webster had, in years past, been known to be quick-tempered. Once, when among several doctors engaging in the young gents' pastime of knocking one another's top hats off, Webster had become so angered that he'd tried to land a blow on the head of Dr. Charles Homans; only a lucky block had saved the surgeon. On another occasion, while Dr. Webster sat in a barber's chair, his fellow physician Dr. Thomas Blatchford passed by and joked, "Did you ever see a man shave a monkey?" Webster seized the barber's knife and narrowly missed stabbing Blatchford.

A procession of supplicants begged the governor and the council for mercy. They received petitions from across the country totaling over eighteen hundred signatures; a letter from Benjamin Greene, the juror who'd initially held out on the premeditation charge and now regretted changing his mind; and a hasty Cambridge petition signed by Webster's neighbors, the town mayor, President Sparks of Harvard, and numerous professors—even the skeptical Benjamin Peirce.

Not everyone was convinced. While the Cambridge petition featured prominent names from the undergraduate college, there was a notable silence from Webster's colleagues on the Boston medical college campus. Three physicians quietly informed the council that the actual likelihood of death in ten minutes was "adverse to the confession." One of them, the young Dr. Henry Bigelow, was blunt in his assessment of the confession: an immediately fatal blow from the wood club was "in the highest degree improbable." Bemis reported later to the attorney general that "Bigelow says that if a man falls off a building & jams his head all to pieces he will generally survive for hours." Nor did it help that in however much of panic he'd killed and carved up Parkman, Webster had been utterly calculating in his months of false insinuations against Ephraim Littlefield.

By July 8, Governor Briggs had heard the professor's confession, pleas from the prisoner's family and spiritual adviser, and statements from medical experts and neighbors alike. Another delay would seem inconceivable—except that the following day, Boston would be convulsed anew—by *another* dead body.

* * * *

THIS TIME the deceased was neither a Boston Brahmin nor an ancient Egyptian princess; it was, in fact, someone whose fame far outshone either at the moment. The *Herald* was one of the first to receive the news, and quickly set it into large type:

Telegraphic to Boston Herald.

Morse's Line.

THE DEATH OF THE PRESIDENT.

ACTION OF THE CABINET.

THE LAST MOMENTS OF THE OLD HERO.

&C., &C.

"Zachary Taylor is dead!" came the cry. The old general had been cut down not by muskets and sabers but by milk and cherries: he'd fallen terribly ill after eating at a Fourth of July reception at the half-built Washington Monument. With Taylor's sudden death and the hasty swearing in of Millard Fillmore, there would be days of mourning to plan around.

Boston's government offices came to a standstill. The flags were lowered to half-mast, the church bells muffled and set to toll hauntingly for an hour at noon, and Boston's courts and State House closed. Newspapers followed the old tradition of laying out their pages with thickly inked borders, as if the very type itself were draped in black.

The committee's recommendation to Briggs would have to wait. The governor's ceremonial work took priority now—and no sooner was that done than Harvard would come calling for *its* ceremonies. Somehow, amid the mourning duties, the college was still to administer its incoming exams on July 15 and 16, and then its graduation procession on July 17. The ritual played out all over again: the calling of names and fathers' professions for sixty-one hopefuls; the exam in Latin; the sweltering summer heat; the anxious wait outside University Hall for the results. With the future Class of 1854 selected, the newly graduating Class of 1850 took over the campus the next day, caps and pages of senior orations in hand.

This year, Professor Webster would be notably missing from the faculty ranks.

The governor, lieutenant governor, and most of the Executive Council made the journey to Cambridge, as always; Harvard was a veritable branch of the state government. The program showed a graduating class well-stocked with the names of the local gentry—Cabot, Channing, Gould, Higginson, Lathrop, Lowell, Quincy—and council members sipped lemonade and sat politely through senior disquisitions on Shakespeare and Milton. Across the river in Boston, though, work continued through the day. Though additional petitions meant one more public hearing the following morning, a subcommittee reviewing the pardon request had already reached its recommendation.

"Friend Clifford," a member wrote confidentially to the attorney general. "The Committee will recommend Friday, August 30th for the Council to have Prof. Webster executed."

24

CLOSING
HOURS

"Is His Excellency the Governor of the Common-wealth in?" the envoy demanded.

The petitioner in the governor's antechamber was so prepossessing and splendidly attired that some wondered whether he could be from the Prussian court; others guessed he might be "some Hungarian or Polish patriot of distinction, come to throw himself on the hospitalities of our patriotic state."

"Is he engaged?" the fellow pressed. "As I have a message for him if he is not particularly engaged."

"I believe he is engaged now, sir," apologized the attendant. But if the visitor might be willing to wait for an appointment at a later—

"Tell His Excellency," the envoy declared. "Tell him to PARDON DOCTOR WEBSTER. Tell him from me, *Antonio Emanuel Knight.* Tell him," he concluded, "that I and the Ancient and Honorable Artillery Company consent that he should be pardoned."

And with that, he bowed deeply, turned on his heel, and departed. "From what mad-house he escaped is not known," sniped a *Daily Mail* reporter. In fact, unknown to the newspaper, the man had indeed been in an asylum—and also in Webster's Class of 1815 at Harvard Medical School.

The hearings by the Executive Council had now dragged on for weeks; its July 18 hearing would be the last chance for final appeals. When the hearing commenced that morning, the panel found itself facing two familiar figures: Reverend John Spear and his brother

Charles Spear, the latter a founder of the Society for the Abolition of Capital Punishment. Charles published the *Prisoners' Friend* and was a zealous speaker at reformist meetings of every variety. After one particularly hectoring peace-rally speech, his fellow pacifist Thoreau drily remarked to Emerson, "Ought he not to be beaten into a plowshare?"

A pardons hearing without the Spear brothers was inconceivable, and this time they were at their most ardent.

I have more petitions for clemency for Dr. Webster, Charles began. These were in addition to the pile of petitions he'd brought to the last meeting. Also: Was the council aware that Michigan had abolished the death penalty four years ago, with excellent results? And that Webster's family, more than Webster himself, would also be made to suffer by this punishment? And that a living Dr. Webster would have greater opportunity for true repentance?

I also have a letter regarding Daniel Pearson, Spears continued.

The lieutenant governor cut him off: *That's not in the purview of this hearing.*

It was worth the try; Pearson, who'd murdered his wife and two children, was due to go to the scaffold in a matter of days. His defense claimed insanity—and, in fact, the Spear brothers had often prevailed at such hearings in the past. Before the execution of Washington Goode, three death sentences in a row had been commuted, and still others had been narrowly avoided in court through the innovative use of a sleepwalking defense. Webster's case was less promising, though, as somnambulism was a less felicitous argument when there were promissory notes and a week of dismemberment involved.

Above all, time was the enemy in death sentence appeals. The irrevocable nature of the punishment meant that neither new evidence nor succeeding governors could undo the mischief of their predecessors. A law had already been proposed in the Massachusetts Senate that all death sentences first be preceded by a year of hard labor—a proposal that, one observer noted, was "presumed to have reference to Professor Webster's case." But it hadn't come to a vote yet.

A few more petitions were put forward; another helpful local brought in a grapevine club, to show that it, and not the missing sledgehammer, could indeed have inadvertently inflicted a deadly blow. "The weapon was knotty and substantial," an *Evening Transcript* reporter admitted, "and altogether had a *murderous* look."

But all of this was not enough.

When Sheriff Eveleth brought the death warrant to the jail cell, the professor had already heard the news: he'd read it, just like everyone else, in the evening newspaper. His fellow condemned prisoner, Pearson, was led onto the scaffold the following week, and asked if he had any final message for Dr. Webster.

"Yes," he said. "Tell him to prepare to meet his God, as I trust I have done."

* * * *

AND SO the preparations began. A few days after Pearson's body was cut down, jailer Andrews led a new visitor into Webster's cell— someone the professor had been asking to see. The prisoner, occupied in no small part these days by his Bible, leapt up and warmly grabbed the visitor's hand.

Mr. Littlefield, he said earnestly. *I have done you a great injustice.*

"I forgive you, Dr. Webster, with all my heart," Ephraim replied. "And I pity and sympathize with you."

The Parkman reward had not brought the janitor much happiness. With the usual summer ravages of illness and mortality afoot, he'd lost a child recently. And his own reputation would never quite recover; after the *Boston Daily Atlas* revealed that he'd been offered $500 to tour with a Parkman and Webster waxworks exhibit, papers across the country repeated the figure as *$5,000*, attacking him as if he'd already taken the offer.

But Dr. Webster was no longer one of his detractors.

"Mr. Littlefield, all that you said was true—you have misrepresented nothing," the professor assured him. One thing from the trial that still bothered Webster, though: the hint by the prosecution that the missing sledgehammer was the murder weapon. "As a dying man," he insisted, "I have no recollection in regard to the sledgehammer."

If Webster and Littlefield had found forgiveness in their hearts for each other, the same was not true for Parkman's family. Webster quietly wrote the Reverend Francis Parkman a letter expressing "sincere contrition and penitence" and explaining that "I had never, until the last two or three interviews with your brother, felt towards him anything but gratitude for his many acts of kindness and friendship." Parkman spurned the condemned man. Fanny Longfellow, well familiar with both, had predicted as much to her father months earlier: "This is asking for more magnanimity than they possess, as the Reverend is very savage, for a reverend." Reverend Parkman had once been a great advocate of the Society for the Abolition of Capital Punishment, yet his voice was now conspicuously missing from the cause. Was abolition only for other people's losses? For a man of the cloth who had once baptized Webster's grandson, there was something unseemly in both his readiness to see the professor executed and his unwillingness to even acknowledge the possibility of forgiveness. Public sympathy for Reverend Parkman curdled. "The response was not what, under the circumstances, it should have been," one newspaper remonstrated, citing its "exhibiting a spirit of unforgiveness."

Such criticism paled, though, beside that of correspondents angry at Governor George Briggs's refusal to commute the death sentence. Each day's mail seemed to bring more abuse, more invective, more unsettling weirdness. Breaking the wax seal on an envelope had become a fraught task in the governor's office.

"The feet of those who have just carried out the President of the United States, are at thy door, thou Governor of Massachusetts, and shall carry thee out," promised one letter, which also accused Briggs of "murder, legalized to be sure, but the none the less murder." And then, a few lines later: "Yes," it helpfully reminded him, "*murderer thou art*." Now that Briggs had executed Washington Goode and Daniel Pearson, and because of the impending execution of Webster, God would speak to the governor in thunder: "It shall be thy death-bed music (if thou art permitted to die in bed) unless thou shalt repent."

God had been in urgent communication with a number of the governor's correspondents; another informed Briggs that "I Rite to inform you that they Had taught me to shut up Webster who killed Parkman *but not Hang Him* For God has told Me so I left home the 15th of July to Come up and se you And I walked the Most of the way to Springfield when I got there they told Me you was yet to Home."

Some letters had traveled even farther; the missive of a "Launcelot English" of New Orleans dubbed Governor Briggs "a hypocrite . . . aye a most oppressive scoundrel." But local writers were the most worrisome: one explained that he personally commanded a band of avengers, and that on August 25 they would "burn your dwelling to the ground and put an end to your damnable life . . . you are a God damned, miserable, lying, thieving, villainous rascal, a sick man for Governor. If Professor Webster is hung there will be a funeral from *your* dwelling." The letter was signed "Bambazilla Frothingham."

Others told the governor, without explanation, to simply drop everything. "You must return to your capital with all speed. The case is urgent," ordered a telegram arriving at his Springfield home on August 28. The correspondent was none other than his "Ancient and Honorable" envoy, Antonio Emanuel Knight.

When, at last, the governor received an envelope that was clearly an ordinary invitation, it might have been a relief. Then he read it:

Dear Sir,

The undersigned begs the pleasure of your company on Friday morning Aug 30 at No. 5 Leverett St to witness a Murder. A dish of tea will be taken after the awful ceremony.

> *Yours with suffocation,*
> *Jackus Netebebus*

N.B. Please to send an answer or a substitute, if you can find one.

In truth, the arrangements for the execution were troublesome. Sheriff Eveleth, upon quietly announcing that he was taking applications for witnesses to the event, was deluged with more than five hundred requests in the first few days alone. The attention created problems for the prisoner and the jail's staff, as they'd done everything they could to hide the date and time from Mrs. Webster and her daughters. The Webster women had long stopped reading the newspapers, and their few visitors were not to mention the August 30 execution date. Although they were aware that it was coming someday, Dr. Webster and his family both felt that the shock of knowing exactly when would be too much for them.

His wife and their daughters made their usual visit to his cell on Thursday, August 29, but found their good-byes a little hurried: visiting hours ended a half hour early. Perhaps that made sense; with the end of summer, soon the days would shorten, with darkness settling over the jail earlier each night.

"Will this be your hour for closing in the future?" Mrs. Webster innocently asked the jailer.

Gustavus Andrews was at a loss for an answer as he showed her out. The jailer couldn't explain the real reason, and nor could her husband: to get them out of the building before they could see the prison yard prepared for the scaffold.

Yes, he finally told Mrs. Webster. *These will be the new closing hours.*

* * * *

A JAIL clerk and a guard sat watching Dr. Webster's fingers carefully follow the curve of a seashell, working at it with a piece of fabric and water until it gained a beautiful shine in the light of his jail cell. It was curious, the comfort to be had cleaning and polishing a shell in some of his final hours on earth; after his decades as a mineralogist, he had reverted back to that most innocent childhood pastime of simply picking something off the ground and treasuring it.

He'd been trying to read, though some books served the occasion better than others. He'd perused Mountford's *Euthanasy, or Happy Talks Towards the End of Life,* a pious young narrator's consolation dialogues with his aging uncle. The youngster's response to the uncle's fear that "death was not meant to be altogether pleasant to us" was itself not altogether reassuring: "No; a skeleton is a skeleton. And a death's head is a death's head; ugly in itself, and without eyes; but then through the eye-sockets there shines the light of God." Webster turned to his other volumes. There was Samuel Longfellow's *Hymns,* by the younger brother of his good neighbor Henry—he'd once nearly landed Samuel a job back in Fayal, come to think of it—and there was Sir John Bowring's *Matins and Vespers.* The professor marked off some particularly fine passages in both, noting which friend they were to be sent to afterward.

And then, at last, he turned to his Bible. The two guards were on a tacit suicide watch, though none called it that; they kept Dr. Webster genial but largely quiet company as he read Scripture—"O death, where is thy sting? O grave, where is thy victory?" The doctor occasionally stopped to pray, or to simply put his head in his hands, deep in thought. Then, as midnight passed, he lay back in his iron prison-issue bedstead, and tried to close his eyes even as the guards continued their watch on him.

The doctor slumbered only awhile, and awoke before dawn. As the sun rose, an insistent noise echoed over the yard outside: *tap, tap, tap.* Mr. Dunbar, the prison's occasional carpenter, led a team in piecing together the scaffold. It was a new spruce one, handily constructed by Dunbar himself according to the latest methods. The crowd already gathering outside the prison walls did not sound very appreciative.

"Stop your infernal clack!" one of them catcalled. "It disturbs the prisoner in his prayers."

In fact, praying sounded like a fine idea to Webster right about now.
May I come in?

It was his confessor, the Reverend Putnam. The two prayed together as a new morning shift of guards stood nearby. Then Webster turned to more immediate practicalities: two cups of tea, breakfast, and a last smoke. He still had some more cigars left, and he wouldn't need them anymore.

Gentlemen, please, he told his keepers. *Take my cigars.*

The doctor was in a philosophical mood. The arriving jail staff had passed through a gauntlet of spectators on Leverett and the surrounding streets—perhaps a thousand were already outside the gates—and more than a hundred police officers and constables were posted to keep the masses at bay. Yet here, in Cell 5, the scene was improbably calm.

Do you know, the prisoner mused to his guards, *that I used to experiment on the bodies from this execution ground? I'd apply galvanic batteries to them.*

He'd seen a great many executions, in fact. During his residency training in London, back when he'd served alongside John Keats, Dr. Webster had been known for his regular attendance at local hangings. He was something of an enthusiast, and classmates could still remember his jaunty invitation each time: "Hang at eight; breakfast at nine!"

He had, of late, become less enthusiastic—and the hour was approaching.

* * * *

THEY ENTERED the prison yard with countless eyes upon them. Reverend Putnam, walking alongside the prisoner, kept his gaze directed at the middle of the field.

"Do not regard any thing about you," he murmured to Webster. "Do not look."

"I do not look," the professor repeated. "My thoughts are elsewhere."

A great mass of Bostonians stretched before them, with boys trying to scale the prison fence to sneak *in*—a rather novel issue in prison security. A cordon of policemen caught the boys and tossed them back like wriggling fish into a swelling sea of men and women. Enterprising locals charged fifty cents, and then a full dollar, for a spot on their rooftops; at 3 Lowell Street, the residents even fashioned some crude benches out of planks, until there were one hundred spectators perched atop their building alone.

"At every possible point (with a few exceptions) from which the gallows or any part of the yard could be seen, might be seen a human face," marveled a *Journal* reporter.

There were some principled holdouts. Sightseers arriving at one building found a simple note posted on its door: "NOT AT HOME, OPPOSED TO CAPITAL PUNISHMENT." Such protestations were promptly ignored as men shinned up the drainpipes to enjoy a prime unoccupied rooftop.

John Webster did not look: he kept his eyes on the scaffold before him, and he mounted the high platform step by step with the sheriff, the deputies, and the minister. Below them in the yard were gathered more than one hundred witnesses invited by the sheriff; in accordance with the state law, he'd asked the "District Attorney, Clerk or Clerks of the County, and twelve respectable citizens," along with the defense team, a surgeon, a minister, and the prison guards. Joining them was Boston's press corps and a contingent of New York reporters that had arrived the night before, poised to telegraph the appalling details back to the eager readers at the *Herald* and the *Sun*.

The professor reached the cross-arm, the August sun bearing down upon his black outfit; up on the rooftops, ladies opened their parasols. The whole affair was running late—it was now going on nine-thirty—for the new gallows had taken a while to erect. It was of a clever design, with a spring-loaded trap door activated by a mere tap of the sheriff's foot.

"It *is* a very ingenious contrivance," one observer allowed.

Sheriff Eveleth drew out the governor's death warrant, and the crowd fell silent.

"Whereas, at the term of the Supreme Judicial Court, begun and holden at Boston, within the county of Suffolk, and for the counties of Suffolk and Nantucket, on the first Tuesday of March, being the fifth day of said month, in the year of our Lord one thousand eight hundred and fifty," he droned, reading the preamble, "JOHN W. WEBSTER, of Cambridge, in the county of Middlesex, was convicted of the crime of murder, and was thereupon by our said Court sentenced to suffer the pains of death, by being hanged by the neck, until he shall be dead . . ."

As the Sheriff read on, Reverend Putnam turned to Dr. Webster and earnestly drew him into discussion, ignoring the sheriff. They'd heard the warrant before; they already knew what was coming. What the prisoner needed was prayer.

". . . agreeably to the provisions of the one hundredth and thirty-ninth chapter of the Revised Statutes, you cause the execution of the said sentence upon our said court, in all respects to be done and performed upon him, the said John W. Webster . . ."

The deputies drew out the leather straps that would bind his feet and hands. Webster had seen enough executions that he'd gone out of his way to ask for the smooth straps, wishing to avoid the coarser ropes that were sometimes used for these jobs.

". . . whereof fail not at your peril, and make return of this warrant, with your doings thereon, into our Secretary's office . . ."

The doctor shook the reverend's hand warmly; then his arms were pinioned.

". . . our seal hereunto affixed, the nineteenth day of July, in the year of our Lord one thousand eight hundred and fifty, and of the Independence of the United States of America, the Seventy-Fifth."

Did the prisoner, the sheriff asked, have any final words?

He did, but not for the sheriff or for the crowd.

"Father," Dr. Webster prayed aloud, "into thy hands I commend my spirit."

He had nothing more to add. The sheriff gently removed the doctor's hat, and as he drew a black cambric hood over his head, Webster turned to look at the Reverend Putnam. His confessor's face would be the last he saw.

"In the name of the Commonwealth of Massachusetts," Sheriff Eveleth called out after the noose was procured, "and in accordance with the Warrant of the Chief Executive, I now proceed to execute the law upon John W. Webster, convicted at the March term of the Supreme Judicial Court, of the murder of Dr. George Parkman."

There was a long, terrible pause; then the sheriff's foot pressed down on the catch.

The trap door sprang open, and Dr. Webster dropped eight feet, with a sudden snap to break his neck. After a minute, involuntary spasms passed through his body that made his shoulders shrug, as if the learned professor had been posed a question that even he could not answer.

Epilogue

WHAT DO YOU MEAN I CAN'T SEE HIM?

The woman stood in the Websters' doorway, uncomprehending and indignant. Her two daughters were still in the carriage on Garden Street, waiting to join the funeral viewing. They were strangers to the Webster family, true. But that hardly mattered now, did it? Dr. Webster was famous, and they were curious, and that meant they had a right to see the man—to see what was left of him.

We came all the way up from New York. The door, as politely as possible, was closed in her face. *Why can't we see him?*

The Websters and their neighbors closed ranks as the streets filled with strange carriages. Sightseers from out of town wheeled around and around, vulturously circling the blocks, hoping to see something, anything, of the infamous Dr. Webster's body. "There has been a morbid curiosity, marked by feelings almost inhuman on the part of some of the populace," observed Harvard librarian John Sibley that weekend.

Inside the parlor, the doctor lay carefully arranged, his features as fully restored as Mr. Peak's mortuary could achieve. Once the crowd outside the prison wall had dispersed, Webster's body had been loaded not into an undertaker's fine polished vehicle, which onlookers would have identified and tailed, but instead into the nondescript lawyer's carriage that his defense counsel had loaned for the trip over the Craigie Bridge and back home. The coffin itself was a regrettable affair, a cheap black-painted pine box from the jail. The professor had wanted mahogany, but the cost was simply too dear. The family remained desperately short of money. They'd quietly sold peaches and pears from their back garden; a friend had taken the fruit into town for sale to buyers unaware of their provenance. Such earnest efforts were, however, nowhere near enough, and now the family was permanently deprived of the doctor's already insufficient Harvard salary.

Working behind the scenes, Longfellow's cousin-in-law, William Appleton, had been quietly arranging matters for Harriet Webster and her daughters. Both Appleton and merchant John Perkins Cushing had pledged $500 to the Webster family as a first step toward a lifetime loan that would revert to the contributors upon the death of the last member of the Webster family. But though Appleton found quick success in raising an initial $5,000 toward the family's crushing debts and future estate, further contributions proved scarce.

"Mr. Appleton tried to raise $20,000 for them," confided Mrs. Webster's sister in a letter, "but he could find no one to second his views."

An auction of the doctor's effects also proved surprisingly unprofitable. His labware sold poorly, and the proceeds from the sale of his library were even more melancholy. The Webster women had naïvely erased the doctor's name from his books, as if removing a stain to clean them for auction; but his name was perhaps the most valuable feature for a collector. As ordinary books, they now held the rather more limited appeal typical of any retiring professor's collection. "It was quite valuable," one visitor commented, "containing many good books in chemistry and medicine, but was more complete in the works of twenty years since than those of the present day."

Still, the efforts did not go entirely for naught. In the end, between the auctions and Appleton's quiet entreaties with friends and creditors, the Websters were left with $450, as well as lodging in a new though smaller home, and the daughters' keepsakes were spared from the auctioneer's hammer. The trusts left by the daughters' grandfather, too, still had some money in them. Of the rest of their learned prosperity—the fine home they had once built, the tasteful library and musical acquisitions, the scientific collections, and the quietly crushing debts and subterfuge that undergirded these attainments—all vanished into the closed ledger of the past. Young Hattie, despite her fortunes being much reduced, was married months later to a man who refused to hear of breaking the engagement, but her mother never really recovered. After Mrs. Webster's death in October 1853, the two remaining daughters, Catherine and Marianne, left town within days, on the next ship for their prosperous in-laws in Fayal—fully intending, a local newspaper reported, "never to return."

Visiting the Azores in 1867, a young Mark Twain was astonished to find the Webster daughters thriving on the island. "I did not recognize them in the fine, matronly, dignified ladies we saw today," he marveled. "Their exile was well chosen. In no civilized land could they have found so complete a retirement from the busy, prying world." They'd even reconciled themselves, if a bit ruefully, to their father's place in history.

"Well," they said, introducing themselves to their American visitors, "I suppose you know who *we* are!"

* * * *

FOR OVER six months, George Bemis's life had been a perfect blank.

"The longest gap perhaps in my journal for ten years," he wrote in its pages in November 1850, "and for reason of the hardest task of 'The Report of the Trial of John W. Webster,' as my title-page now reads."

For a case that Bemis hadn't wanted to get involved with in the first place, Webster's had nearly taken over his life. The associate prosecutor had, in the end, gone forward with editing a transcript for the publisher Little, Brown, and as the task stretched out into months, he repeatedly decided to give up—"four or five times," he recalled—before invariably being drawn back in. "Why has it taken so long?—I have asked myself time and again, & cannot find a satisfactory answer," Bemis admitted in his long-neglected journal.

His care was justified: the case would have an outsized role in American legal history, both for its innovative use of forensic evidence and for Chief Justice Shaw's instructions to the jury on the definition of reasonable doubt. Shaw's formulation became standard usage and a staple of law school instruction across the country; by 1866, the California Supreme Court had deemed it "probably the most satisfactory definition ever given." Though often criticized as law made up on the spot, Shaw's language might be more fairly described as an effective and remarkably durable fusing of existing precedents. Examining the "Webster charge" in 1994, even the U.S. Supreme Court seemed unable to come up with anything better to replace it. "It was commendable for Chief Justice Shaw to pen an instruction that survived more than a century," Justice Anthony Kennedy wrote in bemused exasperation. Even as other states did eventually update the wording of their jury instructions, the "Webster charge" preserved in Bemis's transcript persisted in Massachusetts until 2015, when the state supreme court ruled that "a modernized version of the Webster charge must [now] be given" in criminal trials.

Chronicling the trial did hold some small professional pleasure for Bemis; no longer an adversary, he now interviewed Shaw and the defense attorneys as colleagues, as well as his fellow prosecutor John Clifford, working with each to make sure the wording of their arguments was memorialized correctly. Sometimes his work went beyond correction: Bemis also quietly erased Chief Justice Shaw's careless speculation about whether Webster might have used chloroform on Parkman. Nevertheless, the resulting publication in November 1850 would be the definitive record of the case. As a figure at the sidelines of Transcendentalism, George Bemis might have preferred to write on theology, and to be remembered for that, but he was a busy lawyer, and a trial transcript would be his enduring literary accomplishment.

Other facts of the case would emerge only long after the publication of his transcript, though. Bemis's own role became clear after his death, when his papers, left to the Massachusetts Historical Society, showed that he'd ostensibly been paid $1,000 for his trial services by the attorney general—"tho'," his writing revealed, "really to be paid him by the Parkman family." The Parkmans had secretly funneled their immense wealth into the best and most aggressive government prosecution money could buy—an arrangement that, if not strictly speaking illegal, was still a dismaying example of Boston's ruling class bending the justice system to its own purposes.

Another puzzling aspect of the case became clearer in time as well: the long-rumored refusal of both Daniel Webster and Rufus Choate, the premier attorneys of their time, to serve as John Webster's counsel. "I talked with Daniel Webster about the matter when I was applied to on behalf of Professor Webster," Choate later revealed in his memoirs. "He entirely coincided with me as to the proper line of defense—that it must be *an admission of the homicide.*" To another colleague, Choate explained that he'd have claimed justifiable homicide by self-defense or an insane "visitation of God." Between a forthright confession of homicide and the lack of direct witnesses, he said, "It would have been impossible to convict Professor Webster of murder with that admission." But his would-be client was either too proud or too grasping to admit to anything, even that the body was Parkman's: "Professor Webster would not listen to any such defense as that." Nor would the professor's family, it seemed. And so his fate was sealed.

"Mr. [Daniel] Webster said to me," Choate's law partner later recalled, "some time after he had this conversation with Mr. Choate, that he had not the least doubt of Professor Webster's guilt."

What defense Webster's subsequent lawyers, Merrick and Sohier, did manage, though roundly criticized by many outsiders at the time, makes more sense in retrospect. Those close to the case showed little doubt of their ability; Edward Sohier went on to a long-standing and successful practice in Boston, and Pliny Merrick was appointed associate justice of the state supreme court, as well as to the Board of Overseers at Harvard.

It would not be until the posthumous opening of their papers, too, that the full extent of their professional dilemma became apparent. Webster's complaints about their defense came from the untenable demands he made on them. In hundreds of pages of his notes, Webster strove to prove not just that he couldn't have killed Parkman but—just as importantly—that Ephraim Littlefield likely did. For reputable attorneys like Merrick and Sohier, this posed a problem. Their profession was still grappling with the implications of the 1840 murder trial in London of François Benjamin Courvoisier—in which defense attorney Charles Phillips, even after learning of his client's guilt, still pursued an aggressive strategy that threw suspicion on an innocent chambermaid. Humiliated and shaken, the chambermaid was eventually committed to an asylum. Phillips went public with what had happened only months before the Webster case, and the parallels were troubling. Could Sohier and Merrick in good conscience pin a murder on a humble janitor who, by every indication except Webster's, was guilty of nothing but revealing the truth?

Their hesitation was not misplaced. In a private family letter weeks after Webster's execution, his sister-in-law Amelia Nye revealed that while in jail, Webster had in fact confessed the crime to a cousin, Edward C. Jones—and not out of penance, but because he needed Edward's help.

"He confided to him that he had done the deed," she wrote. "He then wrote him a letter wishing Edward to come to Boston to take the staples out of the ventilator in the College to make it appear that someone had entered and placed the remains where they were found. Edward went to Boston to tell him that he would not do any such thing." Although Mrs. Nye was not to know it, this exact claim—that the ventilation panel in a lab door was loose, and would have allowed entry by Littlefield or others into the room—was indeed a pivotal argument in Dr. Webster's private notes to his counsel. He had even gone to the trouble of sketching the panel for them.

Foiled in his attempt to plant evidence that would frame Littlefield, Nye's letter goes on to reveal, Webster hatched desperate escape plans.

"He then wrote a very long letter to Edward wishing to know when a Whaler would sail and there were in the letter about 40 plans for escape," she wrote. "One was for him to dress in Harriet's clothes, leave her in his place and escape to New Bedford, so poor [cousin] Emma was in a constant state of alarm fearing the Dr. would make his appearance at her house."

Even without the revelations within the family's own papers, the likelihood of Webster's guilt was increasingly taken for granted among the denizens of Cambridge, who allowed that even a reputable Harvard professor might indeed commit a murder. His station in life only proved, as Judge Shaw reflected, that "at such times the glaze of civilization and culture shows very thin in spots." Professor Webster has remained only the second and last Harvard alumnus to be executed in America; the other, George Burroughs, was condemned in 1692 under the altogether less convincing charge of witchcraft.

Attorney General John Clifford's successful conviction of a son of Harvard certainly proved to be no political impediment: just three years after the trial, he was elected governor. By the time Clifford took over George Briggs's old job, though, the governor's duty of considering pardons was evolving; it now occurred amid an increasing unease over the death penalty itself. The one-year-delay law inspired by Webster's case finally passed the legislature in 1852, and the category of second-degree murder was adopted in 1858. But more than a century would pass before the death penalty would be abolished in the state.

At least one person close to Webster, though, remained profoundly untroubled by the doctor's harsh punishment: novelist George Thompson, the doctor's fellow prisoner and erstwhile friendly neighbor in the next jail cell over.

"Probably, in the annals of criminal jurisprudence, there never was seen a more striking instance of equal and exact justice, than was afforded by the trial, conviction and execution of John W. Webster," Thompson later wrote. "Money, influential friends, able counsel, prayers, petitions, the *prestige* of a scientific reputation failed to save him from that fate which he merited as well as if he had been the most obscure individual in existence."

* * * *

PERHAPS IT was only a matter of time before Drs. Parkman and Webster were memorialized as wax figures, counterpoised in perpetual enmity, on display at P. T. Barnum's American Museum in Manhattan. In the end, Ephraim Littlefield did appear in person at one of the wax figure exhibitions, along with a wooden model of the Medical College—and he was met with immediate and vociferous criticism. Littlefield, one newspaper sneered, "is a pure specimen of the money-worshipping hang-dog." Another newspaper deemed the show to have "terribly reduced our general estimate of humanity." Littlefield instantly forswore any involvement with the promoter, explaining that it hadn't been his idea and that he hadn't even done it for pay, but merely for the public's edification. Depending on which newspaper one believed in the years afterward, the much-abused janitor then either retired to a farm in Vermont, ventured to California and "cleared $25,000," or went insane.

The mannequins of Parkman and Webster proved scarcely any less peripatetic. They were perhaps none too realistic in appearance; Webster's sister-in-law later noted that the professor was buried in an unmarked grave, as "it was feared someone would desecrate his tomb for the sake of taking his impression of his features to have a wax figure made." Yet improvised statues of the two were nonetheless spotted in Connecticut, in Maine, and at a cattle show and fair in western Massachusetts, where one reporter found them haphazardly thrust in among the other statues and agricultural exhibits, so that "Dr. Parkman was looking hard at Gen. Taylor, while Professor Webster appeared as if lecturing to a class on the subject of manures." In an inspired poke at an Ivy League rival, the waxen Parkman and Webster also attended Commencement Day festivities at Dartmouth College.

Other jabs at Harvard were not so easily dismissed. A withering committee report in the Massachusetts legislature, issued on the heels of Webster's execution, upbraided the university for an impractical and outdated curriculum. Though the college quickly parried the criticism, this merely delayed reform for another generation. The school was an increasingly elite and moneyed bastion—so that, as Henry Adams later put it, "parents went on, generation after generation, sending their children to Harvard College for the sake of its social privileges." When Oliver Wendell Holmes later described these Boston elite as Brahmins in his novel *Elsie Venner,* the term immediately and permanently stuck. The Brahmins *had* effectively become a caste—and it was, perhaps, no accident that the onetime dean made his story's protagonist a student from a scarcely disguised Harvard.

Yet even as Harvard continued to ossify, its Class of '53 went on to the achievements expected of Boston's favored sons. Edward King, a teenager who had rucksacked through Europe's 1848 revolutions before lodging in Professor Agassiz's home, went on to head the New York Stock Exchange. William Dorsheimer—the uncanny mimic of respectable elders—grew into one himself, and became a congressman. Justin Winsor, who had written a volume of town history in his teens, would preside over a great many more books as head of the Boston Public Library. And Francis McGuire, an unlikely escapee from the Irish potato famine, turned from theology to attend what in that year seemed an even more unlikely destination: the Medical College.

Harvard's year on the front pages had, for better or worse, helped shape the Class of '53. A number went on to notable newspaper careers: Dorsheimer, in his later years, ran the *New York Star,* while the fervently abolitionist Albert Gallatin Browne Jr. would become a *New York Tribune* correspondent and then a *New York Herald* editor. Their classmate Adams Sherman Hill spent years as a D.C. bureau chief before returning to Harvard to create what became the standard for American college writing courses for the next century—a course founded in part, ironically, on Hill's conviction that newspapers were degrading the English language. The man who hired Hill, Charles William Eliot, was himself a '53 classmate, and all too familiar with Webster's story: he trained to become a chemistry professor under

Josiah Cooke, the doctor's own student and successor. In his forty years as Harvard's president—still the longest term in the school's history—Eliot would at last usher in a more diverse student body and a new curriculum that came to epitomize the modern American university.

Sometimes, though, the Harvard of old could unexpectedly reappear. When, many years later, the belfry of Harvard Hall revealed boxes of mineral samples and a dusty piece of discarded apparatus, Professor Cooke immediately recognized the equipment. "That," he mused, "was Webster's volcano"—the pyrotechnic prop that used to nearly set the old doctor's lecture hall on fire.

For generations, Webster's case was recalled whenever a great murder scandal arose, be it Lizzie Borden or Leopold and Loeb. Dr. John Webster and Dr. George Parkman were murderous archetypes, a pair perfectly matched in fatal greed: Webster in his lavish expenditures, and Parkman in his miserly acquisitions. Curiously, while many still remembered Webster with some fondness, if also bafflement at his crime, it was a singular rarity to find anyone who described Parkman as a friend. In a memorial speech at the Medical College, Oliver Wendell Holmes struggled mightily to find something warm to say of their biggest donor. After recalling how Parkman had had "a sententious style of his communications," he added wanly, "Dr. Parkman was a man of strict and stern principles."

In private, Harvard colleagues like mathematician Benjamin Peirce were more blunt. "Dr. Parkman was so harsh and cruel a man with his debtors," Peirce wrote, "that his murder seems almost to have been a retribution of Providence designed to teach us an appalling lesson."

*   *   *   *

THE DEATHS of Dr. Parkman and Dr. Webster were a cautionary tale for some, and for others an important precedent in the use of forensic evidence. Yet their most lasting legacy may have been a literary one. Charles Dickens met Dr. Webster briefly on his first visit to America in 1842, and his crime haunted the author's return trip in

1867–68. During his second trip to Boston, Dickens wrote to his fellow novelist Wilkie Collins, "Longfellow told me a terrific story. He dined with Webster within a year of the murder, one of a party of 10 or 12. As they sat at their wine Webster suddenly ordered the lights to be turned out, and a bowl of some burning mineral to be placed on the table, that the guests might see how ghostly it made them look. As each man stared at all the rest in the weird light, all were horrified to see Webster *with a rope round his neck,* holding it up, over the bowl, with his head jerked on one side, and his tongue lolled out, representing a man being hanged!"

When Dickens asked Oliver Wendell Holmes to take him to Webster's old rooms at the Medical College, he found them much as they had been two decades earlier: "They were horribly grim, private, cold, and quiet; the identical furnace smelling fearfully (some anatomical broth in it I suppose) as if the body were still there." Indeed, the rooms were hauntingly changeless. When the building was torn down in 1911, a local newspaper noted that "Professor Webster's laboratory still remains in the old college building and the vault where the portions of the body were found is still intact."

Dickens promptly commissioned an account of Webster's case for his magazine, *All the Year Round,* but his interest did not end there. After returning to England, he undertook *The Mystery of Edwin Drood,* a novel of a disappearance in which the unlikely perpetrator, a respectable choirmaster, seeks to frame another man. The plot, Dickens told a friend, would pivot on an unidentifiable body in a church vault, nearly destroyed with quicklime—"but all discovery of the murderer was to be baffled till towards the close, when, by means of a gold ring which had resisted the corrosive effects of the lime into which he had thrown the body, not only the person murdered was to be identified but the locality of the crime and the man who committed it." The crucial evidence of Parkman's false teeth, transmuted by literary imagination, at last became the gold ring of Edwin Drood.

Or, that is, it *nearly* did. *Edwin Drood* is famous not just as Dickens's first mystery novel but also as his last, for he died suddenly of a stroke in June 1870, at the end of a full day of working on his story. "I hope his book is finished," Longfellow remarked upon hearing the news. But it was not to be. His readers, who had been following each chapter of *Edwin Drood* in serial form, were left waiting forever for its ending. Like the case that inspired it, some of its secrets will remain a mystery indeed.

Acknowledgments

MUCH OF WHAT YOU'VE READ HERE—AND, JUST AS IMPOR-
tantly, the knotted and tangled sentences you didn't read, because
they were crossed out in the early drafts—is thanks to the love
and guidance of my wife, Jennifer, who is the first reader of all my
work.

My son Bramwell's humor and curiosity reminds me of just why I
write, though I probably won't let Bram read *this* one just yet. Readers
of my previous book about my older son, Morgan, may be startled to
realize that he's gone from a boy to a strapping young man; I owe no
small thanks to his tireless caregiver, Marc Thomas.

My many thanks also go to my agent, Michelle Tessler, and my
editor, John Glusman, for getting this project rolling, and for their
tremendous patience in seeing it through, even when the manuscript
was as confoundingly missing as any Boston miser.

All of my work depends on libraries, and I'm indebted to the Boston Public Library, Harvard University, the Library of Congress, the
Massachusetts Historical Society, and the University of Washington.
I'm especially grateful to Portland State University, which over the
years has endured interlibrary queries from me for everything from
1960s vehicle safety manuals to the transcripts of Victorian chess-
by-telegraph competitions, all without asking what exactly it is that
I do for a living.

In fact, shortly after undertaking this work on an academic murder, I began serving as an English department chair, which per-

haps provided an unintentionally useful perspective on the subject. For my colleagues who so solicitously inquired over the years about how the book was coming along, I can finally tell you: It's in your department mailbox! Also: Can you turn in your office hours for next quarter?

Notes

Abbreviations Used

BA   *Boston Daily Atlas*

BB   *Boston Daily Bee*

BC   *Boston Daily Chronotype*

BH   *Boston Herald*

BJ   *Boston Daily Journal*

BM   *Boston Daily Mail*

BT   *Boston Daily Evening Transcript*

CC   *Cambridge Chronicle*

DJW Defense notes of John Webster (John White Webster Papers, 1837–50, Massachusetts Historical Society)*

JGB Journal of George Bemis (Massachusetts Historical Society)

JHL Journal of Henry Longfellow (Houghton Library manuscript)

LAN Letters of Amelia Nye (Massachusetts Historical Society)

TBH *Trial of Professor John W. Webster* (*Boston Herald* / John A. French trial transcript)

TBJ *The Trial of Prof. John W. Webster* (*Boston Journal* transcript)

TDM *The Parkman Murder* (*Boston Daily Mail* trial transcript)

TGB Bemis, *Report of the Case of John W. Webster*

TJS Stone, *Report of the Trial of Prof. John W. Webster*

TNY *Trial of Professor John W. Webster* (New York *Daily Globe* / Stringer & Townsend transcript)

TTD *The Twelve Days' Trial of John W. Webster* (published in London)

*As Webster's notes to his defense counsel are variously inconsistently numbered and unnumbered, for convenience I've cited the scan numbers assigned to the online copy at mdhistory.net (goo.gl/V7ogji).

Prologue

xv **"Dickenized"**: Longfellow, letter to Charles Sumner, 8 December 1867, *Letters* 5:191.

xv **streets swept for his arrival**: *New York Tribune*, 3 December 1867.

xv **eight thousand tickets**: Dickens, *Letters of Charles Dickens*, 11:492ff.

xv **"our men sit outside the room door"**: Ibid., letter to Mary Dickens, 21 November 1867, 11:480.

xv **"The city has increased enormously"**: Ibid.

xv **"So many years"**: Longfellow, *Works*. 20 November 1867 journal entry, 14:100.

xvi **hiked at least seven miles**: Dickens, letter to Georgina Hogarth, 26 November 1867, *Letters* 11:489.

xvi **Little Nell Cigars and Pickwick Snuff**: *New-York Tribune*, 3 December 1867.

xvi **"Cambridge is exactly as I left it"**: Dickens, letter to John Foster, 22 November 1867, *Letters* 11:485.

xvi **"you couldn't fire a revolver"**: Quoted in Howells, "The White Mr. Longfellow," 328.

xvi **"Boston audiences are proverbially cold"**: Longfellow, letter to Charles Sumner, 8 December 1867, *Letters* 5:191.

xvi **"laughed as if he might crumble to pieces"**: Fields, "Glimpses of Emerson," 459.

xvi **"I thought the roof would go off"**: *New-York Tribune*, 3 December 1867.

xvi **"The manager," he reported**: Dickens, letter to John Foster, 5 January 1868, *Letters* 12:5.

xvi **"I have tried allopathy"**: Ibid.

xvii **"all the spirits ever heard of"**: Dickens, letter to Charles Fletcher, 24 February 1868, *Letters* 12:57.

xvii **Oliver Wendell Holmes Sr. as his visitor**: Payne, *Dickens Days in Boston*, 210.

xvii **the job of a physician, Dr. Holmes would muse**: Howells, "The White Mr. Longfellow," 330.

xvii **they made their way through the snow**: Dickens, letter to Wilkie Collins, 12 February 1868, *Letters* 12:9.

1. The Way into Harvard

3 "ICE! ICE! ICE!": *CC,* 12 July 1849.

3 **one of the hottest weeks of the year**: *CC,* 12 July 1849.

3 **early Monday morning**: Harvard University, *Catalogue,* 40.

3 **tumblers of lemonade**: Hill, *Harvard College,* 90.

4 **"Young men, some standing, others sitting"**: Quoted in Bentinck-Smith, *The Harvard Book,* 168.

4 *John Quincy Adams*: Rantoul, *Report of the Harvard Class of 1853,* 15.

4 *Moses Henry Day*: Ibid., 77.

4 *William Dorsheimer*: Ibid., 78.

4 *Nathan Henry Chamberlain*: Ibid., 56.

4 **Samuel Shaw**: Ibid., 236.

4 **Albert Browne**: Ibid., 46.

4 **John Daves**: Ibid., 74.

4 *Translate those into Latin*: Quoted in Bentinck-Smith, *The Harvard Book,* 169.

5 **he very nearly failed to get in**: *College Courant* (New Haven, CT), 14 January 1871.

5 **"The average number of people that pass"**: Higginson, *Contemporaries,* 174. The brother of Oliver Wendell Holmes Sr., John emerges from Higginson's account as the very model of a Cambridge eccentric: a man whose background, education, and holdings were both impeccable and in utter neglect. He was Harvard '32 and Harvard Law '39 but had no interest in practicing law or indeed in taking any job at all. Instead, he lived with his mother and played whist with the poet James Russell Lowell. His most notable expenditures were the coins he left on his window seat, which he handed out to passing children and tramps.

6 **Cambridge Furniture & Carpet Ware Rooms**: Ford, *The Cambridge Directory and Almanac for 1850,* 168.

6 **students had to provide their own**: Hale, *A New England Boyhood,* 172.

6 **"large, with pleasant, high windows"**: Alpha, "My Room," 349.

6 **"to form groups at the corners of streets"**: "Progress of Cholera," *Boston Medical and Surgical Journal,* 382.

7 **"Death," it announced**: *CC,* 6 September 1849.

7 **ten-cent horse-omnibus ride**: *CC,* 12 July 1849.

7 **poured sulfuric acid**: Vaille and Clark, *The Harvard Book,* 2:142.

7 **arrived in their nightgowns**: Morison, *Three Centuries of Harvard,* 312.

7 **chapel was unheated**: Smith, "Recollections by the Author of 'America,'" 162.
7 **Absence, perversely, only cost two points**: Ibid.
8 **"cooked in a dirty copper boiler"**: Batchelder, "The History of 'Commons' at Harvard—II," 732.
8 **chairs in the dining hall were bolted**: Hale, *A New England Boyhood*, 197.
8 **smashed in an 1818 student fracas**: Morison, *Life and Letters of Harrison Otis Gray*, 1:254.
8 **only one-sixth of the students**: Harvard University, *Twenty-fourth Annual Report*, 9.
8 **Harvard's freshman curriculum**: Ibid., 30.
8 **Schmitz's *A History of Rome***: Ibid., 17.
8 **"Nuper divitiae avaritiam"**: Livy, *Livy: Selections*, 2.
9 **"the fifteen smartest Fellows"**: Emerson, letter to William Emerson, 14 June 1818, *Letters*, 1:85.
9 **the Navy Club**: Vaille and Clark, *The Harvard Book*, 2:357.
9 **regattas held on the Charles River**: "Notes on Our Naval History," 247.
9 **That fall saw four boats**: Ibid., 251.
9 **decked in duck pants**: Ibid., 250.
9 **"Upon these floats"**: *CC*, 30 May 1868.
9 **Society to Discourage the Perpetration**: Morison, *Three Centuries of Harvard*, 183.
9 **production of battling gentleman nitwits**: Garrison, *An Illustrated History of Hasty Pudding Theatricals*, 40.
10 **"Let me get at him"**: Morton, "Slasher and Crasher," 24.
10 **"an annual frolic"**: William Sturgis Bigelow, *A Memoir of Henry Jacob Bigelow*, 9.
10 **"Saw his leg off!"**: Thoreau, Letter from Augustus Peabody to HDT, 30 May 1836, *Correspondence*, 5.
10 **After two college servants were overcome**: Hale, *A New England Boyhood*, 184.

2. On Pins and Crowbars

11 **snowed out for days**: Gallenga, *Episodes of My Second Life*, 152.
11 **nearby was a fresh wreck**: *BT*, 3 November 1849.
11 **bounded up the building's front stairs**: William Sturgis Bigelow, *A Memoir of Henry Jacob Bigelow*, 213.

11 **spacious three-story brick building**: *BA*, 6 November 1846. The layout of the building is noted in this account of its opening; it being made of brick is noted in various later accounts, including Moses King, *King's Handbook of Boston* (Cambridge, MA: Moses King / Harvard College, 1881), 127.

12 **Paul Revere had both a grandson and a great-grandson**: Harvard University, *Catalogue*, 20. The descendants were Edward H. Robbins Revere and John Philips Reynolds.

12 *"Gentlemen of the Medical Class"*: Henry Jacob Bigelow, *An Introductory Lecture*, 3.

12 **Three of the school's seven professors**: Harvard University, *Catalogue*, 61. Specifically, Oliver Wendell Holmes Sr. and John B. S. Jackson in 1847 and Henry Jacob Bigelow in 1849. Their close colleague Jeffries Wyman, though technically not on the Medical College faculty, was also hired by Harvard in 1847.

13 **His lungs had suffered from youthful overindulging**: William Sturgis Bigelow, *A Memoir of Henry Jacob Bigelow*, 15.

13 **"We still linger upon the lower steps"**: Henry Jacob Bigelow, *An Introductory Lecture*, 4.

13 **students also included a number of MDs**: Harvard University, *Catalogue*, 17.

13 **"Pain, but recently an object of insuperable terror"**: Henry Jacob Bigelow, *An Introductory Lecture*, 13.

14 **Roxanna Cook case**: *Emancipator & Republican* (Boston), 15 December 1848.

14 **"Suppose that a severe blow"**: Henry Jacob Bigelow, *An Introductory Lecture*, 14

15 **"tumors, out-growths, or diseased enlargements"**: Advertisement for Henry J. Bigelow, *Boston Medical and Surgical Journal*, 27 April 1853, n.p.

15 **It proved to be a needle**: *CC*, 6 September 1849.

15 **"A good sized crowbar"**: Henry Jacob Bigelow, *An Introductory Lecture*, 15.

15 **clattering down eighty feet away**: *Vermont Mercury*, quoted in Macmillan, *An Odd Kind of Fame*, 36.

15 **"about half a teacupful of the brain"**: Henry Jacob Bigelow, "Dr. Harlow's Case of Recovery," 16.

15 **"in a day or two"**: Ibid., 17.

16 **"inseparable companion"**: Harlow, "Recovery from the Passage," 277.

16 **"no longer Gage"**: Ibid.

16 "WONDERFUL ACCIDENT": quoted in Macmillan, *An Odd Kind of Fame*, 36.

16 "the greasy feel and look of the iron": Henry Jacob Bigelow, "Dr. Harlow's Case of Recovery," 15.

16 a talking mynah bird in his consulting room: William Sturgis Bigelow, *A Memoir of Henry Jacob Bigelow*, 169.

16 Bigelow had nearly been kicked out of Harvard: Ibid., 11.

16 turned rather childish and profane: Harlow, "Recovery from the Passage," 279.

17 life mask: Macmillan, *An Odd Kind of Fame*, 42.

17 "a common skull": Henry Jacob Bigelow, "Dr. Harlow's Case of Recovery," 21.

17 "Remarkable Stalagmite": Macmillan, *An Odd Kind of Fame*, 45

17 over the Smith & Clark pharmacy: Mumford, *The Story of the Boston Society*, 5.

17 the "Med. Fac.": "The First School at Newtowne," 194.

18 even he could be prevailed upon to contribute: "Suspected Murder of George Parkman, M.D.," 367.

18 "The iron entered there and passed through my head": Harlow, "Recovery from the Passage," 275.

18 "The leading feature of this case is its improbability": Henry Jacob Bigelow, "Dr. Harlow's Case of Recovery," 19.

18 "as if it had been a pie-crust": William Sturgis Bigelow, *A Memoir of Henry Jacob Bigelow*, 120.

18 "fell through the decks": Jackson, *A Descriptive Catalogue of the Anatomical Museum*, 16.

19 "very dense and as firm as parchment": Ibid.

19 an essay on the disordered mind of Jonathan Swift: "Suspected Murder of George Parkman, M.D.," 367.

19 conjoined twins from his doctoring days: Jackson, *A Descriptive Catalogue of the Anatomical Museum*, 297.

3. The Skeleton Box

20 the inevitable alkali burns and acid splashes: *TGB*, 258.

20 a long table had been shoved up against a corner window: *TDM*, 24. The illustration in the *Boston Daily Mail* trial transcript shows some minor additional detail beyond the floor plans provided in the Bemis account.

20 **just three professors and a six-week term**: Warren et al., *Report of the Overseers*, 4–5. The respective developments noted are: the stethoscope (1816), the AMA (1847), the *Lancet* (1823), ether (1846), Semmelweis on hand washing and "puerperal fever" (1847), and the graduation of Elizabeth Blackwell (1849).

21 **a tightly wound private staircase**: *TDM*, 24.

21 **Monday, the one weekday when he did not**: *TGB*, 21.

21 **Webster had cut his hand**: *TJS*, 86.

21 *That vault*, **he absently asked**: *TJS*, 60.

21 **"We took up the brick floor"**: *TGB*, 100.

22 **an outing to scout a new cemetery location**: *BB*, 23 November 1849.

22 **"It is not alone when the stench becomes"**: *CC*, 4 October 1849.

22 **"It is a good time now"**: *TGB*, 101.

23 **Webster's lab was tucked**: *TGB*, frontispiece. See also the floor plans accompanying the Bemis volume.

23 **niece up from Connecticut**: *TJS*, 81.

23 **anatomical mannequins, imported**: Sappol, *A Traffic of Dead Bodies*, 192.

23 **While in other cities, corpses could be**: Ibid., 117.

23 **sailors were especially prized**: Ibid., 116.

23 **Harvard had some legal right**: Small, *Oliver Wendell Holmes*, 65.

23 **in bulk on the Manhattan black market**: Sappol, *A Traffic of Dead Bodies*, 115.

23 **five-dollar fee for access**: Harvard University, *Catalogue*, 61.

24 **author being a recent dropout**: Sappol, *A Traffic of Dead Bodies*, 216.

24 **"What possible harm can it do"**: Robinson, *Marietta*, 6.

24 **"visiting relatives in the city"**: Carroll, *The Manchester Tragedy*, 9.

24 **"Her body was carried to Boston"**: *New Hampshire Patriot and State Gazette*, 15 June 1848.

24 **"nature was not sparing in its ornaments"**: Carroll, *The Manchester Tragedy*, 7.

25 **baggage marked GLASS**: Ibid., 12.

25 **"a young girl, 20 years old, perfectly fresh"**: Ibid., 18.

25 **"If I send a man with ten dollars"**: Ibid., 19.

25 **"Never in my practice have I seen anything like this puncture"**: Ibid., 20.

25 **"Bury it"**: Ibid., 20.

26 **"No exertions are spared"**: Harvard University, *Catalogue*, 61.

26 **"He said I should feel very badly indeed"**: Hoar, *Autobiography of Seventy Years*, 101.

26 **You could show the absorption of gases**: Webster, *A Manual of Chemistry*, 119.

26 **you could separate out the serum**: Ibid., 493.

26 **cook down that serum into pink crystals**: Jones, *On Animal Chemistry*, 29.

27 **Webster, as a hired expert**: *New Hampshire Sentinel*, 30 September 1847. The example noted here is the poisoning trial of Stephen Harris Jr., though Webster testified in a number of others as well.

27 **"as much as a pint"**: *TGB*, 101.

27 **The shelf by the stairs**: *TDM*, 24.

27 **"Get it full, if you can"**: *TGB*, 101.

27 **Littlefield gently set the jar down**: Ibid., 101.

27 **"a gentleman's hands are clean"**: Holmes, *Puerperal Fever as a Private Pestilence*, 60.

27 **a tape measure in his pocket to measure tree trunks**: Holmes, "The Autocrat of the Breakfast-Table," 361. Though this account is rendered in Holmes's narrative guise of the "Autocrat," decades later he would describe the same activity in his 1887 travelogue *Our Hundred Days in Europe*.

28 **"Professor Bones"**: Tilton, *The Amiable Aristocrat*, 197.

28 **"My subject this afternoon"**: Ibid., 196.

28 **"Here, take the bone!"**: Kennedy, *Oliver Wendell Holmes*, 121.

28 **skeleton boxes maintained for checkout**: Ibid., 122.

28 **John Hathaway worked in the apothecary shop**: "Trial for Malpractice," 16. Hathaway's name is inconsistently and often incorrectly identified in various trial transcripts; he is John Eaton Hathaway, Harvard Medical Class of 1852. Cf. D. Hamilton Hurd, compiler, *History of Worcester County, Massachusetts* (Philadelphia: J. W. Lewis, 1889) 2:1568.

29 **auditing all of Webster and Holmes's lectures**: *TGB*, 140.

29 **"I think we shall bleed someone tomorrow morning"**: *TGB*, 101.

4. The Great World Goes Clanging On

30 **back to his Cambridge home by two**: *TGB*, 253.

30 **finishing *The Seaside and the Fireside***: JHL, 19 November 1849.

30 **"the place we have selected for ourselves"**: JHL, 22 November 1849.

31 **"Harvard Hill"**: Dearborn, *Guide Through Mount Auburn*, 4.

31 **Lot 580 on Indian Ridge Path**: King, *Mount Auburn Cemetery*, 100.

31 **"without one feeling of dread"**: Longfellow, letter to George Washington Greene, 31 May 1837, *The Letters of Henry Wadsworth Longfellow*, 1:27.

31 **"The foliage all gone"**: JHL, 22 November 1849.

31 *"Take them, O Grave!"*: Longfellow, *The Seaside and the Fireside*, 50.

31 **"again the great world goes clanging on"**: JHL, 6 August 1849.

32 **Ground had been broken three weeks earlier**: *CC,* 1 November 1849.

32 **just north of Harvard Yard**: Lovet, "The Harvard Branch Railroad," 31.

32 **railway's board still hadn't even voted**: Ibid., 33.

32 **"He says," Longfellow recalled**: JHL, 27 October 1849.

32 **a $1,000 check in the mail**: Ibid., 28 November 1849.

2 **gift from his father-in-law**: Charles Calhoun, *Longfellow: A Rediscovered Life*, 167.

33 **were Harvard men themselves**: Story, *The Forging of an Aristocracy*, 81, 84.

33 **A typical Harvard professor's net worth**: Ibid., 84.

33 **language instructors had earned a stingy $500**: Doyle, "Poets Can Be Professors," 89.

33 *"four-in-hand* **of outlandish animals"**: Longfellow, letter to Stephen Longfellow, 29 October 1837, *The Letters of Henry Wadsworth Longfellow*, 1:46.

33 **firing of a German instructor for abolitionism**: Johnson, *Professor Longfellow of Harvard*, 9.

33 **piled many of their former classes into Longfellow's**: Ibid., 38.

33 **"a cloud of mystery in his life"**: Quoted in La Piana, *Dante's American Pilgrimage*, 46.

33 **real name was Bartolo**: Gallenga, *Episodes of My Second Life*, 62.

34 **"given up to pawnbrokers, gin-shops"**: Ibid.

34 **"I never drink more than is good for me"**: Ibid., 65.

34 **"like a horse that has once fallen on its knees"**: Ibid., 102.

34 **president of the Boston chapter of the Italian Charitable**: *BA,* 19 July 1842.

34 **"Mr. Everett cold!"**: Gallenga, *Episodes of My Second Life,* 105.

34 **"not to be trifled with"**: Doyle, "Poets Can Be Professors," 89.

35 **"Poor Bachi!"**: La Piana, *Dante's American Pilgrimage*, 48.

35 **piano and violin soiree**: JHL, 30 October 1849.

35 **idly wishing that he'd taken up music**: Ibid., 10 March 1862.

35 **treatise on the science of sound**: Peirce, *An Elementary Treatise on Sound*.

35 **played French horn and attacked the drums**: Thorndike, "Henry J. Bigelow," 233.

35 **local dancing master led his seven-thirty class**: *CC*, 8 November 1849.

35 **the town still had no streetlamps**: *CC*, 25 October 1849.

36 **a stone perron column**: JHL, 22 April 1848.

36 **the attire of a thirteenth-century feudal lord**: Homer, *Nahant, and Other Places*, 48.

36 **His wife's grandfather had risen**: Wilson, *The Aristocracy of Boston*, 28.

36 **"a chateau as Monte-Christo might have lavished"**: *Hartford Daily Courant*, 4 February 1871.

36 **animal rugs, a fountain of cologne**: Kirker and van Zanten, "Jean Lemoulnier in Boston," 207.

36 **"young cherubs tumbling about"**: Woolson, *Browsing Among Books*, 228.

36 **Deacon had bought the furnishings**: Kirker and van Zanten, "Jean Lemoulnier in Boston," 205.

37 **Gobelin tapestries on the landing**: Woolson, *Browsing Among Books*, 220.

37 **"It haunts me like a vision"**: JHL, 22 April 1848.

37 **midnight prank of rolling cannonballs**: Muzzey, "College Life Under President Kirkland," 138.

5. A Bad Business

41 **long, vertiginous spiral staircase**: The trapezoidal steps and spiderweb transom are still visible in the house today.

41 **his manservant, Patrick**: *TGB*, 42.

41 **stopping by before the clock had chimed nine**: *TJS*, 30.

41 **"I will be there at half past one o'clock"**: *TDM*, 8.

42 **Beacon Hill Reservoir, opened its valves**: Bradlee, *History of the Introduction of Pure Water*, 117.

42 **population had already more than doubled**: Gibson, *Population of the 100 Largest Cities*, unpaginated. Boston's population was 61,392 in the 1830 census and 136,881 in the 1850 census.

42 **"procuring elastic pipes"**: *CC*, 12 July 1849.

42 **"a perpetual supply of pure water"**: Bradlee, *History of the Introduction of Pure Water*, 108.

42 **wooden benches had been replaced**: Barber, *Boston Common*, 158.

42 **throw out the scruffy boys bathing in the Frog Pond**: Ibid., 159.

42 **"Some of the patients bathe six times a day"**: *Historic Americana Auc-*

tion, Shaw letter dated 18 July 1849, in Lot 573, "Robert Gould Shaw Archive."

43 **"stimulating diet is fuel to their disease"**: George Parkman, *Management of Lunatics,* 18.

43 **gentlemen parted by the Merchant Bank on State Street**: *TGB,* 42.

43 *tens* **of thousands of dollars at a time**: *Final Report of the Committee on the Erection of the New Jail,* 38.

43 **the imposing exterior columns**: Drake, *Old Landmarks and Historic Personages,* 94.

43 *"The devil you have!"*: *TGB,* 104.

43 **a sizable fortune from his father**: *Records of Proceedings of the City Council of Boston,* entry for 27 December 1909, 784–85.

44 **a proposed new bridge, he lobbied against**: *Salem Gazette,* 13 January 1826.

44 **extending a wharf, he lobbied for it**: *BA,* 23 February 1846.

44 **for 111 real estate transactions**: Sullivan, *The Disappearance of Dr. Parkman,* 4.

44 **hired his own agent, Mr. Kingsley**: *TGB,* 33.

44 **"I should think"**: Ibid., 162.

44 **Merchant's Bank was still an outpost**: Drake, *Old Landmarks and Historic Personages,* 94.

44 **whipping post, a brutally stout wooden beam**: Ibid., 93.

44 **inaugurated by the carpenter who built them**: Winsor and Jewett, *The Memorial History of Boston,* 1:506.

44 **"SYMPATHY FOR MURDERERS"**: *BB,* 23 November 1849.

44 **he'd sent a fellow to prison**: *BA,* 24 August 1849.

44 **an Irishman who'd stolen**: *BH,* 3 August 1849.

44 **$1,500 in cash, plus over $300 in checks**: *Weekly Messenger* (Boston), 23 May 1849.

45 **Officer Clapp discovered**: *BT,* 18 May 1849.

45 **as he reported to work in the morning**: *Weekly Messenger* (Boston), 23 May 1849.

45 **"Never go to law"**: *BH,* 20 December 1849.

45 **cart was loaded with pig iron**: *TGB,* 55.

45 **Two horses could be expected to steadily**: "Notes on Roads and Railways," 180.

46 **hauler being named Marsh**: *TGB,* 55.

46 **stopped for a moment to gawk**: Ibid., 54.

46 **driver at least showed enough forbearance**: *TJS*, 35.

46 **rolling their heavy castings**: Ibid., 55.

46 **donated it for the new Medical College**: Holmes, *The Benefactors of the Medical School*, 31.

46 ***Parkman George, physician, house 8 Walnut***: *The Boston Directory* (1849), 225.

47 **He'd suffered poor health in his own childhood**: Holmes, *The Benefactors of the Medical School*, 17.

47 **Harvard at scarcely fifteen**: Ibid., 19.

47 **the local rate for house calls**: Boston Medical Association, *Boston Medical Police*, 17.

47 **surgeon for the Massachusetts militia**: Holmes, *The Benefactors of the Medical School*, 21.

47 **offered some of his many homes as field hospitals**: Ibid., 28–29.

47 **a riverside lot he'd sold to the city**: *Final Report of the Committee on the Erection of the New Jail*, 38.

47 **the death of a prostitute, Pamela Percy**: *Salem Gazette*, 17 April 1821.

47 **Jonathan Houghton**: *Haverhill Gazette*, 21 January 1826.

47 **"I have no doubt but that the deceased died"**: *Masonic Mirror* (Boston), 21 January 1826.

48 **in the doorway of the local corner grocer**: *TDM*, 10.

48 **some thirty-two pounds of it**: *TGB*, 57.

48 **cut off a six-pound portion**: Ibid.

48 **"any time in the afternoon"**: *TTD*, 10.

48 **"We cannot find fault with such weather"**: *TGB*, 52.

48 ***Might I leave this with you for five minutes?***: W. E. Bigelow, *The Boston Tragedy*, 5. This very early account, published after Webster's arrest, cites Holland recalling "five" minutes; later accounts of the trial show Holland recalling it as either "five" or "a few."

49 **grocer finally peeked inside**: *TGB*, 57.

6. A Gentleman Unknown

50 **thirteen years of working for George Parkman**: *TTD*, 7.

50 **Kingsley had come by at three p.m.**: *TGB*, 30.

50 **Word was sent a block over to Robert Gould Shaw**: Ibid., 31

51 **Bowdoin Square, where the Reverend Francis Parkman**: *The Boston Directory* (1849), 225.

51   **now in the railway shipping business**: *BB*, 24 February 1848.

51   **served as city marshal**: *The Boston Almanac for the Year 1843*, 31.

52   **their fears were immediate and blunt**: *TGB*, 31.

52   **to the office of John C. Park, Esq.**: Ibid., 43.

52   **he'd added four counterfeiters to his rolls**: *Emancipator & Republican* (Boston), 29 November 1849.

52   **an assault case between two stage actors**: Gill, *Selections from Court Reports*, 94.

52   **served side by side with Blake**: *BA*, 31 October 1849.

52   *Impossible*, **the lawyer replied**: *TGB*, 31.

52   **he wouldn't be out for another fourteen months**: *BA*, 24 August 1849.

53   **simple silver jug**: *BA*, 18 August 1848.

53   **the dramatic collapse the summer before**: *BT*, 26 June 1848.

53   **Tukey had also carried a printer's apprentice**: *Daily Crescent* (Baton Rouge), 21 March 1848.

54   **"a voice of cast-iron"**: *San Francisco Bulletin*, 19 June 1863.

54   **dark and piercing eyes**: Bungay, *Crayon Sketches and Off-hand Takings*, 102.

54   **profession it was rumored he'd worked**: *A Narrative of the Life and Adventures of Francis Tukey*, 10. This can at best be called a rumor, as the publication was an anonymously authored ("By One Who Knows Him") hatchet job published by the *Boston Herald*, which vehemently opposed Tukey.

54   **Madam Hufeland**: *BT*, 21 November 1849. Hufeland advertised herself as "The Celebrated German Female Physician" through local ads (e.g. *BH*, 18 September 1848), most notably selling "Female Monthly Pills" as a "remover of menstrual obstructions," while cautioning "married ladies against the use of these pills during pregnancy"—common code words in nineteenth-century advertisements to sell abortifacients.

54   **petitioned the city council to throw Tukey out**: *Springfield Republican*, 9 May 1849.

54   **his house had had its linens burgled**: *BT*, 25 July 1849.

55   **trains would be arriving by two p.m.**: *TGB*, 47.

55   **improper ash disposal**: *BT*, 7 May 1847.

55   **insufficient snow removal from sidewalks**: *BT*, 28 November 1846.

55   **"DR. GEORGE PARKMAN"**: *BT*, 24 November 1849. Though many accounts note the later ads, which included a physical description of Parkman and a reward, perusing that evening's newspapers shows that this more minimal notice without a reward was what initially ran.

56   a *Journal* reporter who had been loitering: *TGB*, 47.
56   Charles Kingsley waited at Dr. Parkman's mansion: Ibid., 33.
56   He picked up the doctor's trail on Bromfield: Ibid., 34.
56   feather selling and shade painting: *The Boston Directory* (1849), 75.
56   Paine & Newcomb's Fruit and Refreshments: Ibid., 51.
57   habitually stopped at Kingsley's: *TBH*, 10.
57   Half a dozen police officers: *TJS*, 26.
57   descended into one damp cellar after another: *TGB*, 34.
57   Grove Street Murder: *BH*, 30 October 1849.
57   "Old fellow, are you following me?": *BB*, 30 October 1849.
58   the last unequivocal sighting: *TGB*, 57.
58   *Can you take the lettuce:* Ibid., 34.

7. The Yellow Envelope

59   the day constable roster was called: Edward Savage, *A Chronological History*, 376.
59   *Derastus Clapp . . . Lucian Drury*: *The Boston Directory* (1849), 19.
59   "the Police were not usually overstocked": Savage, *A Chronological History*, 375.
59   "Officers north of City Hall": Ibid., 376.
60   spreading fifty to sixty miles: *TGB*, 47.
60   ban the pernicious modern practice: *BT*, 26 January 1850. This became known in Massachusetts (and in many other cities) as the "Sunday Train Bill," and arguments over implementing or repealing the ban on Sunday travel persisted well into the twentieth century.
60   "The general enquiry": *BB*, 26 October 1849.
60   houses and vacant lots, sweeping over the half-constructed: *TGB*, 34.
60   the cold was creeping back in: Ibid., 94.
60   "There comes one of our professors now": Ibid., 106.
61   "I never knew that Dr. Parkman had disappeared": Ibid., 127.
62   a crony from the local customhouse: *TJS*, 166.
62   gravel spread over its planking: Bowen, *Bowen's Picture of Boston*, 85.
62   peered in through the window: *TGB*, 33.
62   men took to searching around the docks: *Boston Courier*, 26 November 1849.
63   rumor placed Dr. Parkman in Salem: Ibid.
63   "Both had on green pants": *BB*, 26 November 1849.

63 **All of 48 South Russell Street**: *The Boston Directory* (1849), 278.

63 **reputed to be haunted**: *BH,* 5 May 1848.

63 **last week he'd hosted a friend's funeral**: *BA,* 17 November 1849.

63 **the scene of an ax murder**: *Life of Michael Powers,* 8.

64 **newly cleaned ax**: *Hampshire Gazette* (Northampton MA), 14 March 1820.

64 **"large enough to pass his finger into"**: *Weekly Messenger* (Boston), 13 April 1820.

64 **pitched face-first into the fire**: *Hampshire Gazette* (Northampton, MA), 14 March 1820.

64 **"The most he could say"**: *Life of Michael Powers,* 15.

64 **unearthed a sum of over $1,000**: *BB,* 11 May 1848.

65 **another house reputed to be haunted**: *Vermont Phoenix,* 1 September 1848.

65 **up and down Leverett Street**: *Awful Disclosures and Startling Developments,* 8.

65 **"We want to look around this college"**: *TNY,* 26. This entire exchange with Littlefield is drawn from this trial transcript.

66 **a fifteen-dollar French silver watch**: *BB,* 27 November 1849.

66 **waxed twine for candlewicks**: *BT,* 28 November 1849.

66 **a grubby yellow envelope**: *TJS,* 122.

8. Some Aberration of Mind

67 **"The supposition of those who know him"**: *Boston Courier,* 26 November 1849.

67 **engaged in subtle blackmail**: Jackson, "Digging for Dirt." Jackson notes that this was a specialty of William Joseph Snelling, a previous editor of the *Boston Herald.*

67 **successfully lobbied for new furnishings**: *BT,* 27 November 1849.

68 **"subject to depression"**: Frothingham, *Boston Unitarianism,* 162.

68 **breakdown for a substantial part of 1844**: Sprague, *Annals of the American Unitarian Pulpit,* 451.

68 **"conditions of the nervous system"**: Francis Parkman, *The Francis Parkman Reader,* 10.

68 **He'd begged his friends to warn him**: Farnham, *A Life of Francis Parkman,* 317.

68 **he'd visited insane asylums**: *Boston Commercial Gazette,* 21 July 1814.

68 **A week after graduating from the Medical College**: *Portland Gazette* (Maine), 2 July 1814; *Columbian Centinel* (Boston), 13 July 1814.

68 **"salutary exercise and employments"**: George Parkman, *Proposals for Establishing a Retreat*, 9.

68 **the design of its beds**: George Parkman, *Management of Lunatics*, 28.

68 **"a mile from Boston, on a gravelly eminence"**: Ibid., 36.

69 **"Temperaments, features, humors, are transmitted"**: "Evidences of Insanity," *Boston Medical Journal*, 14 January 1835, 368.

69 **"Almost everybody is occasionally indifferent to life"**: George Parkman, *Remarks on Insanity* (Boston, 1818), 3.

69 **"SPECIAL NOTICE!"**: *BT*, 27 November 1849.

70 **as much as one of the city's detectives earned**: *BH*, 18 August 1849.

70 *I saw him at six o'clock*: *BH*, 26 November 1849.

70 **"Henri Le Rennet"**: Quinn, *Edgar Allan Poe*, 116.

70 **sixteen-year-old boy who vanished**: *Salem Register*, 22 January 1849.

71 **"her friends feel much alarmed"**: *BT*, 15 November 1848.

71 **Tukey once found a sixteen-year-old girl**: *Constitution* (Middletown, CT), 10 February 1847.

71 **ticket masters at railroads were also the eyes**: *BH*, 26 November 1849.

71 **a drunken carpenter recently found**: *BH*, 26 September 1849.

71 **desperate friends even consulted mesmerists**: *BT*, 15 September 1849. The missing man in question was one James G. Perkins; he was the subject of a number of local articles at the time.

72 **the deliveryman finally turned up**: *BH*, 18 September 1849.

72 **the open case of Franklin Taylor**: *BT*, 12 February 1850.

72 **stopped by the offices of a religious newspaper**: *BH*, 26 November 1849.

73 **He'd been on the force for some twenty years**: *Boston Patriot*, 30 October 1829.

73 **The only person with much enthusiasm**: *TGB*, 37.

73 **Rumors had him begging**: Macmillan, *An Odd Kind of Fame*, 96.

73 **"Show them everything"**: *TGB*, 109.

73 **officers snickering at him**: Ibid., 37.

73 **"Let us go into Dr. Webster's apartments"**: Ibid., 109.

74 **"We can't believe"**: Ibid., 154.

74 **"That's where I keep my dangerous articles"**: Ibid., 109.

74 **"What place is this?"**: Ibid., 171.

75 **"If we search the college first"**: Ibid., 154.

75 **improbable array of patent-office contraptions**: *BB*, 26 November 1849.

75 **two seven-year stretches in prison**: *BT*, 24 December 1849.

75 **machinery for brick manufacturing**: *BB*, 26 November 1849.

75 **he'd be caught stealing again**: *BH*, 23 April 1857. The thief, Daniel Lombard Jr., did in fact get seven years, and he reoffended almost immediately in 1857 by stealing $500 from a stationery shop. His interest in inventions appears genuine, though: someone by the same name in Boston patented a "rice hulling machine" in 1860 (*BT*, 25 October 1860).

76 **Clapp had worked for years as an auctioneer**: *Boston Daily Advertiser*, 11 February 1820.

76 **tracking down auction room swindlers**: *Boston Patriot*, 12 August 1826.

76 **"$100 REWARD"**: *TGB*, 48.

76 **more unconfirmed leads**: *BC*, 29 November 1849.

9. Thanksgiving by the Fire

81 **twelve thousand on Boston Common**: *CC*, 20 July 1849.

81 **converting half the inmates**: *CC*, 6 September 1849.

81 **fond as he was of staying up late, dancing**: *TGB*, 115.

81 **a new deck of cards**: Ibid., 124.

81 **acknowledgment of the new day**: *Trenton State Gazette*, 25 March 1850.

81 **they'd stowed a load of soft coal**: *TGB*, 112.

81 **"a cold-feeling kind of man"**: Ibid., 129.

82 **not just on time but *early***: Ibid., 112.

82 **experiments the doctor didn't want disturbed**: Ibid.

82 **had a trusty utility knife**: Ibid., 129.

82 **thin section of partitioning**: *TNY*, 19 The *Globe* transcription specifies that the partition was wood.

82 ***Come back!***: *TGB*, 136.

83 **lay down on the cold brick floor**: Ibid., 129.

83 **Only the professor's legs were visible**: Ibid., 112. Details of the remainder of this section come from the same source.

84 ***Do you know where Mr. Foster's is***: Ibid., 111.

84 **"Take that order, and get you a nice turkey"**: *TJS*, 65. Trial transcripts vary about whether Littlefield went out for his turkey on Tuesday or Wednesday, and Littlefield's own recollection changed on this point. However, all the transcripts note a long shopping trip with Mrs. Littlefield on Wednesday, and a number of them (including the *Boston Her-*

ald transcript) peg the visit to Foster's as being on Wednesday. Earlier sources, such as the *Pittsfield Sun* of 6 December 1849, also note this day.

84 **corner police watch box**: Stark, *Stark's Antique Views*, 347.

84 **sign announcing A. A. FOSTER & CO.**: Bergen, *Old Boston in Early Photographs*, 95.

84 **occupied by the Millerite**: Drake, *Old Landmarks and Historic Personages*, 367.

84 **farce titled *The Irish Secretary***: *BA*, 27 November 1849.

84 **Harvard students there**: Rantoul, *Report of the Harvard Class of 1853*, 213.

84 **seventy-five-cent box seats**: *BB*, 26 November 1849. There were cheap seats there, too—just twelve and a half cents.

84 **lard, pork, butter, and turkey**: *Boston Traveler*, 9 February 1858.

84 ***Pick whichever turkey you like***: *TJS*, 65.

84 **order for a bushel of sweet potatoes**: *TGB*, 134.

85 **made the run out to Cambridge hundreds**: Ibid., 147.

85 ***I want a piece about as big as your head***: Ibid., 114.

85 **felt a curious warmth**: Ibid., 112.

85 **ran into the chemistry lecture hall**: Ibid., 113.

86 **muddy tidal flats**: W. E. Bigelow, *The Boston Tragedy*, 8.

86 **double windows to the lab**: *TJS*, 66.

86 **Littlefield had never broken into**: *TTD*, 28.

86 **pitch pine kindling he'd brought in on Friday**: *TGB*, 113.

86 **furnace was out but still radiated heat**: Ibid., 130.

86 **a broom from the corner of the coal pen**: *TBJ*, 21.

86 **one was empty, the other nearly so**: *TGB*, 113.

86 **up the back stairs to the lecture hall**: Ibid., 113.

86 **hard pine steps**: *Awful Disclosures and Startling Developments*, 10.

87 **days since he'd washed any glassware**: *TDM*, 22.

87 **perhaps fifteen minutes or more**: *TBJ*, 22.

87 **probing the frigid and murky water**: *TGB*, 47.

10. The Final Reward

88 **Dr. Webster had returned unexpectedly**: *TGB*, 253.

88 **in the Garden Street home for only two weeks**: Ibid., 253.

88 **two parlors, six bedrooms, sumptuous carpeting**: Burnett, Amelia Burnett Diary, n.d., Folder 1.

88 **up every morning at five o'clock**: Ibid., 22 March 1847.
88 **Websters kept their house stoked so warm**: Ibid., n.d., Folder 1.
88 **illustrated edition of Milton's pastoral "L'Allegro"**: *TGB*, 252.
89 **Hattie had even built herself a little studio**: Burnett, Amelia Burnett Diary, 18 August 1848.
89 **none shared the doctor's enthusiasm**: Ibid., 22 March 1847.
89 **installed an open-air gym on Harvard's grounds**: *Portsmouth Journal of Literature and Politics*, 6 May 1826. This was very much an undertaking of the moment; gymnastics were a new fitness craze in 1826, and Webster was joined in the effort by his friend and colleague Dr. Charles Follen. Along with painstakingly keeping track of weights and repetitions, they set up a "a dynamometer . . . by which the strength of every part of the body can be ascertained."
89 **nectarines, pears**: *Newburyport Herald*, 21 September 1830.
89 **currants**: Burnett, Amelia Burnett Diary, 3 July 1847.
89 **provided fruit and floral displays**: *Newburyport Herald*, 21 September 1830; *BT,* 24 November 1833.
89 **carefully packed boxes of precious bulbs**: *TDM*, 42.
90 **they'd been flying in formations overhead**: *BC*, 29 November 1849.
90 **"a very porous wood"**: *TGB*, 567.
90 **a new method of tanning leather**: Ibid., 570.
90 **missed the rush of the gutta-percha trade**: Burnett, Amelia Burnett Diary, December 1847.
90 **his knife had slipped**: *TDM*, 36.
90 **boarded the six-twenty p.m. omnibus**: *TGB*, 252.
90 **Mrs. Webster and daughter Hattie both stayed home**: Ibid., 252.
90 **Hattie had recently become engaged**: Jarnagin, *A Confluence of Transatlantic Networks*, 103.
90 **Sarah and Hattie who took after their father**: Burnett, Amelia Burnett Diary, n.d., Folder 1.
91 **Mrs. Cunningham's house on Vine Street**: *The Boston Directory* (1849), 109.
91 **a tangle of maritime trading clans**: Jarnagin, *A Confluence of Transatlantic Networks*, 103. Jarnagin's study is especially helpful and comprehensive in explaining the web of familial and commercial relationships between these families.
91 **"dignified and severely polite"**: State Street Trust Company, *Some Merchants and Sea Captains of Old Boston*, 17.
91 **Andrew and Charles sat atop fortunes**: *Our First Men*, 19.

91   **through a hole cut into**: State Street Trust Company, *Some Merchants and Sea Captains of Old Boston*, 17.

91   **with little economies visible**: Burnett, Amelia Burnett Diary, 24 November 1846.

91   **an inordinate love of Italian opera**: Ibid., 22 March 1847

91   *is trying to bring over Jenny Lind*: *CC*, 22 November 1849.

91   **imported Sicilian lemons and Portuguese Madeira**: State Street Trust Company, *Some Merchants and Sea Captains of Old Boston*, 17.

92   **"They think only professional men"**: LAN, Amelia Nye letter to Marianne Ivens, 4 October 1850.

92   **engaged to yet another Dabney brother**: Jarnagin, *A Confluence of Transatlantic Networks*, 102.

92   **The very doors and sheds of the college**: *TTD*, 29.

92   **"you were the last person"**: LAN, Amelia Nye letter to Marianne Ivens, 4 October 1850.

92   **The Websters left at ten-thirty**: *TGB*, 252.

92   **the theater omnibus, it was called**: *TDM*, 59.

93   **"livery stable keepers, omnibus proprietors"**: *BT*, 30 November 1849.

93   **piggybacked up to the tollbooth**: *CC*, 29 November 1849.

93   **craning to look up at yet another new handbill**: *TGB*, 254.

93   **"$1000 REWARD"**: Ibid., 48.

94   **railroad to Cambridge would not be ready**: *BC*, 29 November 1849.

94   **the remains of the old Cow Common**: Howe, "The History of Garden Street," 37.

94   **Mr. Sanderson**: *TDM*, 59.

94   **Hattie hadn't stayed up**: *TGB*, 252.

94   **a devotee of the *Evening Transcript***: Ibid., 251.

94   **shifted into his nightgown and stayed up**: Ibid., 252.

94   **"How many circles have been thinned"**: *BT*, 28 November 1849. The remainder of this section, except as noted, draws from that day's *Evening Transcript*.

95   **oyster sauce**: Howland, *The New England Economical Housekeeper*, 72. Oyster sauce, along with some other dishes no longer associated with the holiday—chicken pie and turnip sauce, for instance—is noted under this 1845 book's entry for "Thanksgiving Dinner." (Cranberry sauce and pumpkin pie, though, are indeed reassuringly present.)

11. Wickedness Takes Eleven

96 **"What a contrast"**: *BT,* 28 November 1849.

96 **one man upbraiding another's son**: *Christian Watchman* (Boston), 19 July 1846.

96 **The officers were trampled**: Ibid.

96 **"his knowledge-box"**: Savage, *A Chronological History,* 323.

97 **running a bakery in Salem**: *Salem Gazette,* 31 October 1834.

97 **he was hauled before a judge**: *Newark Daily Advertiser* (New Jersey), 22 October 1839.

97 **declared himself insolvent**: *Law Reporter* 2 (February 1840): 319.

97 **a new charge of selling liquor**: *Boston Traveler,* 9 July 1841.

97 **"nobody, probably, but Tukey"**: *A Narrative of the Life and Adventures of Francis Tukey,* 15.

97 **passed the bar in 1844**: *BT,* 18 March 1844.

97 **city marshal job in 1846**: *BT,* 23 June 1846.

97 **"a more promising candidate"**: *Salem Register,* 25 June 1846.

97 **an embezzler**: *A Narrative of the Life and Adventures of Francis Tukey,* 24.

97 **a necrophiliac**: Ibid., 6.

97 **a seducer of Sunday school teachers**: Ibid., 17.

97 **had in fact later died**: Ibid., 15.

97 **"a three-cent rumseller"**: *BH,* 11 September 1848.

97 **Tukey declared insolvency again**: *Law Reporter* 10 (June 1847): 48.

97 **"that he might go to hell"**: *BH,* 11 September 1848.

98 **Officer Burnham**: *BH,* 1 December 1849.

98 **Burnham was clobbered with a brick**: *BT,* 30 November 1849. The shopbreaker, one Michael Murphy, was finally hauled in and charged, and the wielder of the brick that injured Burnham proved to be none other than his would-be lookout, Dennis McCarty. When searched, McCarty was jangling with curious bits of metal that turned out to be barber's tools—peculiar things to take out on a holiday stroll, but much more explicable when a Broad Street barber's shop was found to have been broken into as well.

98 **window pried open and some $700**: *BT,* 30 November 1849.

98 **picked a house on Lexington Street**: *BB,* 1 December 1849.

98 **"I fought in Mexico"**: *BC,* 1 December 1849.

98 **still trying their luck at dragging the river**: Ibid.

99 **a missing Bostonian**: Ibid.

99 **this one down in Braintree**: Ibid.

99 "an honest old cobbler": Ibid.

99 Their turkey sat uneaten: *TGB*, 412.

99 they'd had turkey every Thanksgiving: Ibid., 140.

99 *Just as much as I am standing here*: Ibid., 135.

99 "What makes you think so?": Ibid., 23.

100 children had been scattering them: Ibid., 24.

100 three small pine boxes marked, in red chalk: Ibid., 148.

100 "You see?": Ibid., 24.

100 "He never gave me a present before this time": *TNY*, 26.

100 He'd had a sledgehammer: *TGB*, 102.

101 *hammer on the floor four times*: Ibid., 114.

101 slid down the trap door: Ibid.

101 member of the Geological Society of London: Davies, *Whatever Is Under the Earth*, 66.

102 *"Nature requires five"*: *CC*, 25 October 1849.

102 out dancing until four in the morning: *TGB*, 115.

102 his wife had been waiting an hour: Ibid., 115.

102 managed to remove only a few bricks: Ibid.

102 "Is there any more news?": Ibid.

102 plenty of news that day: *BB*, 29 November 1849.

103 taken the omnibus into the city with a friend: *BA*, 3 December 1849.

103 stopped by Mr. Henchman's: *TGB*, 115.

103 decreed the licensing and numbering: Hobson, *Uneasy Virtue*, 42.

103 *It was covered*: *TGB*, 137.

103 "There are a great many stories": Ibid.

103 *He knows more than he lets on*: Ibid.

12. "I Shal Be Kiled"

104 "the whole region of animal propensities": Jackson, *A Descriptive Catalogue of the Warren Museum*, 714.

104 Madeline Albert: Ibid., 727. The catalog is a fascinating work in itself. Among its entries is one for a mask of a man named Hey: "A gentleman who considered if he tried, could ruin the government by gaining all the prizes in the lotteries; constantly inventing machines; immense hope" (718). Another intriguing entry is for "Abraham Courtney, a blind man, and formerly well known in this city. Remarkable for his sense of travelling, and faculty of finding places; being familiar with all the streets and

lanes in Boston, Cincinnati, and New York. He travelled by himself in nearly every state in the Union, after he became blind. Locality uncommonly large" (725).

104 **hauling plaster busts into Dr. Holmes's anatomy lecture**: *TGB*, 115.

104 **acquired the immense holdings in plaster heads**: Warren, "The Collection of the Boston Phrenological Society," 1.

105 **gentle suggestion of this emeritus**: Holmes, letter of Oliver Wendell Holmes Sr. to John Collins Warren, 28 February 1850.

105 **a $5,000 donation**: Harvard University, *Twenty-third Annual Report*, Treasurer's Statement (unpaginated). As noted elsewhere in the text, for a few years Harvard, largely at its president's behest, called itself the University at Cambridge.

105 **"diffident to approach the subject"**: Holmes, letter of Oliver Wendell Holmes Sr. to John Collins Warren, 28 February 1850.

105 **"degenerates and celebrated criminals"**: Warren, "The Collection of the Boston Phrenological Society," 1.

105 **He took the doctor aside**: *TGB*, 115.

105 **about to become engaged to Dr. Parkman's son**: *Milwaukee Sentinel*, 21 May 1850.

105 **"Go ahead with it"**: *TGB*, 115.

106 **Jackson who'd been among the first**: *BH*, 14 June 1848.

106 **"Go to Dr. Holmes"**: *TGB*, 116.

106 **book of poetry coming out**: *BT*, 1 December 1849.

106 **"Go to the elder Dr. Bigelow"**: *TGB*, 116.

107 **"which poured a feeble stream of cold water"**: Lawrence, *Old Park Street and Its Vicinity*, 99.

107 **produced many of the cast-iron pipes**: *American Traveller* (Boston), 21 November 1846.

107 **"I guess you do"**: *TGB*, 116.

107 **a letter addressed to Marshal Tukey**: Ibid., 196.

108 **"Dr Parkman was took on Bord"**: Ibid., 210.

108 *Herculean*—**and it had set sail**: *Boston Courier*, 29 November 1849.

108 **unremarkable cotton runs**: *Boston Daily Advertiser*, 15 March 1841.

108 **save a sinking ship's crew**: *Whalemen's Shipping List and Merchant's Transcript* (New Bedford, MA), 20 January 1849.

108 **it didn't budge**: *TGB*, 37.

108 *Clink*: Ibid., 138.

108 **overalls muddy**: Ibid., 57.

109 **"I've made a fool of you this time"**: Ibid., 116.

109 "Let us go into his laboratory": Ibid.

109 "Can we not get in, then?": Ibid., 181

109 Littlefield had known George: Ibid., 144.

109 he pointed out the entryway: Ibid.

110 "You have just saved your bacon": Ibid., 117.

110 collected the long-neglected grapevines: Ibid., 137.

110 "What about that twenty-dollar bill?": Ibid., 144.

110 A draft was pulling cold air: Ibid., 117.

111 water could collect to the height of a man: Ibid., 118.

13. Pistols Drawn

115 sitting down to his dinner: William Sturgis Bigelow, *A Memoir of Henry Jacob Bigelow*, 117.

115 "a whole bushel of locks": Ibid., 295. The remainder of this scene is drawn from William Sturgis Bigelow's account.

116 the marshal, Kingsley, the lawyer James Blake: *TGB*, 49.

116 highwaymen had held up a cab up: *BA*, 3 December 1849.

116 Trenholm had already beat them to the scene: *TGB*, 145.

117 he asked the detective to pass him the lamp: Ibid., 49.

117 water had been left running: Ibid., 50.

117 *was this, a human?*: Ibid., 50.

117 "No": *TNY*, 11.

117 every single one of them had descended: *TGB*, 145.

117 "That is Webster": Ibid., 50.

117 Webster kept a loaded pistol in the lab: Ibid., 122.

118 Tukey toward the lab: Ibid., 50.

118 professor's hidden store of wine and liquor: *TNY*, 43.

118 sloping auditorium rows: Ibid., 50.

118 keep it slightly out of sight: *TJS*, 89.

119 still in his slippers: *TNY*, 38.

119 show a visitor to the gate: *TGB*, 155.

119 "How do you do, Mr. Clapp?": *BB*, 3 December 1849.

119 must be in great pain: *BA*, 3 December 1849.

119 into the professor's study: Ibid.

119 "I should like to go back": *TGB*, 155.

119 one favorite trick at the omnibus stops: Savage, *A Chronological History*, 237.

120 **sweethearts who hanged themselves**: Ibid., 72.

120 **Rat-fighting matches in saloons**: Ibid., 166.

120 **crackled over the Craigie Bridge**: *TGB*, 156.

120 **"There is a lady over there"**: Ibid.

120 **She'd apparently also seen Dr. Parkman**: *TNY*, 43.

120 **"Suppose we ride over there?"**: *TGB*, 156.

121 **"Dr. Webster, it is no use to disguise our purpose"**: *BJ*, 3 December 1849. Starkweather's and Clapp's trial accounts of the arrest give similar if slightly varied versions of this speech; Clapp's is the more florid of the two. This particular line, though, is not in either's trial recollections four months later—but it was noted by both the *Boston Daily Journal* and the *Boston Daily Evening Transcript* at the time of the arrest.

121 **"You recollect that I called your attention"**: *TGB*, 156.

121 **a writ of mittimus to be drawn**: Ibid., 178.

121 **"You are now in custody"**: Ibid., 156.

14. A Ruined Man

122 **"What!" Dr. Webster blurted**: *TGB*, 128.

122 **an inventory taken**: Ibid., 157.

122 **"Don't commit the doctor"**: Ibid.

122 **"Have they found Dr. Parkman?"**: Ibid., 179.

123 **old cannonballs had deliberately been embedded**: Drake, *Old Landmarks and Historic Personages*, 375.

123 **"My children, what will they do!"**: Ibid.

124 **Despite the cold of the jail**: Ibid., 38.

124 **Should they call a doctor?**: Ibid., 179.

124 **something like five thousand prisoners**: *BT*, 8 August 1849. There is a more specific breakdown in this report. For instance, Andrews reported to an inspection of county commissioners that between 4 December 1848 and 23 July 1849, the Leverett Street Jail had taken in "2177 criminals, 106 Commonwealth and United States witnesses, [and] 527 debtors."

124 **"I expected this"**: *TGB*, 192.

124 **he'd known John Webster and his father**: Ibid., 190.

124 **alumni secretary for the Class of '35**: "News from the Classes," 732.

124 **"my wife and children!"**: *TGB*, 109.

125 **"We do not come here to distress you"**: *BJ*, 3 December 1849.

125 *There isn't anything to explain*: *TGB*, 38.

125 "We've got Dr. Webster here!": Ibid., 119.
126 "is the coat that I lecture in": Ibid., 192.
126 "This is where I make examinations": *BA*, 3 December 1849.
126 discovered a parcel wrapped in paper: *TGB*, 179.
126 "Force the door!": Ibid., 119.
126 "You will find nothing but some bottles": Ibid., 59.
126 a set of filed keys: Ibid., 181.
126 "Where is the chimney that was so heated?": Ibid., 60.
127 "Don't disturb the bones": Ibid., 120.
127 a right calf, a right thigh, and a pelvis: Ibid., 38.
127 Tears were now streaming down his face: *TDM*, 21.
127 "I have nothing to say": *TGB*, 193.
127 body parts into the privy: Ibid., 146.
127 drove a nail halfway into the door frame: Ibid., 147.
127 folded the pants into the semblance of a pillow: Ibid., 257. Though some caution was already being exercised—as in Coroner Pratt telling officers to leave Webster's furnace alone—it would be nearly fifty years before the work of Hans Gross more widely popularized the idea of securing a crime scene.
128 arms and legs had stiffened: Ibid., 194.
128 his pants and coat both now soaked: *TJS*, 110.
128 dapper counterfeiters to the wild murderer: *BT*, 27 April 1846; and *Nantucket Inquirer*, 3 May 1848.
128 "I pity you": *TJS*, 110.
129 bolstered Webster's head: *TGB*, 194.
129 three scraps of paper: Ibid., 153. The alternate readings of "ale" and "axe" are noted in the court transcript.

15. Old Grimes Is Dead

131 Mrs. Webster's in-law Charles Cunningham: *TGB*, 158.
131 signature of the Cambridge town judge: *TDM*, 28.
131 "I thought it would be a disagreeable business": *TGB*, 158.
131 they'd sent out invitations: *Trenton State Gazette*, 6 December 1849.
131 checkbook for the Charles River Bank: *TGB*, 158.
132 "STRANGE RUMOR": *BH*, 1 December 1849.
132 "DISCOVERY OF THE BODY OF DR. PARKMAN": *BB*, 1 December 1849.

133 **"This is atrocious"**: Willard, *Half a Century with Judges and Lawyers*, 152.

133 **father had once been the president**: Winsor, *Biographical Contributions*, 52:33.

133 **"I always knew Dr. Webster"**: Willard, *Half a Century with Judges and Lawyers*, 152.

133 **His partner had been screaming**: *TGB*, 172.

134 **officials at eight-thirty that morning**: *TJS*, 90.

134 **teeth spilled out from between the gridirons**: *TGB*, 61.

134 **earthenware plate with dried black ink**: Ibid., 173.

134 **chiastolite, spodumene, green feldspar**: "Additions to the Cabinet of Minerals at Cambridge," 299.

134 **His fingers sank into another object**: *TGB*, 172.

134 **"Starkweather!"**: Ibid., 180.

134 **"There's something more in there"**: *TDM*, 30.

135 **roughly turned it onto its side**: *TJS*, 59.

135 **a jackknife came clattering out**: *TNY*, 7.

135 **a human torso**: *TGB*, 172.

135 **handle was decorated with hunting figures**: *BT*, 3 December 1849.

135 **newly cleaned and oiled**: *TGB*, 50.

135 **slid the knife into his pocket**: *TJS*, 98.

135 **walking stick to scrape the bark**: Ibid., 99.

135 **twine around the back**: *TGB*, 39.

135 **bared ribs were poking into it**: Ibid.

135 **showed some medical knowledge**: Ibid., 68.

136 ***Boston Herald* stood at the laboratory window**: *BH*, 3 December 1849.

136 **one could find the printing offices**: *The Boston Directory* (1849), 40.

136 **was not the most popular**: *BH*, 15 December 1849. The *Herald* commissioned independent circulation audits and ran the results on December 12, 13, and 15, 1849. They showed the following circulations among the penny papers:
Herald 11,253
Boston Times 7,794
Bee 5,628
Mail 3,500

136 **"Our office was thronged"**: *BB*, 3 December 1849.

136 **"Can it be true?"**: *BT*, 1 December 1849.

136 **the story stoutly denied**: *BC*, 3 December 1849.

137 **the *Bee* had the jump**: *BB*, 3 December 1849.

137   *Perley's Pic-nic*: Ibid.

137   **"The sight of the water crazed him!"**: Ibid.

137   **"I nursed the baby as I listened"**: Dall, *Daughter of Boston*, 123.

137   **"The excitement, the melancholy, the aghastness"**: Sibley, Diary 1 December 1849.

137   **He'd made it off-campus and partway**: JHL, 1 December 1849. Aside from the suicide rumor, the remainder of this section is drawn from Longfellow's journal entry. It's worth noting that this is from the original handwritten journal in the Houghton Library at Harvard; the version of the journal published later by Longfellow's son is bowdlerized throughout, and in this case lacks mention of Webster or Farrar's comment about Parkman's thigh.

138   **Webster, it was said, had killed himself**: *BH*, 1 December 1849.

138   *You're fine*: *BH*, 3 December 1849.

138   **sitting up on his cot**: *TGB*, 194.

138   **netted 660 fake quarters**: *Weekly Messenger* (Boston), 12 March 1851. Andrews did indeed eventually get the chunk of metal cast into the prison dinner bell.

139   **"I never liked the looks of Littlefield"**: *TGB*, 194.

139   **He wasn't willing to talk with them**: *BH*, 3 December 1849.

139   **"REPORTED SUICIDE"**: *BH*, 1 December 1849.

139   **"It is supposed the building will be torn down"**: Ibid.

139   **local Irish poor, scapegoated**: *BH*, 1 December 1849.

139   **A local urchin**: *BH*, 3 December 1849.

140   *I saw Dr. Parkman enter this college*: Ibid.

140   **"scarcely less criminal"**: *BC*, 3 December 1849.

140   **"were a good deal magnified"**: Ibid.

140   **City Guards, New England Guards, and the Artillery**: *BB*, 3 December 1849.

140   **more peaceable group emerged**: *BH*, 3 December 1849.

140   **"Old Uncle Ned"**: Foster, "Old Uncle Ned."

140   *"Old Grimes is dead"*: Greene, "Old Grimes Is Dead," in *Old Grimes*. There are numerous earlier references to "Old Grimes Is Dead," including in the 3 December 1849 coverage of the crowd in the *Boston Herald*. But Greene's later 1867 edition is one of the first to preserve the wording.

141   **Wentworth, a provisioner with a store on Lynde Street**: *TGB*, 268.

141   **humbugs like Dalley's Magical Pain Extractor**: *BC*, 7 December 1849.

141   **he'd seen him there at about three p.m.**: *TGB*, 268.

16. A Lifetime of Uprightness

142 **"It is with deep regret"**: *BT,* 5 December 1849.

142 **police permission to come inside**: Small, *Oliver Wendell Holmes,* 66.

142 **prying up floorboards and planing off samples**: *BH,* 14 December 1849.

142 **"to the present excited state"**: *BT,* 5 December 1849.

143 **evidence was quickly parceled out**: *TGB,* 62.

143 **"the fleshy portions of the body"**: Ibid.

143 **He knew, for instance, that Dr. Parkman**: Noble, "Incidents Connected with the Trial," 43. Dr. Lester Noble had been Dr. Nathan Keep's dental assistant.

143 **announcing the discovery of the African gorilla**: Savage and Wyman, "Notice of the External Characters."

144 **"professor of obstetrics and medical jurisprudence"**: Harvard University, *Catalogue,* 61.

144 **or even by vinegar**: Taylor, *Medical Jurisprudence,* 59.

144 **"Let us bow"**: *BT,* 5 December 1849.

144 **cousins had been footing the bill**: Gardiner, *William Hickling Prescott,* 294.

144 **enjoyed some oysters**: *BH,* 3 December 1849.

145 **waited for another delivery**: *TGB,* 195.

145 **"His numerous friends will be rejoiced"**: *BH,* 3 December 1849.

145 **the lowest floor of the jail**: *BH,* 5 December 1849.

145 **dim but whitewashed and clean**: JHL, 12 January 1850.

145 **He needed a little rug**: *BT,* 14 December 1849.

145 **Professors ... Peirce and Eben Horsford**: *TGB,* 195.

145 **the dread pirate Don Pedro Gilbert**: *BH,* 25 December 1849.

145 **Holmes had consulted with**: Small, *Oliver Wendell Holmes,* 65–66.

146 **"The professor has been embarrassed for money"**: *BB,* 3 December 1849.

146 **inheritance he'd received from his late father**: *Daily Globe* (Washington, DC), 8 December 1849.

146 **"expensive habits and a love of luxury"**: *Sun* (Baltimore), 5 December 1849.

146 **a nine-dollar check returned**: *BT,* 6 December 1849.

146 **"A lifetime of uprightness forbids it"**: *CC,* 6 December 1849.

146 **"We are at perfect liberty to suppose"**: *BC,* 4 December 1849.

146 **"Of course we cannot believe Dr. Webster guilty"**: Frances Longfellow,

Mrs. Longfellow: Selected Letters, 4 December 1849 letter to Mary Longfellow Greenleaf, 161.

146 **"the anti-Webster and the anti-Littlefield parties"**: *BJ*, 7 December
1849.

147 **Littlefield had offered one of them seventy dollars**: *BB*, 3 December
1849.

147 **"to throw a deed of blood"**: *Trenton State Gazette*, 6 December 1849.

147 **He'd requested a private arraignment**: *TGB*, 195.

147 **"His whole mind seems to be running upon his food"**: Quoted in
Hogan, *Of the Human Heart*, 143

147 **normally have been abandoned**: *BB*, 4 December 1849.

147 **Two lucky reporters made it in**: *BC*, 4 December 1849.

148 **"The color of a man's skin makes a mighty difference"**: Ibid.

148 **Madame O'Connor . . . a miscreant**: *BJ*, 3 December 1849.

148 **Webster occupied his wait with a newspaper**: *BB*, 4 December 1849.

148 **"ASTOUNDING DISCLOSURES!"**: *BB*, 3 December 1849.

148 **bounties of up to fifty dollars**: *BT*, 7 December 1849.

148 **illustration of George Parkman's remains**: *BH*, 3 December 1849.

148 **urchins were stealing them**: *BT*, 12 December 1849.

148 **weekend storm knocking out Boston's lines**: *BT*, 4 December 1849.

149 **"looks no more like that gentleman"**: Quoted in Chaney, *The Parkman
Tragedy*, 52.

149 **"upon search of said Medical College"**: *BB*, 4 December 1849.

149 **turkey and rice arrived from Parker's**: *TGB*, 195.

150 **"They send much more than I can eat"**: Ibid.

150 **At nine-thirty on Thursday morning**: *BJ*, 6 December 1849.

150 **A brass plate**: *BT*, 7 December 1849.

151 **donated both an organ and a piano**: Holmes, *The Benefactors of the Medical School*, 30.

151 **"the value of electricity in producing"**: *BJ*, 6 December 1849.

151 **politician had asked him to donate ten dollars**: *BJ*, 6 December 1849.
This story, or very close variants of it, was repeated throughout the local
press in the early weeks of coverage.

151 **an astronomical twelve-fold markup**: *Final Report of the Committee on
the Erection of the New Jail*, 14. I am indebted to Robert Sullivan's 1970
account *The Disappearance of Dr. Parkman* for noting both the unsuit-
ability of the land and the unusually high price the city paid for it. He
does not quite connect the dots between this jail deal and the involvement of the Quincys in both it and the Harvard donation, though. Fur-

ther, the *Final Report* makes it clear that city committees recommended different sites altogether, not once but *twice*: a South Boston site in an 1845 committee (14), and a rebuilding of the Leverett Street Jail by the 1848 committee (17). Instead, the city purchased Parkman's lot at a price that works out to about $1.20 per square foot. The Boston City Council *Reports of Proceedings* (27 December 1909, 785) notes that Parkman's original purchase of the West End tracts cost 10 cents per square foot.

151 **nearly $50,000 more in municipal funds**: *Final Report of the Committee on the Erection of the New Jail*, 38.
152 **for months he halted construction**: Ibid., 36
152 **George had helped his brother Samuel**: *BT,* 5 December 1849.
152 **"Naughty Sam"**: Doughty, *Francis Parkman*, 8.
152 **a murky scandal involving forgeries**: *Our First Men*, 35.
152 **living in debauchery in Paris**: Doughty, *Francis Parkman*, 8.
152 **procession of five carriages**: *BT,* 7 December 1849.
152 **"Day by day"**: JHL, 6 December 1849. Longfellow also used "Cambridge Tragedy" in his 4 December 1849 letter to Richard Henry Dana (Longfellow, *Letters*, 3:231); his wife, Fanny, used it in an undated autumn 1850 letter as well (Frances Longfellow, *Mrs. Longfellow: Selected Letters*, 173).

17. In the Dead House

155 **the "dead house"**: *BJ,* 7 December 1849.
155 **"SECRET INQUISITION"**: *Sun* (Baltimore), 12 December 1849.
155 **"pre-occupying and misdirecting public opinion"**: *BB,* 6 December 1849.
156 **"From the beginning"**: *Ibid*.
156 **"17,000,000 columns of reading matter"**: *CC,* 29 November 1849. The item was reprinted from the *Boston Weekly* of 5 June 1841.
156 **Washington Monument reaching the fifty-foot mark**: *CC,* 13 December 1849.
156 **"lovers of horrors"**: *Savannah Daily Republican*, 13 December 1849.
156 **"The Northern papers teem"**: *Daily Picayune* (New Orleans), 13 December 1849.
156 **run in the Honolulu *Polynesian***: *Polynesian,* 2 March 1850.
156 **the *New Zealand Spectator***: *New Zealand Spectator,* 3 August 1850.
156 **east to the *Illustrated London News***: *Illustrated London News,* 5 January 1850.

156 **"the Bermondsey Horror"**: *BT,* 3 December 1849.

157 **"He was exceedingly sorry"**: *Boston Post,* 7 December 1849.

157 **"WHO was caught in the dead house?"**: *BH,* 7 December 1849.

157 **"The owl is killed"**: *BB,* 17 December 1849.

157 **"Murder-Worship"**: *BT,* 2 January 1850.

157 **had run in *Punch***: "Murder-Worship," *Punch,* 201.

158 **sleigh rides in the moonlight**: *BT,* 1 January 1850.

158 **inaugural journey of the rail line**: *CC,* 10 January 1850.

158 **"What stupendous discoveries"**: *BT,* 1 January 1850.

158 **"very pleasant, though it leaves down by North End"**: JHL, 16 January 1850.

158 **"sat the doctor reading"**: Ibid., 12 January 1850.

158 **copies of the *Advertiser* and the *Courier***: *BH,* 25 December 1849.

158 **Charlotte Brontë's *Shirley***: *BT,* 20 December 1849.

158 **Irving's biography of Mohammed**: *BH,* 25 December 1849.

159 **"imagination is so wrought upon"**: *Springfield Republican,* 12 January 1850.

159 **"public mind inflamed—blind to truth"**: DJW, no. 361.

159 **"Hesperian Gardens of college life"**: JHL, 30 September 1849.

159 **hours building snow forts**: Ibid., 8 January 1850.

159 **"was really in want"**: Ibid., 5 January 1850.

159 **might have gained entry to his lab**: DJW, no. 420.

159 **"Dr. Lawrence hired Littlefield"**: Ibid., no. 362.

160 **"The body was probably brought to the college"**: Ibid., no. 367.

160 **"Would it not be well"**: Ibid., no. 418.

160 **"He talked freely about his case"**: JHL, 12 January 1850.

160 **turned the streets into treacherous sheets of ice**: *BT,* 15 December 1849.

160 *I've got something*: *BH,* 24 January 1850.

161 **"Found the hands of Dr. Parkman"**: Ibid.

161 **"a rather good-looking young girl"**: *BH,* 10 January 1850.

161 **turned up alive in a South Boston workhouse**: *BH,* 14 January 1850.

161 **"THE PARKMAN TRAGEDY in the glow"**: *BH,* 30 January 1850.

161 **unload its stock**: *BT,* 15 December 1849.

162 **ads for the latest**: *BB,* 5 February 1850.

162 **"evidence of the blackest character"**: W. E. Bigelow, *The Boston Tragedy,* 14.

162 **publisher . . . claimed that twenty thousand copies**: *BB,* 12 February 1850.

162 **"for gratuitous circulation, or nearly so"**: Edward Everett journal entry for 20 December 1849, quoted in Chaney, *The Parkman Tragedy,* 72

162 **"The University at Cambridge"**: Morison, *Three Centuries of Harvard,* 276.

162 **"HIGHLY IMPORTANT!"**: *BH,* 28 February 1850.

163 **News of the discovery was halfway**: E.g., *Daily Missouri Republican* (St. Louis), 11 March 1850.

163 **a missing thirty-eight-year-old carriage-smith**: *Trenton State Gazette,* 4 March 1850.

163 **"the Parkman Hoax"**: *Sun* (Baltimore), 5 March 1850.

163 **"We never wantonly trifle with the feelings"**: *BH,* 4 March 1850.

163 **scarcely lasted over an hour**: Papers of John White Webster, 1840–1969, John W. Webster letter to John A. Lowell, 21 December 1849.

163 **besieged by letters from attorneys**: *BH,* 26 January 1850.

163 **barely fifty dollars a month**: Papers of John White Webster, 1840–1968, John W. Webster letter to John A. Lowell, 21 December 1849.

163 **fashionable straw hats and stockings**: Ibid. Avoidance of duties, some of which were quite steep, was no small advantage in this era. One importer, for instance, was discovered circumventing the high tariffs on lead ingots by having the stuff fashioned into solid (and presumably very weighty) busts of Shakespeare, which were then promptly melted back into raw material after making it through customs (*BT,* 26 December 1849).

164 **one of Sarah and her baby**: Dabney Family Papers, 1825–1915, letter of Harriet Webster to Sarah Dabney, 1 March 1847.

164 **"There are also some good pictures"**: Papers of John White Webster 1840–1968, letter of John White Webster to John A. Lowell, 12 December 1849.

164 **A carriage came by each morning**: *Trenton State Gazette,* 20 January 1850.

164 **"Skyrocket Jack"**: *Sun* (Baltimore), 17 December 1849.

165 **"Dear Sir: It is with difficulty"**: *Daily Missouri Republican* (St. Louis), 24 January 1850. The letter is referred to, though not quoted, as early as January 19 in the *Boston Daily Evening Transcript.*

165 **One from Philadelphia claimed that Parkman**: *BH,* 25 January 1850.

165 **a mysterious man from Boston's suburbs**: *Springfield Republican,* 15 March 1850.

165 **Some maintained that the news couldn't**: *Constitution* (Middletown, CT), 6 March 1850.

166 **appeared in Boston twenty-one days after**: *BT,* 19 January 1850.

18. Good Men and True

168 reporters gathered in the empty courtroom: *BH*, 19 March 1850.

168 all weekend Sheriff Eveleth had had carpenters: *BH*, 18 March 1850.

168 back downstairs, out through the cellar: Willard, *Half a Century with Judges and Lawyers*, 153.

168 New York papers had reporters there: *BH*, 19 March 1850.

168 "This, without question, will be the most exciting trial": *BB*, 7 March 1850.

168 "one of the fastest presses": *BH*, 18 March 1850.

169 "Daguerreotypes by Steam": E.g., *BB*, 25 February 1850.

169 magic lantern show of "dissolving views": *BB*, 16 February 1850.

169 "from a daguerreotype by Mr. Whipple": *BT*, 20 March 1850. It is possible that the ad refers to Daniel Webster; however, its timing and its placement next to the trial coverage make the more obvious (and more commercial) interpretation likely. Engravings of Dr. Webster from this period, as well as the photograph reproduced in this volume, also make it clear that there was indeed an extant daguerreotype of Dr. Webster to draw upon.

169 talk of moving the trial: *Emancipator & Republican* (Boston), 21 February 1850.

169 could have filled the room twelve times over: *BT*, 18 March 1850.

169 special priority in applying for trial passes: Ibid.

169 carpenters had even built some press tables: *BH*, 18 March 1850.

170 "I don't know what else can be done": *BB*, 19 March 1850.

170 "That's him!": *BM*, 20 March 1850.

170 bronze-sheathed doors: Sullivan, *The Disappearance of Dr. Parkman*, 64.

170 "to keep at bay the unfavored multitude": *BT*, 19 March 1850.

170 "All stretched forward to scan his looks": *TDM*, 3.

170 cushioned armchair: *BT*, 19 March 1850.

170 smiled at several friends: *BB*, 20 March 1850.

170 "The countenance of the prisoner": *TNY*, 3.

170 Capital cases required a majority: *TGB*, 4.

171 disputed will by one Edward Phillips: *CC*, 19 July 1849.

171 clerk called out, taking roll: *TGB*, 5.

171 Of the sixty men in the jury pool: Ibid.

172 "Prisoner, look upon the juror": Ibid., 6.

172 "it is necessary that we know": *BJ*, 19 July 1850.

172 a buzz passed through the assembled crowd: *TNY*, 3.

172 a printer named Thomas Barrett: *TGB*, 8.

173 **His hand trembled slightly**: *TNY*, 3.

173 **"To this indictment"**: *TGB*, 8.

173 **his duties as the state's attorney general**: Ibid., 9. Though Sullivan (*Disappearance*, 57) presents this arrangement as being rather dodgy—and, indeed, the financing of it would prove to be so—the addition of Bemis to the prosecution team had in itself been publicly known for at least one month (*BH*, 18 February 1850).

173 **mingled in the same circles as Longfellow**: E.g. JGB, 17 February 1850.

174 **distracted by his father**: Ibid., 10 March 1850.

174 **extracting a promise**: Ibid., 31 March 1850.

174 **"in the clear, calm light of justice"**: *TJS*, 6.

174 **"That presentment involves two general propositions"**: Ibid., 8.

174 **"Notices were published"**: Ibid., 9.

175 **"On the 30th of November"**: Ibid., 10.

175 **"Of the bones found in the furnace"**: Ibid., 11.

175 **"you will have placed for your inspection"**: Ibid., 12.

176 **The jury selection had gone better than he'd**: JGB, 31 March 1850.

176 **"if Dr. Parkman was murdered"**: *TJS*, 13.

176 **"*This* was the relation of those parties"**: Ibid., 15.

176 **"The last time I saw Dr. Parkman"**: *TGB*, 42.

177 **unimpressed with Sohier**: JGB, 31 March 1850.

177 **"What appearances," he asked Shaw**: *BM*, 20 March 1850.

177 **"I saw appearances about these remains"**: *TGB*, 43.

177 **"well dressed females"**: *New-York Commercial Advertiser*, 27 March 1850.

177 **"Shall I relate the circumstance?"**: *TJS*, 31.

177 **"He came to my house early"**: *TGB*, 43.

177 **"On the 18th of April, 1848"**: *TJS*, 31.

178 **"Subsequently to this"**: *TGB*, 44.

179 **Abbot and Amos Lawrence, had also made a $1,500 loan**: *BB*, 20 December 1850. A few additional details also appeared in the *Emancipator & Republican* (Boston) of 27 December 1850.

179 **"He said that he would see Dr. Webster"**: *TGB*, 45.

19. The Catalog of Bones

180 **the waiting prison carriage**: *BM*, 20 March 1850.

180 **"So much for one nob"**: Ibid.

180 **betting pools were already forming**: *BM*, 21 March 1850.

180 **"Public opinion is divided"**: Ibid.

180 **They'd spent the night sequestered**: Crosby, *Notes of James Crosby*, 20 March 1850.

180 **"seem like a pleasant set of men"**: Ibid., 19 March 1850.

181 **arrived at the courthouse at nine-thirty**: Ibid., 20 March 1850.

181 *a member of the bar*: *BM*, 22 March 1850.

181 **ticket was a forgery**: *BM*, 21 March 1850.

181 **"If tickets were ever at a premium"**: *BM*, 22 March 1850.

181 **"I am the City Marshal"**: *TGB*, 46.

181 **"It would have been impossible to make"**: Ibid., 47.

181 **a wooden model of the college**: *American Traveller* (Boston), 23 March 1850. Hobbs went on to be the primary carver for the fittings for the Vermont State House, where they can still be seen today; see *Vermont Legislative Directory* (1898), 212.

181 **Each floor lifted out**: *BT*, 20 March 1850.

182 **"When we arrived, from Mr. Littlefield's apartments"**: *TGB*, 49.

182 **"various other things, which I now produce"**: Ibid., 50.

182 **setting the gallery abuzz**: *BH*, 20 March 1850.

182 **Professor Webster was laughing**: Crosby, *Notes of James Crosby*, 21 March 1850.

182 **Dr. Woodbridge Strong was rather amused**: *BH*, 21 March 1850.

183 **"no expression of surprise"**: *TGB*, 96.

183 **painstaking catalog of bones**: Ibid., 89.

183 **"I am a practicing physician in this city"**: Ibid. 69.

183 **"If I see a man with one shoulder higher"**: *BB*, 21 March 1850.

184 **"I had a pirate given to me"**: *TGB*, 69.

184 **"Sickening," one juror wrote**: Crosby, *Notes of James Crosby*, 20 March 1850.

184 **"I was afraid of a visit by the police"**: *TGB*, 69.

184 **"After death, the elasticity of a body is gone"**: Ibid., 70.

184 **the windows were thrown open**: *BM*, 21 March 1850.

185 **"These remains were *unusually bloodless*"**: *TGB*, 70.

185 **"a monstrous size, a perfect barricade"**: *BM*, 21 March 1850.

185 **a triple-sized run of 37,880 copies**: *BH*, 21 March 1850.

185 **he was earnestly taking notes**: *BB*, 20 March 1850.

185 **Jackson was also a frustrated inventor**: "Sketch of Dr. Charles T. Jackson," 404–5.

185 **"I knew the late Dr. George Parkman"**: TGB, 73.

186 **quarter-sized pieces**: *BJ*, 21 March 1850.

186 **a seemingly exonerating circumstance**: E.g., *BC*, 6 December 1849.

186 **"I think that with the proper quantity of acid"**: *TGB*, 79.

186 **"The largest kettle which I saw"**: Ibid., 76.

186 **nearly 174 grains, or $6.94 worth**: Ibid., 77.

187 **pioneering use of ether during Fanny Longfellow's**: Keep, "The Letheon Administered in a Case of Labor," 226.

187 **"artificial teeth of the most approved materials"**: *Columbian Centinel* (Boston), 12 May 1824.

187 **Dental evidence had never before been used**: Senn, *Forensic Dentistry*, 13.

187 **Paul Revere had used his metalworking sideline**: Ibid., 13.

187 **"These blocks, now shown before me"**: *TGB*, 80.

188 **"to have the set finished"**: Ibid.

188 **"The two sets were connected together by spiral springs"**: Ibid., 83.

188 **City hall wildly rang its bell**: *BH*, 22 March 1850.

188 *he* **was staying at the Tremont**: *BM*, 21 March 1850. This is also noted in Bemis's journal entry of 31 March 1850, as where he and Clifford worked in the previous week to prepare for the case.

188 **Was it arson?**: *BH*, 21 March 1850.

189 **"we ought to have that model"**: Frances Longfellow, *Mrs. Longfellow: Selected Letters*, 25 March 1850 letter to Nathan Appleton, 188.

189 *I fear some could misinterpret your testimony*: *BH*, 21 March 1850.

189 **"It would be very difficult to make a man's life"**: *BC*, 4 December 1849.

189 **"***I*** employed Keep in my family"**: DJW, no. 498.

189 **a half hour later, his papers and bags moved**: *BT*, 21 March 1850.

189 **only people arrested were half a dozen pickpockets**: *BH*, 21 March 1850.

190 **"They hung along the stairs and lobbies"**: *BM*, 20 March 1850.

190 **knocked two officers off their feet**: *BH*, 21 March 1850.

190 **"He called on me the day before his disappearance"**: *TGB*, 84.

191 **"sat as unmoved as a rock"**: *BA*, 22 March 1850.

191 **"I have known such explosions to take place in new teeth"**: *TGB*, 85.

191 **crying into his handkerchief**: *BH*, 21 March 1850.

191 **"When Dr. Lewis showed the teeth to me"**: *TGB*, 85.

20. Mesmeric Revelation

192 **a blue frock coat**: *BH*, 22 March 1850.

192 **"I have no middle name"**: Ibid.

192 "I am janitor of the Medical College": *TGB*, 99.

193 he'd given Littlefield something just last year: DJW, no. 518.

194 "Dr. George Hayman can say something": Ibid., 380.

194 "Captain Stacy of the Custom House": Ibid., 424.

194 *His wife's got a reputation*: Ibid., 380.

194 "Where were you": *BH*, 25 March 1850. Unusually for any of the trial coverage, the *Herald*'s coverage on this date included Sohier's cross-examination of Littlefield in transcript form, rather than consolidating the witnesses' responses into long paragraphs, as was typically done in both newspapers and subsequent trial transcripts. The remainder of this section of the chapter therefore draws on the *Herald*'s version, which does not differ substantively from Bemis's but is more conversational.

195 "Every appearance has been in his favor": Crosby, *Notes of James Crosby*, 23 March 1850.

196 Reverend Huntington's in the morning: *BT*, 25 March 1850. The details in the remainder of this paragraph are drawn from this account.

196 "Been stared at to my heart's content": Crosby, *Notes of James Crosby*, 24 March 1850.

196 weather had turned improbably beautiful: Ibid.

196 Hawthorne's new novel had landed: *BJ*, 25 March 1850.

196 "in the best vein of the author of *Typee*": *BT*, 25 March 1850.

196 *David Copperfield* had arrived: Crosby, *Notes of James Crosby*, 28 March 1850.

196 "a hearty laugh": Crosby, *Notes of James Crosby*, 23 March 1850. The *Herald*, for instance, had claimed that day that Greene was violently ill.

197 ad for his Waterman's Patent Refrigerators: *Boston Post*, 22 March 1850.

197 "I have in my possession": *TGB*, 194.

197 "I am a resident of this city": Ibid., 197.

197 A trained violinist, Gould: Wilson and Fiske, *Appleton's Cyclopaedia of American Biography*, 2:695.

198 handwriting guides and patent writing paper: *BT*, 13 February 1850. This was a notice for the latest edition of his various guides, which had been running for decades (e.g., in Boston's *Daily American Statesman*, 12 June 1827).

198 "I know the prisoner by sight": *TGB*, 197.

198 an alumnus of the medical school: Wyman, *Biographical Memoirs*, 95.

198 "I *am* familiar with his signature": *TGB*, 197.

198 **Gould himself had been one of the handwriting experts**: *BH*, 12 October 1848.

199 **the "Charlestown Incendiaries"**: *BH*, 6 December 1849.

199 **"has always been considered admissible"**: *TGB*, 200.

199 **engraver and calligrapher who published a popular**: *BT*, 10 March 1846.

199 **"I am acquainted with the defendant's signature"**: *TGB*, 208.

200 **The carriage's front axle had snapped**: *BB*, 25 March 1850.

200 **Franklin Dexter had turned him down**: Willard, *Half a Century with Judges and Lawyers*, 153.

200 **the renowned Rufus Choate**: Parker, *Reminiscences of Rufus Choate*, 218.

200 **Sohier's quiet manner hid a droll**: Willard, *Half a Century with Judges and Lawyers*, 331.

201 **"May it please Your Honor"**: *TGB*, 213.

201 **Sohier walked quickly and with a habitual stoop**: Willard, *Half a Century with Judges and Lawyers*, 194.

201 **He hadn't even *wanted* to be a jury foreman**: *TGB*, 8.

201 **"speaking in all frankness"**: Ibid., 215.

203 **"I reside in Cambridge"**: Ibid., 246.

203 **"his lucid manner of communicating"**: Calhoun, *The Papers of John C. Calhoun*, Jared Sparks letter of 11 May 1824 to Calhoun, 9:85.

203 **"No delicacy as to the college ought to interfere"**: DJW, no.379.

203 **running through ten of them in a single hour**: *BB*, 28 March 1850.

203 **appearance of the professor's three daughters**: *BB*, 29 March 1850.

203 **"On Friday the 23rd, Father was home"**: *TGB*, 250.

204 **"I think one subject broached with Dr. Wyman"**: Ibid., 249.

204 **a onetime collaborator of Nathan Keep's**: Gay and Jackson, *A Statement of the Claims of Charles T. Jackson*, xvii.

204 **"I mentioned it to my sister"**: *TGB*, 262.

205 **"I am a clerk"**: Ibid., 263.

205 **laughter began to run through the crowd**: *BH*, 29 March 1850.

205 **"I do not carry a magnifying glass"**: *TGB*, 266.

206 **"Reverend" Theophilus Fiske**: *BH*, 31 January 1850. Fiske's decidedly checkered career apparently later included getting sacked from a job in the Dead Letter Office, on account of his stealing money from the letters (*Portland Daily Advertiser* [Maine], 16 August 1861).

206 **"Professor" J. S. Grimes**: *BB*, 23 January 1850.

206 **trendily renamed and using zinc-plated copper**: Winter, *Mesmerized*, 281.

206 **"for exhibiting for the public amusement"**: *BB*, 8 February 1850.

206 **"Rheumatism, Neuralgia, Deafness, Dimness of Sight"**: *BH*, 6 February 1850. An additional example, of a different acolyte altogether, can be seen in *BB*, 16 March 1850.

206 **"I simply carried the glass for others to use"**: *TGB*, 266.

206 **"appeared to be regularly purblind"**: *BH*, 29 March 1850.

21. Twelve Men in Massachusetts

209 **law offices on Court Street**: *The Boston Directory* (1849), 261.

209 **bearing a Boston postmark**: *TGB*, 598.

209 **"Important Notice"**: *BH*, 29 March 1850.

210 **"Did you hear what they said"**: *BB*, 30 March 1850.

210 **"It was the regular practice"**: Webster, John White Webster Papers, 1837–1850, letter of James Edward Oliver to Pliny Merrick, 27 March 1850.

210 **one fumbled the evidence box**: *BH*, 29 March 1850. The damage is also noted in other accounts, including *TJS*, 165.

210 **"that there was an individual"**: *TJS*, 167.

211 **"a gentleman distinguished in railroad enterprises"**: *BM*, 29 March 1850.

211 **more than seven thousand spectators**: *BH*, 29 March 1850.

211 **walking down the exit stairs with a bloody nose**: *BH*, 2 April 1850.

211 **"They may indeed be mistaken"**: *TGB*, 298.The remainder of this section is drawn from the Bemis transcript, pp. 282–374.

213 **"a quantity of old brass"**: *BJ*, 27 March 1850.

213 **"Gentlemen of the jury"**: *TGB*, 380. Except where noted, the remainder of the prosecution's closing argument is from Bemis's transcript.

216 **the possibility that Dr. Parkman was insane**: DJW, no. 380.

216 **"Dr. Bell's Lunatic Asylum perhaps knows something"**: DJW, no. 397.

216 **"Gentlemen . . . there is resting upon you"**: *TGB*, 448.

216 **Shaw began, and his voice broke**: *BJ*, 1 April 1850.

216 **"Before committing this cause"**: *TGB*, 449.

217 **Dr. Webster stood up, trembling**: *BJ*, 1 April 1850.

217 **"I am much obliged to Your Honors"**: *TGB*, 449.

217 **His voice turned scornful**: *Ohio Statesman*, 1 April 1850.

217 **"But in their *superior wisdom*"**: *TGB*, 449.

219 **a relatively modern standard**: Waldman, "Origins of the Legal Doctrine of Reasonable Doubt," 299.

219 **Enlightenment philosophy epitomized**: Ibid., 301.

219 **"a fantastical incredulous fool"**: Quoted in ibid., 303.

219 **"To acquit upon light, trivial and fanciful suppositions"**: Quoted in ibid., 314. The quote is from Starkie's *A Practical Treatise of the Law of Evidence* (1824).

220 **"This is to be proved beyond reasonable doubt"**: *TGB*, 470. The remainder of this section is from the Bemis transcript.

221 **"God help us to judge aright"**: Crosby, *Notes of James Crosby*, 28 March 1850.

221 **Jones led Dr. Webster to an anteroom**: *BJ*, 1 April 1850.

221 **tickets to the island of Fayal**: *BT*, 1 April 1850.

221 *Do you want some tea?*: *BJ*, 1 April 1850.

221 **knots of attorneys now formed**: *BA*, 1 April 1850.

222 **"definite character of the judge's charge"**: Ibid.

222 **dead silence within**: *BJ*, 1 April 1850.

222 **ad began with the words "MURDER! MURDER!"**: *BH*, 29 March 1850.

222 **"PROFESSOR WEBSTER'S FATE"**: *BM*, 29 March 1850.

222 **transcripts that were already being hurriedly**: *BM*, 30 March 1850.

222 **getting the windows open**: JGB, 31 March 1850.

223 **"The jury have agreed"**: *BA*, 1 April 1850.

223 **the county coroner, slipping**: JGB, 31 March 1850.

223 **"He's convicted"**: *BA*, 1 April 1850.

223 **"Ah! Do they?"**: *BJ*, 1 April 1850.

223 **judges entered through one side door**: *TDM*, 63.

223 **"Gentlemen of the jury, have you agreed"**: *TGB*, 497.

223 **"We have"**: *TNY*, 73.

223 **"Hold up your right hand!"**: *TGB*, 497.

22. Law Manufactured for the Occasion

224 **"started as if shot"**: Nathaniel Parker, quoted in Sullivan, *The Disappearance of Dr. Parkman*, 148.

224 **fell to the bar with a dull thud**: *Boston Courier*, 1 April 1850.

224 **the sound of weeping**: *BH*, 1 April 1850.

224 **Merrick grasped Webster's hand**: *Boston Courier*, 1 April 1850.

224 **his spectacles slightly askew**: *BT*, 1 April 1850.

224 **"Gentlemen of the jury, hearken to your verdict"**: *TGB*, 497.

224 **"What do you want to keep me here for?"**: *BJ*, 1 April 1850.

224 **"If I was conscious of having uttered one single word"**: *BA*, 1 April 1850.

225 **"I suppose I shall have meals"**: *BJ*, 1 April 1850.

225 **their old friend Judge Fay**: Ibid.

225 **His wife's sister was chosen to deliver**: Sibley, Diary, 31 March 1850.

225 **sixty thousand visitors**: *TGB*, 604.

226 **seemed the greatest of all**: *BJ*, 1 April 1850.

226 **His eyelids grew heavy**: *BT*, 1 April 1850.

226 *"Every person who shall commit the crime"*: *TGB*, 500.

226 **Officer Spurr showed**: *Trenton State Gazette*, 8 April 1850.

226 **voted to invite the public in**: *BA*, 8 April 1850.

227 **women could be spotted quietly slipping splinters**: *BT*, 15 April 1850.

227 **"another Eugene Aram"**: JHL, 31 March 1850.

227 **"an unbroken chain of indubitable proof"**: *Boston Courier*, 1 April 1850.

227 **the *Mail* agreed, the inevitable conclusion**: *BM*, 2 April 1850.

227 **In the view of the *Evening Transcript***: *BT*, 1 April 1850.

227 **"the murderer and mangler"**: *BB*, 6 April 1850.

228 **"We have never seen an example of such baseness"**: *BH*, 6 April 1850.

228 **Webster had confessed to taking strychnine**: *Richmond Enquirer*, 9 April 1850.

228 **a medical student saw Webster's crime**: *BM*, 8 April 1850.

228 **recanted her testimony**: *BT*, 1 April 1850.

228 **abandoned a woman in Edinburgh**: *BH*, 8 April 1850.

228 **Webster had tried triple-selling his mineral cabinet**: *BH*, 6 April 1850.

228 **"This is an utter falsehood"**: Webster, John White Webster Papers, 1837–1850, letter of John W. Webster to Dr. Winslow Lewis, 11 April 1850.

229 **Six competing editions**:
1. James W. Stone, ed., *Report of the Trial of Prof. John W. Webster* (Boston: Phillips, Sampson)
2. *The Parkman Murder: Trial of Prof. John W. Webster* (Boston: Daily Mail Office)
3. *Trial of Professor John W. Webster . . . Reported Exclusively for the New York Daily Globe* (New York: Stringer & Townsend)
4. *The Trial of Prof. John W. Webster, Indicted for the Murder of Dr.*

> *George Parkman*, reported for the *Boston Journal* (Boston: Redding & Co.)

5. John A. French, ed., *Trial of Professor John W. Webster* (Boston: Boston Herald Steam Press, 1850).

6. *The Twelve Days' Trial of Dr. John W. Webster* (London: James Gilbert)

There would be later editions as well, not least George Bemis's that fall.

229 **"superior Engravings"**: *BH,* 1 April 1850.

229 **thirty thousand copies printed**: *BM,* 8 April 1850.

229 **educational reformers like Horace Mann**: "Reading Reform," 27.

229 **"most of our unhappy arguments had already been cast in stereotype"**: Webster, John White Webster Papers, 1837–1850, Edward Sohier letter [to Pliny Merrick], [April 1850]. From its context, and its reference to communicating with Clifford, Sohier's letter is clearly one to Merrick written in early April.

229 **"will have a monopoly"**: Ibid., John Clifford letter to Edward Sohier, 7 April 1850.

230 **angry newspaper notices by the lawyers**: *BH,* 13 April 1850.

230 **"NO ADMITTENCE"**: *Barre Patriot,* 12 April 1850.

230 **fifty thousand, by one estimate**: *BT,* 15 April 1850.

230 **snipping off locks of his hair**: *Trenton State Gazette,* 8 April 1850.

230 **collect the $3,000**: *BT,* 11 April 1850.

230 **"Dr. Parkman stands in the attitude of a creditor!"**: *BT,* 30 May 1850.

231 **"the mercy of the Executive may be extended"**: *BT,* 4 April 1850.

231 **petitions were circulating in Philadelphia**: *Constitution* (Middletown, CT), 15 April 1850.

231 **Dayton**: *Ohio State Journal,* 30 April 1850.

231 **Richmond**: *Sun* (Baltimore), 4 May 1850.

231 **Louisville**: *Sun* (Baltimore), 22 April 1850.

231 **Augusta**: *BH,* 20 April 1850.

231 **"that most disgusting of all bipeds"**: Quoted in *BH,* 8 April 1850.

231 **"so fully had the evidence pointed to the prisoner"**: *BM,* 3 April 1850.

231 **"the prayers of devout Puritans"**: "The Webster Case," 10.

231 **"I am no fanatic—no bigot"**: *BT,* 20 April 1850.

232 **he wanted to talk to someone unassociated**: *BT,* 9 April 1850.

232 **Webster began promising to say grace**: LAN, Amelia Nye letter to Marianne Ivens, 14 June 1850.

232 **"We are quite astonished in Boston"**: Benjamin Peirce letter to A. D. Bache, 7 April 1850; quoted in Hogan, *Of the Human Heart*, 142.

232 **Webster had ordered a *dozen***: JGB, 31 March 1850.

232 **"There is a very faint hope"**: Hogan, *Of the Human Heart*, 142.

232 **"after a stormy and most tedious passage"**: Dabney Family Papers, 1825–1915, John Dabney letter to Sarah Dabney, 7 May 1850.

233 **the guards had run a needle through the paper**: *New Hampshire Gazette*, 18 April 1850.

233 **George Thompson, imprisoned in the next cell**: Thompson, *Venus in Boston*, 370.

233 **"He is the victim of circumstances"**: *BH*, 13 April 1850.

233 **On April 24, Dr. Webster had filed**: *TGB*, 560.

234 **"certain errors in the proceeding and judgment of the court"**: *TGB*, 503.

234 **"silence and timidity of cross-examination"**: Hall, *A Review of the Webster Case*, 14.

234 **hadn't bothered to read the defense's more aggressive closing**: Borowitz, "The Janitor's Story," 1544. Borowitz's story is notable because he chanced across a particularly interesting memento: Hall's own notes and annotated copy of the Stone transcript.

234 **"law manufactured for the occasion"**: Upton, *A Statement of Reasons*, 32.

23. A Man in Error

235 **"DR. PARKMAN FOUND!"**: *BM*, 1 April 1850.

235 **construction revealed more remains**: *Springfield Republican*, 20 April 1850.

235 **"the intact coffin, unopened for 30 centuries"**: *BT*, 25 May 1850.

235 **"She may have witnessed the ten plagues"**: Ibid.

236 **Chief Justice Shaw subscribed**: *BT*, 7 May 1850.

236 **"in beautiful condition"**: *BT*, 3 June 1850.

236 **dust kicked up into the crowd**: *BT*, 5 June 1850.

236 **"The daughter of the high priest of Thebes"**: JHL, 7 June 1850.

236 **"Dr. Bigelow blushed"**: Marvel, *The Opera Goer*, 2: 101.

236 **Gliddon stammered out an explanation**: *BT*, 7 June 1850.

237 **rhymed "mummy" with "dummy"**: *BH*, 7 June 1850.

237 **"SUPPOSE YOUR AUNT"**: *CC*, 27 June 1850. The mummy itself, one of a pair possessed by Gliddon—the other, ironically, was indeed a woman—

eventually wound up at Tulane University, where for a decades it was stored under the bleachers of Tulane Stadium. Gliddon's aspersions on the Egyptian mortuary's record keeping were, as it turns out, quite unfair: "Inscriptions on his coffin indicate he was Djed-Thoth-iu-ef-ankh, a priest and overseer of craftsmen at the Temple of Amun in Thebes" (Carol J. Schlueter, Tulane University press release, 15 November 2015).

237 **This time all five state supreme court justices**: *TGB*, 502.

237 **"May it please Your Honors"**: Ibid., 503.

237 **he'd unsuccessfully run for mayor in 1847**: *Salem Observer*, 11 December 1847.

237 **he excelled in "chamber practice"**: Bell, *The Bench and Bar of New Hampshire*, 398.

238 **"My experience in the courts"**: *TGB*, 537.

238 **"The human remains found in the Medical College"**: Ibid., 562.

238 **"My acquaintance with Dr. Webster"**: Ibid.

239 **The minister had delivered the election sermon**: *Springfield Republican*, 11 January 1845.

239 **narrowly missed being appointed to Harvard's Board**: *Weekly Messenger* (Boston), 28 February 1844.

239 **offered him its Hollis Chair**: *New-York Spectator*, 21 January 1846.

239 **"On the 23rd of May"**: *TGB*, 562. Modern musings that Webster's confession document was a hoax are merely fanciful. It was presented by a respected clergyman to the governor—a career-ending and pointless stunt, if a hoax—and neither Webster nor his family disavowed the document. Indeed, Webster chose to have Putnam accompany him to the scaffold. Nor did his friends find the confession out of character: as Fanny Longfellow notes in her 11 July 1850 letter to Emmeline Austin Wadsworth: "Dr. Webster's confession is very awful, is it not? But to me credible knowing the nature of the man" (*Mrs. Longfellow: Selected Letters*, 173).

239 **"He came in at the lecture-room door"**: Ibid. The remainder of this section was drawn from Bemis's transcript.

242 **"the very picture of distress and sorrow"**: *BH*, 6 June 1850.

242 **they'd refused visitors**: LAN, Amelia Nye letter to Marianne Ivens, 4 October 1850.

242 **"How could I believe my husband to be guilty"**: quoted In Buescher, *The Remarkable Life of John Murray Spear*, 56.

243 **"We feel assured of that"**: *BT*, 6 July 1850.

243   **moved that date to July 16**: *BT,* 8 July 1850.

244   **"adverse to the confession"**: *BT,* 6 July 1850.

244   **"in the highest degree improbable"**: quoted in Sullivan, *The Disappear-
      ance of Dr. Parkman,* 198.

245   **"Telegraphic to Boston Herald"**: *BH,* 10 July 1850.

245   **Boston's government offices came to a standstill**: *BT,* 10 1850.

245   **incoming exams on July 15 and 16**: *CC,* 27 June 1850.

246   **sixty-one hopefuls**: *BT,* 17 July 1850.

246   **most of the Executive Council made the journey**: *BT,* 18 July 1850.

246   **a graduating class well-stocked**: *BT,* 17 July 1850.

246   **"Friend Clifford"**: Papers Related to the Trial of John White Webster,
      1814–1937, letter of Samuel Wood to John Clifford, 17 July 1850.

24. Closing Hours

247   **"Is His Excellency the Governor"**: *BT,* 9 July 1850. I have taken the lib-
      erty of correcting the name. *BT*'s account, reprinted from the *Mail,* has
      the reporter overhearing it as "Anto Emanuel Hunt." Another account,
      in the *Boston Herald* of 8 July, presents his name as Antonio Emanuel
      Dwight. Their respective renderings hint at the visitor almost certainly
      being *Antonio Emanuel Knight,* an eccentric figure memorialized in John
      J. Currier's *History of Newburyport, Mass.: 1764–1909* (2: 441–45). Knight
      was a member of John White Webster's Class of 1815 but never grad-
      uated; and, like Webster, he went on to practice medicine—though, as
      Currier puts it, "he was never overburdened with patients" (441). Knight
      had a fondness for issuing imperative declarations to governors and pres-
      idents. After a spell in an insane asylum in 1834, he existed somewhere
      between being a ward of the state and the master of his only partially
      imaginary domains in Newburyport—a sort of a spiritual heir to the
      previous reigning town eccentric, Lord Timothy Dexter.

248   **founder of the Society for the Abolition of Capital Punishment**:
      Buescher, *The Remarkable Life of John Murray Spear,* 42.

248   **published the *Prisoners' Friend***: Ibid., 46.

248   **"Ought he not to be beaten into a plowshare?"**: 24 January 1843 letter
      by H. D. Thoreau to R. W. Emerson, quoted in Buescher, *The Remarkable
      Life of John Murray Spear,* 20.

248   *I have more petitions for clemency*: *BT,* 18 July 1850.

248 **Spear brothers had often prevailed**: Buescher, *The Remarkable Life of John Murray Spear*, 55.

248 **A law had already been proposed**: *Trenton State Gazette*, 25 April 1850.

249 **"The weapon was knotty and substantial"**: *BT*, 18 July 1850.

249 **the professor had already heard the news**: *BT*, 19 July 1850.

249 **"Yes. Tell him to prepare"**: *Worcester Palladium*, 31 July 1850.

249 **"I forgive you, Dr. Webster"**: *Emancipator & Republican* (Boston), 1 August 1850.

249 ***Boston Daily Atlas* revealed that he'd been offered $500**: *BA*, 5 August 1850.

249 **repeated the figure as *$5,000***: *Sun* (Baltimore), 5 August 1850.

250 **"Mr. Littlefield, all that you said"**: *Emancipator & Republican* (Boston), 1 August 1850.

250 **"sincere contrition and penitence"**: *BT*, 31 August 1850.

250 **"This is asking for more magnanimity than they possess"**: Frances Longfellow, *Mrs. Longfellow: Selected Letters*, 8 April 1850 letter to Nathan Appleton, 169.

250 **advocate of the Society for the Abolition of Capital Punishment**: Buescher, *The Remarkable Life of John Murray Spear*, 56.

250 **"The response was not what, under the circumstances"**: *Boston Times*, quoted in *Trenton State Gazette*, 13 September 1850.

251 **"The feet of those who have just carried out"**: Briggs, Letters Received by George N. Briggs, unsigned letter to Governor George Briggs, n.d.

251 **"I Rite to inform you"**: Ibid., letter of James Rollins to Governor George Briggs, 10 August 1850.

251 **"aye a most oppressive scoundrel"**: Ibid., letter of Launcelot English to Governor George Briggs, 15 August 1850.

251 **"burn your dwelling to the ground"**: Ibid., letter of William Web [indecipherable] a.k.a. Bambazilla Frothingham to Governor George Briggs, 12 August 1850.

251 **"You must return to your capital"**: Ibid., letter of Antonio Emanuel Knight to Governor George Briggs, 28 August 1850.

252 **"*The undersigned begs the pleasure*"**: Ibid., letter of Jackus Netebebus to Governor George Briggs, 27 August 1850.

252 **deluged with more than five hundred requests**: *BT*, 20 August 1850.

252 **hide the date and time from Mrs. Webster**: *BB*, 29 August 1850. The arrangement is also noted in other newspapers and in Amelia Nye's letter

of 4 October 1850 (LAN). The Webster hometown paper (*Cambridge Chronicle*) notably avoids any mention of the next day's execution in its issue of 29 August 1850.

252   **"Will this be your hour for closing"**: *BB*, 31 August 1850.

253   **cleaning and polishing a shell**: Willard, *Half a Century with Judges and Lawyers*, 155.

253   **perused Mountford's *Euthanasy***: *BT*, 8 August 1850.

253   **"death was not meant to be altogether pleasant"**: Mountford, *Euthanasy*, 37.

253   **Longfellow's *Hymns***: *BT*, 31 August 1850.

253   **stopped to pray, or to simply put his head**: *BT*, 30 August 1850.

253   **Mr. Dunbar, the prison's occasional carpenter**: *BB*, 31 August 1850.

254   **new spruce one, handily constructed by Dunbar**: *Boston Traveler*, 13 April 1866.

254   **"Stop your infernal clack!"**: *BM*, 31 August 1850.

254   **two cups of tea, breakfast, and a last smoke**: *BT*, 30 August 1850.

254   **more than a hundred police officers**: *BB*, 30 August 1850.

254   *I used to experiment on the bodies*: Willard, *Half a Century with Judges and Lawyers*, 155.

254   **"Hang at eight; breakfast at nine!"**: *BT*, 4 September 1850.

255   **"Do not regard any thing about you"**: *BT*, 31 August 1850.

255   **boys trying to scale the prison fence**: *BJ*, 20 August 1850.

255   **charged fifty cents**: *BM*, 31 August 1850.

255   **fashioned some crude benches**: *BB*, 30 August 1850.

255   **"At every possible point"**: *BJ*, August 1850.

255   **"NOT AT HOME, OPPOSED TO CAPITAL PUNISHMENT"**: *BH*, 31 August 1850.

255   **"District Attorney, Clerk or Clerks"**: Webster, John White Webster Papers, 1837–1850, form letter [invitation] of Sheriff Eveleth, 23 August 1850.

255   **a contingent of New York reporters**: *Springfield Republican*, 31 August 1850.

255   **upon his black outfit**: *BM*, 31 August 1850.

256   **"It *is* a very ingenious contrivance"**: *Springfield Republican*, 31 August 1850.

256   **"Whereas, at the term of the Supreme Judicial Court"**: *TGB*, 590.

256   **gone out of his way to ask for the smooth straps**: Willard, *Half a Century with Judges and Lawyers*, 155.

256 **"into thy hands"**: *BT,* 31 August 1850.

257 **Webster turned to look at the Reverend Putnam**: *BM,* 30 August 1850.

257 **"In the name of the Commonwealth of Massachusetts"**: *BB,* 30 August 1850.

257 **made his shoulders shrug**: *BJ,* 30 August 1850.

Epilogue

259 **The woman stood in the Websters' doorway**: LAN, Amelia Nye letter to Marianne Ivens, 4 October 1850.

259 **"There has been a morbid curiosity"**: Sibley, Diary, 30 August 1850; see also following entries.

259 **Mr. Peak's mortuary**: LAN, Amelia Nye letter to Marianne Ivens, 4 October 1850.

259 **black-painted pine box**: *BT,* 30 August 1850.

259 **The professor had wanted mahogany**: *Pittsfield Sun,* 5 September 1850.

259 **They'd quietly sold peaches**: LAN, Amelia Nye letter to Marianne Ivens, 4 October 1850.

260 **merchant John Perkins Cushing had pledged $500**: Ibid., Amelia Nye letter to Marianne Ivens, 9 February 1851.

260 **Appleton found quick success**: Appleton, *Selections from the Diaries of William Appleton,* entry for 4 September 1850, 140.

260 **"Mr. Appleton tried to raise $20,000"**: LAN, Amelia Nye letter to Marianne Ivens, 4 October 1850.

260 **His labware sold poorly**: *Trenton State Gazette,* 31 March 1851.

260 **"It was quite valuable"**: *Springfield Republican,* 17 March 1851.

260 **the Websters were left with $450**: LAN, Amelia Nye letter to Marianne Ivens, 9 February 1851. I do not find any primary source for the widely repeated assertion that George Parkman's widow was atop the list of contributors to Mrs. Webster. Its appeal is understandable, as a reassuring proof of forgiveness and mercy. Yet the earliest version of this story I have found appears eighty years later in Sir William Hale White's article "John White Webster: The Guy's Ghoul" in *Guy's Hospital Reports* (1930). Hale's claim is unsourced. Perhaps I have overlooked a line in a primary source; if a reader notices one, I'll gladly give Mrs. Parkman her due in a future edition.

261 **Young Hattie, despite her fortunes**: *Trenton State Gazette,* 11 April 1851.

261 **Mrs. Webster's death in October 1853**: *Boston Recorder,* 13 October 1853.

261 **Catherine and Marianne, left town**: *BH,* 14 October 1853.

261 **"I did not recognize them"**: Twain, *Notebook and Journals,* 341n.

261 **"I suppose you know who *we* are!"**: Ibid., entry of 21 June 1867, 341.

261 **"The longest gap perhaps"**: JGB, 3 November 1850.

262 **"probably the most satisfactory definition ever given"**: Quoted in *Victor v. Nebraska,* 9.

262 **effective and remarkably durable fusing**: Rogers, *Murder and the Death Penalty,* 100101.

262 **"It was commendable for Chief Justice Shaw"**: *Victor v. Nebraska,* 23.

262 **"a modernized version of the Webster charge"**: Ellement, "SJC Rewrites a Judicial Tradition."

262 **he now interviewed Shaw**: JGB, 3 November 1850.

262 **paid $1,000 for the trial**: Ibid., 31 March 1850. Bemis was later paid an additional $150 for his appeals work.

263 **"I talked with Daniel Webster"**: Parker, *Reminiscences of Rufus Choate,* 272.

263 **"visitation of God"**: Neilson, *Memories of Rufus Choate,* 18.

263 **"Mr. [Daniel] Webster said to me"**: Parker, *Reminiscences of Rufus Choate,* 273.

263 **Merrick was appointed associate justice**: *Dictionary of American Biography* (1879 ed.), 617.

264 **the murder trial in London of François Benjamin Courvoisier**: Borowitz, "The Janitor's Story," 1544.

264 **"He confided to him that he had done the deed"**: LAN, Amelia Nye letter to Marianne Ivens, 4 October 1850.

264 **that the ventilation panel in a lab door was loose**: DJW, no. 421 and no. 423. On the same page, Webster also proposes impugning specific police officers: "Cannot Clapp and Starkweather['s] character be impeached?"

264 **"He then wrote a very long letter to Edward"**: LAN, Amelia Nye letter to Marianne Ivens, 4 October 1850.

265 **"at such times the glaze of civilization"**: Chase, *Lemuel Shaw,* 189.

265 **George Burroughs**: Sibley, *Biographical Sketches of Graduates of Harvard University,* 2:331. The dubious distinction of becoming the third executed Harvard alumnus was narrowly avoided in 1998 by "Unabomber" Ted Kaczynski, who instead drew eight life terms without parole.

265 **The one-year-delay law**: Rogers, *Murder and the Death Penalty,* 102.

265 **second-degree murder**: Ibid., 112.

265 **"Probably, in the annals of criminal jurisprudence"**: Thompson, *Venus in Boston*, 370.

266 **on display at P. T. Barnum's**: *Trenton State Gazette*, 23 May 1851. This was later spoofed by Charles Farrar Browne in his showman persona of Artemus Ward, who claimed to have "wax figgers of G. Washington, Genl. Taylor, John Bunyan, Captain Kidd, and Dr. Webster, besides several miscellanyous wax statoots of celebrated piruts and murderers" (Hingston, *The Genial Showman*, 137).

266 **"is a pure specimen"**: *New Hampshire Gazette*, 8 October 1850.

266 **"terribly reduced our general estimate of humanity"**: *Trenton State Gazette*, 2 October 1850.

266 **Littlefield instantly forswore**: *Trenton State Gazette*, 7 October 1850.

266 **retired to a farm in Vermont**: *Savannah Daily Republican*, 17 April 1851.

266 **"cleared $25,000"**: *Weekly Herald* (New York), 12 February 1853.

266 **went insane**: *BA*, 23 April 1854.

266 **"it was feared someone would desecrate his tomb"**: LAN, Amelia Nye letter to Marianne Ivens, 15 February 1854.

266 **spotted in Connecticut**: *Constitution* (Middletown, CT), 13 November 1850.

266 **in Maine**: *Portland Daily Advertiser*, 25 May 1850.

266 **"Dr. Parkman was looking hard at Gen. Taylor"**: *Springfield Republican*, 3 October 1850.

266 **Commencement Day festivities at Dartmouth**: *New Hampshire Sentinel*, 1 August 1850.

266 **committee report in the Massachusetts legislature**: Morison, *Three Centuries of Harvard*, 288. Namely a committee led by George S. Boutwell, who became the state's governor soon thereafter. Notably, Boutwell—later a senator and then secretary of the Treasury under Grant—was self-taught and did not attend college at all.

267 **"parents went on, generation after generation"**: Adams, *The Education of Henry Adams*, 65.

267 **described . . . as Brahmins**: Holmes, *Elsie Venner*, 13.

267 **Edward King**: Rantoul, *Report of the Harvard Class of 1853*, 167.

267 **William Dorsheimer**: Ibid., 78.

267 **Justin Winsor**: Ibid., 283.

267 **Francis McGuire**: Ibid., 178.

267 **Dorsheimer, in his later years, ran the** *New York Star*: Ibid., 80.

267 **Albert Gallatin Browne Jr.**: Ibid., 46.

267 **Adams Sherman Hill**: Ibid., 133.

267 **Charles William Eliot**: Ibid., 95.

268 **"was Webster's volcano"**: Cohen, *Some Early Tools of American Science*, 19.

268 **Lizzie Borden**: *Tacoma Daily News*, 14 June 1893.

268 **Leopold and Loeb**: *BH*, 20 June 1924. Readers of my book *The Murder of the Century* may take note that Dr. Webster's case was also duly mentioned during the feverish coverage of the murder of William Guldensuppe—for example, in the *Philadelphia Inquirer* of 1 July 1897.

268 **"a sententious style"**: Holmes, *The Benefactors of the Medical School*, 27.

268 **"Dr. Parkman was a man of strict and stern"**: Ibid., 35.

268 **"Dr. Parkman was so harsh and cruel"**: Benjamin Peirce letter to A. D. Bache, 7 April 1850; quoted in Hogan, *Of the Human Heart*, 143.

269 **"Longfellow told me a terrific story"**: Letter to Wilkie Collins, 12 January 1868, in Dickens, *Letters of Charles Dickens*, 12:9.

269 **"They were horribly grim"**: Letter to Lord Lytton, 13 January 1868, in Dickens, *Letters of Charles Dickens*, 12.

269 **"Professor Webster's laboratory still remains"**: *BJ*, 21 April 1911.

269 **"but all discovery of the murderer was to be baffled"**: Forster, *The Life of Charles Dickens*, 3: 426.

270 **at the end of a full day of working on his story**: Ibid., 3: 428.

270 **"I hope his book is finished"**: Ibid., 3: 427.

Sources

Adams, Henry. *The Education of Henry Adams: An Autobiography*. Boston: Houghton Mifflin, 1918.

"Additions to the Cabinet of Minerals at Cambridge." *Boston Journal of Philosophy and the Arts* 2 (1826): 299.

Alpha [pseud.]. "My Room." *Harvard Magazine* (October 1856): 346–52.

Appleton, William. *Selections from the Diaries of William Appleton, 1786–1862*. Boston: privately printed, 1922.

Awful Disclosures and Startling Developments in Relation to the Late Parkman Tragedy: With a Full Account of the Discovery of the Remains of the Late Dr. George Parkman and the Subsequent Arrest of Professor John W. Webster. Boston: n.p., 1849.

Barber, Samuel. *Boston Common: A Diary of Notable Events, Incidents, and Neighboring Occurrences*. Boston: Christopher Publishing House, 1916.

Batchelder, Samuel. "The History of 'Commons' at Harvard—II," *Harvard Alumni Bulletin* 23 (12 May 1921): 727–35.

Bell, Charles Henry. *The Bench and Bar of New Hampshire: Including Biographical Notices of Deceased Judges of the Highest Court, and Lawyers of the Province and State, and a List of Names of Those Now Living*. Boston: Houghton, Mifflin, 1894.

Bemis, George, ed. *Report of the Case of John W. Webster*. Boston: Charles C. Little and J. Brown, 1850.

Bentinck-Smith, William. *The Harvard Book: Selections from Three Centuries*. Cambridge: Harvard University Press, 1960.

Bergen, Philip. *Old Boston in Early Photographs, 1850–1918: 174 Prints from the Collection of the Bostonian Society*. New York: Dover, 1990.

Bigelow, Henry Jacob. "Dr. Harlow's Case of Recovery from the Passage of an Iron Bar Through the Head," *American Journal of the Medical Sciences* 20 (1850): 13–22.

————. *An Introductory Lecture, Delivered at the Massachusetts Medical College, November 6th, 1849*. Boston: B. B. Mussey and Co. 1850.

Bigelow, W. E. *The Boston Tragedy! An Exposé of the Evidence in the Case of the Parkman Murder!* Boston: n.p., 1850.

Bigelow, William Sturgis. *A Memoir of Henry Jacob Bigelow*. Boston: Little, Brown, 1900.

Borowitz, Albert. "The Janitor's Story." *ABA Journal* (December 1980): 1540–45.

The Boston Almanac for the Year 1843. Boston: John P. Jewett, 1842.

The Boston Directory for the Year Commencing 1849. Boston: George Adams, 1849.

Boston Medical Association. *Boston Medical Police*. Boston: Sewell Phelps, 1820.

Bowen, Abel. *Bowen's Picture of Boston, or The Citizens and Stranger's Guide to the Metropolis of Massachusetts, and Its Environs*. Boston: Otis, Broaders & Co., 1838.

Bradlee, Nathaniel J. *History of the Introduction of Pure Water into the City of Boston, with a Description of Its Cochituate Water Works*. Boston: A. Mudge, 1868.

Briggs, George. Letters Received by George N. Briggs, 1850. Archive. Massachusetts Historical Society.

Buescher, John B. *The Remarkable Life of John Murray Spear: Agitator for the Spirit Land*. Notre Dame, IN: University of Notre Dame Press, 2006.

Bungay, George W. *Crayon Sketches and Off-hand Takings*. Boston: Stacy and Richardson, 1852.

Burnett, Amelia. Amelia Burnett Diary (transcript), 1846–48. Archive. Massachusetts Historical Society.

Calhoun, Charles C. *Longfellow: A Rediscovered Life*. Boston: Beacon, 2004.

Calhoun, John C. *The Papers of John C. Calhoun*. Vol. 9, *1824–1825*. Edited by W. Edwin Hemphill. Columbia: University of South Carolina Press, 1976.

Carroll, George. *The Manchester Tragedy: A Sketch of the Life and Death of Miss Sarah H. Furber, and the Trial of Her Seducer and Murderer*. Manchester, NH: Fisk & Moore, 1848.

Chaney, Karen Elizabeth. "The Parkman Tragedy: A Story of Murder, the Penny Press, and the Elite Community in 1850 Boston." ALM thesis, Harvard University, 2002.

Chase, Frederic Hathaway. *Lemuel Shaw: Chief Justice of the Supreme Judicial Court of Massachusetts, 1830–1860*. Boston: Houghton Mifflin, 1918.

Cohen, I. Bernard. *Some Early Tools of American Science: An Account of the Early*

Scientific Instruments and Mineralogical and Biological Collections in Harvard University. Cambridge, MA: Harvard University Press, 1950.

Costigan, George P. *Cases and Other Authorities on Legal Ethics*. St. Paul, MN: West, 1917.

Crosby, James. "Notes of James Crosby Concerning Testimony in the Trial of John W. Webster for the Murder of George Parkman, March 1850." Archive. Harvard Law School Library.

Dabney Family Papers, 1825–1915. Archive. University of Washington, Special Collections.

Dall, Caroline Wells Healey, and Helen Deese. *Daughter of Boston: The Extraordinary Diary of a Nineteenth-Century Woman*. Boston: Beacon, 2005.

Davies, G. L. Herries. *Whatever Is Under the Earth: The Geological Society of London, 1807 to 2007*. Bath: Geological Society of London, 2007.

Dearborn, Nathaniel. *Guide Through Mount Auburn*. Boston: Nathaniel Dearborn, 1847.

Dickens, Charles. *Letters of Charles Dickens*. Edited by Madeline House and Graham Storey. Oxford: Clarendon, 1965.

Doughty, Howard. *Francis Parkman*. New York: Macmillan, 1962.

Doyle, Henry Grattan. "Poets Can Be Professors." In *Report of the Third Annual Round Table Meeting on Linguistics and Language*, edited by Salvatore J. Castiglio, 81–89. Washington, DC: Georgetown University Press, 1952.

Drake, Samuel Adams. *Old Landmarks and Historic Personages of Boston*. Boston: James Osgood, 1873.

Ellement, John. "SJC Rewrites a Judicial Tradition." *Boston Globe*, 26 January 2015.

Emerson, Ralph Waldo. *The Letters of Ralph Waldo Emerson*. Edited by Ralph Rusk and Eleanor M. Tilton. New York: Columbia University Press, 1939.

Farnham, Charles Haight. *A Life of Francis Parkman*. Boston: Little, Brown, 1901.

Farr, Samuel. *Elements of Medical Jurisprudence*. London: J. Callow, 1814.

Fields, Annie Adams. "Glimpses of Emerson." *Harper's New Monthly Magazine* (February 1884): 457–67.

Final Report of the Committee on the Erection of the New Jail, in the Board of Mayor and Alderman, November 10, 1851. City Document No. 61. Boston: [City of Boston,] 1851.

"The First School at Newtowne," *Harvard Magazine* 10 (March 1864): 189–99.

Ford, John. *The Cambridge Directory and Almanac for 1850*. Cambridge, MA: Cambridge Chronicle, 1850.

Forster, John. *The Life of Charles Dickens*. London: Chapman and Hall, 1874.

Foster, Stephen. *Old Uncle Ned*. New York: Millet's Music Salon, 1848.

Frothingham, Octavius Brooks. *Boston Unitarianism, 1820–1850: Study of the Life and Work of Nathaniel Langdon Frothingham*. New York: G. P. Putnam's Sons, 1890.

Gallenga, Antonio Carlo Napoleone. *Episodes of My Second Life*. London: Chapman and Hall, 1884.

Gardiner, C. Harvey. *William Hickling Prescott: A Biography*. Austin: University of Texas Press, 1969.

Garrison, Lloyd McKim. *An Illustrated History of the Hasty Pudding Club Theatricals*. Cambridge, MA: Hasty Pudding Club, 1897.

Gay, Martin, and Charles T. Jackson. *A Statement of the Claims of Charles T. Jackson, M.D., to the Discovery of the Applicability of Sulphuric Ether to the Prevention of Pain in Surgical Operations*. Boston: D. Clapp, 1847.

Gibson, Campbell. *Population of the 100 Largest Cities and Other Urban Places in the U.S., 1790–1990: Population Division Working Paper No. 27*. Washington, DC: U.S. Bureau of the Census, 1998.

Gill, Thomas. *Selections from the Court Reports Originally Published in the Boston Morning Post, from 1834 to 1837*. Boston: Otis & Broaders, 1837.

Greene, Albert G. *Old Grimes Is Dead*. Providence, RI: Sidney Rider & Brother, 1867.

Hale, Edward Everett. *A New England Boyhood*. Boston: Little, Brown, 1898.

Hall, Abraham Oakey. *A Review of the Webster Case, by a Member of the New York Bar*. New York: J. S. Redfield, 1850.

Harlow, John W. "Recovery from the Passage of an Iron Bar Through The Head." 1868. Reprinted in the *History of Psychiatry* 4 (1993): 274–81.

Harvard University. *Catalogue of the Officers and Students of Harvard College, for the Academical Year 1849–1850*. Cambridge, MA: Metcalf & Co., 1849.

———. *The Class of 1844, Harvard College, Fifty Years After Graduation*. Edited by Edward Wheelwright. Cambridge, MA: John Wilson & Son, 1896.

———. *Laws of Harvard University, Relative to Undergraduates*. Cambridge, MA: Metcalf & Co., 1845.

———. *Twenty-third Annual Report of the President of the University at Cambridge to the Overseers, Exhibiting the State of the Institution for the Academical Year 1847–48*. Cambridge, MA: Metcalf & Co., 1849.

———. *Twenty-fourth Annual Report of the President of Harvard College to the Overseers, Exhibiting the State of the Institution for the Academical Year 1848–1849*. Cambridge, MA: Metcalf & Co., 1850.

———. *Twenty-fifth Annual Report of the President of Harvard College to the*

Overseers, Exhibiting the State of the Institution for the Academical Year 1849–50. Cambridge, MA: Metcalf & Co., 1851.

Higginson, Thomas Wentworth. *Contemporaries*. Boston: Houghton, Mifflin, 1899.

Hill, George Birkbeck Norman. *Harvard College, by an Oxonian*. New York: Macmillan, 1894.

Hingston, Edward Peron. *The Genial Showman: Being Reminiscences of the Life of Artemus Ward; and Pictures of a Showman's Career in the Western World*. London: J. C. Hotten, 1871.

Historic Americana Auction, June 6 & 7, 2007. Auction catalog. Cincinnati, OH: Cowan's Auctions, 2007.

Hoar, George Frisbie. *Autobiography of Seventy Years*. Charles Scribner's Sons, 1903.

Hobson, Barbara Meil. *Uneasy Virtue: The Politics of Prostitution and the American Reform Tradition*. Chicago: University of Chicago Press, 1990.

Hogan, Edward R. *Of the Human Heart: A Biography of Benjamin Peirce*. Bethlehem, PA: Lehigh University Press, 2008.

Holmes, Oliver Wendell, Sr. "The Autocrat of the Break-fast Table." *Atlantic* (August 1858): 360–69.

———. *The Benefactors of the Medical School of Harvard University, with a Biographical Sketch of the Late Dr. George Parkman*. Boston: Ticknor, Reed & Fields, 1850.

———. *Elsie Venner*. Boston: Ticknor & Fields, 1861.

———. Letter of Oliver Wendell Holmes Sr. to John Collins Warren, 28 February 1850. Warren Library of the Harvard Medical Library. Online.

———. *Puerperal Fever as a Private Pestilence*. Boston: Ticknor & Fields, 1855.

Homer, James Lloyd. *Nahant, and Other Places on the Northshore: Being a Continuation of Notes on the Sea-shore*. Boston: William Chadwick, 1848.

Howe, Lois Lilley. "The History of Garden Street." *Proceedings of the Cambridge Historical Society* 33 (1953): 37–57.

Howells, W. D. "The White Mr. Longfellow." *Harper's New Monthly Magazine* (August 1896): 327–43.

Howland, E. A. *The New England Economical Housekeeper, and Family Receipt Book*. Worcester, MA: S. A. Howland, 1845.

Jackson, J.B.S. *A Descriptive Catalogue of the Anatomical Museum of the Boston Society for Medical Improvement*. Boston: Ticknor & Co., 1847.

———. *A Descriptive Catalogue of the Warren Anatomical Museum*. Boston: A. Williams, 1870.

Jackson, Leon. "Digging for Dirt: Reading Blackmail in the Antebellum Archive." *Common-place* 12, no. 3 (April 2012). http://www.common-place-archives.org/vol-12/no-03/reading/.

Jarnagin, Laura. *A Confluence of Transatlantic Networks: Elites, Capitalism, and Confederate Migration to Brazil.* Tuscaloosa: University of Alabama Press, 2013.

Johnson, Carl Leonard. *Professor Longfellow of Harvard.* Eugene: University of Oregon, 1944.

Jones, H. Bence. *On Animal Chemistry in Its Application to Stomach and Renal Diseases.* London: John Churchill, 1850.

Keep, Nathan Cooley. "The Letheon Administered in a Case of Labor." *Boston Medical and Surgical Journal* 36 (1847): 226.

Kennedy, William Sloane. *Oliver Wendell Holmes: Poet, Littérateur, Scientist.* Boston: S. E. Cassino & Co., 1883.

King, Moses. *Mount Auburn Cemetery: Including Also a Brief History and Description of Cambridge, Harvard University, and the Union Railway Company.* Boston: Moses King, 1883.

Kirker, Harold, and David van Zanten. "Jean Lemoulnier in Boston, 1846–1851." *Journal of the Society of Architectural Historians* (October 1972): 204–08.

La Piana, Angelina. *Dante's American Pilgrimage: A Historical Survey of Dante Studies in the United States, 1800–1944.* New Haven: Published for Wellesley College by Yale University, 1948.

Lawrence, Robert Means. *Old Park Street and Its Vicinity.* Boston: Houghton Mifflin, 1922.

Life of Michael Powers: Now Under Sentence of Death for the Murder of Timothy Kennedy. Boston: Russell & Gardner, 1820.

Livy. *Selections from the First Five Books: Together with the Twenty-first and Twenty-second Books Entire.* Translated by Karl Alschefski and John Lincoln. New York: Appleton, 1849.

Longfellow, Frances. *Mrs. Longfellow: Selected Letters of Fanny Appleton Longfellow.* Edited by Edward Wagnerknecht. New York: Longmans Green, 1956.

Longfellow, Henry Wadsworth. Henry Wadsworth Longfellow Papers. Journal [1 January 1849–31 October 1850]. Houghton Library, Harvard University.

———. *The Letters of Henry Wadsworth Longfellow.* Edited by Andrew R. Hilen. Cambridge, MA: Belknap Press, 1967.

———. *The Seaside and the Fireside.* Boston: Ticknor & Fields, 1850.

————. *The Works of Henry Wadsworth Longfellow: With Bibliographical and Critical Notes and His Life, with Extracts from His Journals and Correspondence*. Boston: Houghton, Mifflin, 1886.

Lovet, Robert W. "The Harvard Branch Railroad, 1849–1855." *Proceedings of the Cambridge Historical Society* 38 (1958): 23–50.

Macmillan, Malcolm. *An Odd Kind of Fame: Stories of Phineas Gage*. Cambridge, MA: MIT Press, 2002.

Marvel, Ik. [Donald Grant Mitchell.] *The Opera Goer, or Studies of the Town*. London: Thomas Cautley Newby, 1852.

Morison, Samuel Eliot. *The Life and Letters of Harrison Gray Otis, Federalist, 1765–1848*. Boston: Houghton Mifflin, 1913.

————. *Three Centuries of Harvard, 1636–1936*. Cambridge, MA: Harvard University Press, 1936.

Morton, James Madison. "Slasher and Crasher." *New York Drama* [9] (1848): 24.

Mountford, William. *Euthanasy, or Happy Talk Towards the End of Life*. Boston: Crosby & Nichols, 1849.

Mumford, J. G. *The Story of the Boston Society for Medical Improvement*. Boston: Damrell & Upham, 1901.

"Murder-Worship." *Punch*, 16 (17 November 1849): 201.

Muzzey, Artemas Bowers. "College Life Under President Kirkland." *Harvard Register* (March 1881): 136–39.

A Narrative of the Life and Adventures of Francis Tukey, Esq., City Marshal of Boston: By One Who Knows Him. Boston: Boston Herald Office, 1848.

Neilson, Joseph. *Memories of Rufus Choate: With Some Consideration of His Studies, Methods, and Opinions, and of His Style as a Speaker and Writer*. New York: Houghton Mifflin, 1884.

"News from the Classes." *Harvard Graduates' Magazine* (June 1908): 732–65.

Noble, Lester. "Incidents Connected with the Trial of Professor Webster." *International Dental Journal* (January 1894): 41–43.

"Notes on Our Naval History." *Harvard Magazine* (July 1858): 247–59.

"Notes on Roads and Railways." *Practical Mechanic* (April 1845): 180–81.

Oliver, James Edward. Letter of James Edward Oliver to Pliny Merrick, 27 March 1850. Papers Related to the Trial of John White Webster, 1814–1937. Archive. Massachusetts Historical Society.

Our First Men: A Calendar of Wealth, Fashion and Gentility; Containing a List of Those Persons Taxed in the City of Boston, Credibly Reported to Be Worth One Hundred Thousand Dollars; With Biographical Notices of the Principal Persons. Boston: Published by All the Sellers, 1846.

Papers Related to the Trial of John White Webster, 1814–1937. Archive. Massachusetts Historical Society.

Parker, Edward G. *Reminiscences of Rufus Choate, the Great American Advocate.* New York: Mason Brothers, 1860.

Parkman, Francis. *The Francis Parkman Reader.* Edited by Samuel Eliot Morison. New York: Da Capo, 1998.

Parkman, George. *Management of Lunatics: With Illustrations of Insanity.* Boston: John Eliot, 1817.

———. *Proposals for Establishing a Retreat for the Insane.* Boston: John Eliot, 1814.

The Parkman Murder: Trial of Prof. John W. Webster for the Murder of Dr. George Parkman. Boston: Daily Mail Office, 1850.

Payne, Edward F. *Dickens Days in Boston: A Record of Daily Events.* Boston: Houghton Mifflin, 1927.

Peirce, Benjamin. *An Elementary Treatise on Sound.* Boston: J. Munroe, 1836.

"Progress of Cholera." *Boston Medical and Surgical Journal* (13 June 1849): 382–83.

Quinn, Arthur Hobson. *Edgar Allan Poe: A Critical Biography.* 1969. Reprint, Baltimore: Johns Hopkins University Press, 1998.

Rantoul, Robert S. *Report of the Harvard Class of 1853: 1849–1913.* Cambridge, MA: University Press, 1913.

"Reading Reform." *Phonetic Journal* (22 January 1853): 27.

Records of Proceedings of the City Council of Boston, for the Year Commencing January 1, 1909. Boston: City of Boston, 1910.

Robinson, J. H. *Marietta, or The Two Students: A Tale of the Dissecting Room and "Body Snatchers."* Boston: Jordan & Wiley, 1846.

Rogers, Alan. *Murder and the Death Penalty in Massachusetts.* Amherst: University of Massachusetts Press, 2008.

Sappol, Michael. *A Traffic of Dead Bodies: Anatomy and Embodied Social Identity in Nineteenth-Century America.* Princeton, NJ: Princeton University Press, 2002.

Savage, Edward H. *A Chronological History of the Boston Watch and Police, from 1631 to 1865, Together with the Recollections of a Boston Police Office, or Boston by Daylight and Gaslight, from the Diary of an Officer Fifteen Years in the Service.* Boston: Edward Savage, 1865.

Savage, Thomas S., and Jeffries Wyman. "Notice of the External Characters and Habits of Troglodytes Gorilla, a New Species of Orang from the Gaboon River." *Boston Journal of Natural History* (December 1847): 417–42.

Senn, David R., and Paul G. Stimson. *Forensic Dentistry*. Boca Raton, FL: CRC Press, 2010.

Sibley, John Langdon. Diary ["Sibley's Private Journal"], 1846–1882. Harvard University Archives. Online.

————, et al. *Biographical Sketches of Graduates of Harvard University: In Cambridge, Massachusetts*. Cambridge, MA: C. W. Sever, 1873.

"Sketch of Dr. Charles T. Jackson." *Popular Science Monthly* (July 1881): 404–07.

Small, Miriam Rossiter. *Oliver Wendell Holmes*. New York: Twayne, 1963.

Smith, S. P. "Recollections by Author of 'America.'" *Harvard Graduate* (February 1893): 161–70.

Sprague, William B. *Annals of the American Unitarian Pulpit, or Commemorative Notices of Distinguished American Clergymen of the Unitarian Denomination in the United States, from its Commencement to the Close of the Year Eighteen Hundred and Fifty-five*. New York: Robert Carter and Brothers, 1865.

Stark, James Henry. *Stark's Antique Views of Ye Towne of Boston*. Boston: J. H. Stark, 1901.

State Street Trust Company. *Some Merchants and Sea Captains of Old Boston: Being a Collection of Sketches of Notable Men and Mercantile Houses Prominent During the Early Half of the Nineteenth Century in the Commerce and Shipping of Boston*. Boston: State Street Trust, 1918.

Stone, James W., ed. *Report of the Trial of Prof. John W. Webster, Indicted for the Murder of Dr. George Parkman: Before the Supreme Judicial Court of Massachusetts, Holden at Boston, on Tuesday, March 19, 1850*. Boston: Phillips, Sampson, 1850.

Story, Ronald. *The Forging of an Aristocracy: Harvard and the Boston Upper Class, 1800–1870*. Middletown, CT: Wesleyan University Press, 1980.

Sullivan, Robert. *The Disappearance of Dr. Parkman*. Boston: Little, Brown, 1971.

"Suspected Murder of George Parkman, M.D." *Boston Medical and Surgical Journal* (5 December 1849): 366–67.

Taylor, Albert Swaine. *Medical Jurisprudence*. 3rd ed. London: John Churchill, 1849.

Thompson, George. *Venus in Boston: And Other Tales of Nineteenth-Century City Life*. 1854. Reprint, edited by David S. Reynolds and Kimberly R. Gladman. Amherst: University of Massachusetts Press, 2002.

Thoreau, Henry David. *The Correspondence of Henry David Thoreau*. Edited by Walter Harding and Carl Bode. New York: New York University Press, 1958.

Thorndike, T. W. "Henry J. Bigelow: A Sketch." *St. Paul Medical Journal* (April 1902): 227–39.

Tilton, Eleanor. *The Amiable Aristocrat: A Biography of Dr. Oliver Wendell Holmes*. New York: Henry Shulman, 1947.

"Trial for Malpractice." *Boston Medical and Surgical Journal* (5 February 1857): 9–23.

Trial of Professor John W. Webster for the Murder of Dr. George Parkman. Boston: John A. French / Boston Herald Steam Press, 1850.

The Trial of Prof. John W. Webster, Indicted for the Murder of Dr. George Parkman. Reported for the *Boston Journal*. Boston: Redding & Co., 1850.

Trial of Professor John W. Webster for the Murder of Doctor George Parkman: Reported Exclusively for the N.Y. Daily Globe. New York: Stringer & Townsend, 1850.

Twain, Mark. *Notebook and Journals*. Vol. 1: *1855–1873*. Berkeley: University of California Press, 1975.

The Twelve Days' Trial of Dr. John W. Webster. London: James Gilbert, 1850

Upton, Francis. *A Statement of Reasons Showing the Illegality of That Verdict Upon Which Sentence of Death Has Been Pronounced Against John W. Webster for the Alleged Murder of George Parkman*. New York: Stringer & Townsend, 1850.

Vaille, Frederick Ozni, and Henry Alden Clark. *The Harvard Book: A Series of Historical, Biographical, and Descriptive Sketches*. Cambridge, MA: Welch, Bigelow, 1875.

Victor v. Nebraska. 511 U.S. 1 (1994).

Waldman, Theodore. "Origins of the Legal Doctrine of Reasonable Doubt." *Journal of the History of Ideas* 20, no. 3 (1959): 299–316.

Warren, John Collins, et al. *Report of the Overseers of Harvard College, Appointed to Visit the Medical School in 1849*. Boston: John Wilson, 1849.

Warren, John J. "The Collection of the Boston Phrenological Society: A Retrospect." *Annals of Medical History* (Spring 1902): 1–11.

"The Webster Case." *Monthly Law Reporter* (May 1850): 1–16.

Webster, John White. John White Webster Papers, 1837–1850. Archive. Massachusetts Historical Society.

———. The Papers of John White Webster, 1840-1968 (inclusive) 1840–1850 (bulk). Archive. Harvard University Archives.

———. *A Manual of Chemistry on the Basis of Professor Brande's*. Boston: Richardson & Lord, 1828.

Willard, Joseph A. *Half a Century with Judges and Lawyers*. Boston: Houghton, Mifflin, 1895.

Wilson, James Grant, and John Fiske. *Appleton's Cyclopaedia of American Biography*. New York: D. Appleton & Co., 1888.

Wilson, Thomas L. V. *The Aristocracy of Boston; Who They Are and What They Were: Being a History of the Business and Business Men of Boston, for the Last Forty Years, by One Who Knows Them*. Boston: published by the author, 1848.

Winsor, Justin, ed. *Biographical Contributions*: No. 52, The Librarians of Harvard College 1667–1877. Cambridge, MA: Library of Harvard University, 1897.

———, and C. F. Jewett. *The Memorial History of Boston: Including Suffolk County, Massachusetts, 1630–1880*. Boston: Ticknor, 1880.

Winter, Alison. *Mesmerized: Powers of Mind in Victorian Britain*. Chicago: University of Chicago Press, 1998.

Woolson, Abba Goold. *Browsing Among Books: And Other Essays*. Boston: Roberts Brothers, 1881.

Wyman, Jeffries. *Biographical Memoir of Augustus Addison Gould, 1805–1866*. Revised by William Healey Dall. Washington, DC: National Academy of Sciences, 1905.

Illustration Credits

All illustrations are from the 1879 Frederick D. Linn & Co. reprint of George Bemis's *Report of the Case of John W. Webster* (1850), with the exception of the photograph of John W. Webster, which is reproduced courtesy of the Houghton Library of Harvard University.

Index

Page numbers followed by *n* refer to endnotes.